CARTOGRAPHIES

Cartographies of the Absolute takes
perspectivalism and flat ontolog   ⎯⎯ (and
often quietistic) formulae that a⌐⎯ ⎯ ⎯⎯ow capitalism's modern
complexities must remain forever beyond human grasp.
Bringing vital insights to a range of aesthetic practices – and
recognising the torsions, refractions and ruses required to
puncture the reified social forms before us – Toscano and Kinkle
elaborate a praxis of dissident totalisation to counter capital's
limited horizons.

Gail Day, author of *Dialectical Passions: Negation in Postwar Art
Theory*

Culture, in the last decade, has had a simple duty: to be the
dreamlife of the bust. It has answered this call in ways uneven,
tawdry, messed up, beautiful – but it has finally not failed to
make a veiled reading of this obscene catastrophe. But how then
to wake from the purling images, how to leap from dream to
map of the present? Here we need ideal readers of culture's
readings, and none have come closer than Alberto Toscano and
Jeff Kinkle. Their bravura cleavings of spectacular representation
and the transformations of global capital become themselves a
kind of new knowledge, a kind of psychelocation from which we
might take an orientation and a sense of possibility.

Joshua Clover, author of the *Totality for Kids* and *1989*

How this complex, chaotic, vicious system of exploitation called
capitalism has been rendered by TV writers, Hollywood
directors, and glamorous or struggling artists forms the theme of
this book. From box sets to boxes floating across the seas, from
dialectical thinking to diabolical reckoning: it is all here, laid out,

picked out and unpicked, absorbed and turned over. Rubbish practices are called out, whether they originate in governments or the artworld. Cognitive mapping, which may be the poor analyst's conspiracy theory, gets its abstractions made real. Read it and move more consciously and dialectically through the globe.

Esther Leslie, author of *Walter Benjamin and Synthetic Worlds: Nature, Art and the Chemical Industry*

A grand tour de force of western cognitive maps and a searching dérive through anti-capitalist dimensions of theory, media and art – now pulsing on the rotting flesh of the world system. With critical acumen, serious political commitment and more than a modicum of erudite cool, Toscano and Kinkle revisit Jameson's landmark work on cognitive mapping and, by drawing extensively on the Marxist critical tradition, forward the life and death project of teaching readers to read in a dialectical mode. Grasping the aesthetic as at once program and battleground, they clearly manifest the necessity, the stakes, and the fine-grained resolution of a radical critical practice.

Jonathan Beller, author of *The Cinematic Mode of Production*

Cartographies
of the Absolute

Cartographies
of the Absolute

Alberto Toscano & Jeff Kinkle

Winchester, UK
Washington, USA

First published by Zero Books, 2015
Zero Books is an imprint of John Hunt Publishing Ltd., Laurel House, Station Approach,
Alresford, Hants, SO24 9JH, UK
office1@jhpbooks.net
www.johnhuntpublishing.com
www.zero-books.net

For distributor details and how to order please visit the 'Ordering' section on our website.

Text copyright: Alberto Toscano & Jeff Kinkle 2014

ISBN: 978 1 78099 275 4

A CIP catalogue record for this book is available from the British Library.

Design: Stuart Davies

Printed and bound by CPI Group (UK) Ltd, Croydon, CR0 4YY

We operate a distinctive and ethical publishing philosophy in all
areas of our business, from our global network of authors to
production and worldwide distribution.

CONTENTS

This book is dedicated to the memory of Allan Sekula (1951-2013) and Harun Farocki (1944-2014).

Acknowledgements

This book has taken shape over several years and many people have given us invaluable feedback, support and inspiration at various stages of the process. Thanks especially to Brenna Bhandar, Gail Day, Benjamin Noys, Steve Edwards, Evan Calder Williams, Go Hirasawa, Harry Harootunian, Jason Smith, Christopher Connery, Matteo Mandarini, Emanuel Almborg, Kate Sennert, Dan Fetherston, and Jane and Jeff E. Kinkle.

Early versions of arguments and ideas that have found their way into the book appeared in *Infinite Thought*, *Dossier*, *Film Quarterly*, *Mute*, *The Sociological Review*, the *Taipei Biennial* journal and the forthcoming book *ECONOMY*. Thanks to Nina Power, Rob White, Benedict Seymour, Josephine Berry-Slater, Anthony Iles, Nirmal Puwar, Brian Kuan Wood, Les Back, and Angela Dimitrakaki for their intellectual hospitality and engagement. We are grateful too to our hosts and audiences at the Auguste Orts gallery, the Tate Modern, University of Wolverhampton, University of Alberta, Phaidon Bookshop, Simon Fraser University, the University of Shanghai, and the Marxist Literary Group conference in Vancouver. In particular we remain indebted to the *Marxism in Culture* seminar and the *Historical Materialism* conference, where the earliest versions of this project were delivered, for their unique combination of comradeship and ruthless criticism of all that exists.

Alberto would also like to thank the several cohorts of students of his *Mapping Capitalism* graduate course, for having engaged with these ideas, and introducing him to artists and projects he was unaware of, some of which have found their way into this book.

Finally, we are immensely grateful to Allan Sekula and Sally Stein, Trevor Paglen, Patrick Keiller and Martha Rosler for allowing us to reproduce their images in these pages, and to

Trevor Barnes and Nik Heynen for the Bunge cover image. The Paglen images are courtesy of Metro Pictures, New York; Altman Siegel, San Francisco; Galerie Thomas Zander, Cologne. We hope the inevitably limited quality of the reproductions will be an added incentive for our readers to immerse themselves in the inspiring contributions of these artists to an aesthetics in and against capitalism.

List of Illustrations

Today we have to realise that the worldwide and worldness, with their hazardous and unforeseen features, constitute the 'revolution' itself, instead of concluding it.
Henri Lefebvre

Kant said he had no time to travel precisely because he wanted to know so much about so many countries.
Hannah Arendt

A few other clues / we mull them over as we go to sleep, the skeletons of dollarbills, traces of dead used up / labour, lead away from the death scene until we remember a quiet fit that everywhere / is the death scene.
Amiri Baraka, 'Das Kapital'

Everything comes down to Aesthetics and Political Economy.
Stéphane Mallarmé

Introduction

The Limits of the Known Universe, or, Cognitive Mapping Revisited

The movements of the stars have become clearer; but to the mass of the people the movements of their masters are still incalculable.
Bertolt Brecht, *The Life of Galileo*

Views from above

Charles and Ray Eames's short film *Powers of Ten* (1977) opens on a young couple recumbent on a picnic blanket in a park on the Chicago lakefront. The pair are captured in an overhead shot; the narrator informs us that the camera is a meter above them, and that every ten seconds it will ascend a power of ten. The frame

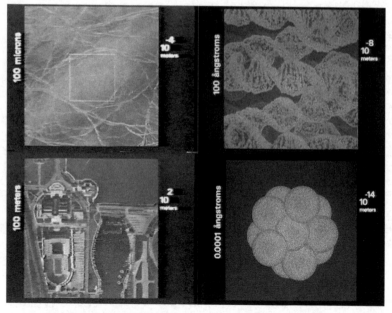

Charles and Ray Eames, *Powers of Ten*, 1977

1

Alan J. Pakula, *All the President's Men*, 1976

rises exponentially through the atmosphere, into outer space, leaving our solar system and then galaxy as it travels 10^{24} meters from the surface of the earth. From this point, deep in the emptiness of space, the 'camera' (itself a painstakingly composite simulation[1]) starts a rapid descent back to the couple on the blanket. Once it reaches them, it focuses on the man's hand before zooming in, getting ninety-percent closer every ten seconds until it ends up at 10^{-16}, inspecting the quarks of a carbon atom. In just under nine minutes, the short film displays the upper and lower bounds of the then known universe.

A kindred god's-eye-view shot, spanning nano and macro, occurs midway through Alan Pakula's thriller *All the President's Men* (1976), as Bob Woodward and Carl Bernstein's journalistic investigation into the burglary in the Watergate complex leads them to the Library of Congress, where, sitting at a table in the main reading hall, they sift through a gigantic pile of call slips. This celebrated shot begins with a high-angle close-up of the protagonists' hands, only to shakily climb to the ceiling of the world's largest library, revealing the concentric arrangement of reading tables below, with their barely discernible occupants. Oft-interpreted as a symbolic representation of the immensity of the reporters' task – looking for a needle in a haystack, armed only with mundane materials like pencils, library cards, and public records, as they try to expose some of the country's most powerful men[2] – it is given a more speculative reading by Fredric Jameson, for whom it embodies at once a social metaphysics and a political aesthetic:

> The mounting camera shot, which diminishes the fevered researches of the two investigators as it rises to disclose the frozen cosmology of the reading room's circular balconies, confirms the momentary coincidence between knowledge as such and the architectural order of the astronomical totality itself, and yields a brief glimpse of the providential, as what organizes history but is unrepresentable within it.[3]

Jameson compares the shot to a series of views from the French New Wave director Alain Resnais's short essay-film, *Toute la Mémoire du Monde* (1956). That film – an exploration of France's Bibliothèque Nationale which doubles as a general meditation on human memory and knowledge – ends with an overhead shot of the Parisian library's reading room, the narrator telling us that the activities of the readers, each focused on his own small segment of knowledge, 'each working on his slice of universal memory, will have laid the fragments of a single secret end to end, perhaps a secret bearing the beautiful name of "happiness".' Jameson remarks that 'happiness' may not be the best term for this secret, as for us in the present, 'the ultimate referent, the true ground of being in our time', is capital.[4]

Overviews such as these dramatise, in the most general way, the processes of inquiry and sight involved in the endeavour to understand the world, and the magnitude of the ambition behind such an all-encompassing will-to-know. They also introduce us to tensions in how we approach the cognisability of nature and society, cosmos and capital. In the thirty-five years since the Eames made their film, increasingly sophisticated technologies have allowed cartographers to map the world, astronomers to map the universe, molecular biologists to map genomes, and atomic physicists to map the building blocks of the universe with every greater precision (the smallest measurement, planck length, being 10^{-35} and the size of the known universe being 46 billion light years in any direction, or about 10^{27} metres). In the time since the works by Pakula and Resnais, and especially with the recent shift into the age of 'Big Data', the vastness of these national collections has grown apace (the Library of Congress adds about 10,000 items to its collection per day).[5] Yet, to echo our epigram from Brecht, what do these filmic sequences – depicting knowledge as an overview, a vertical scaling-up and scaling-down, a modern *scientia dei*, or God's eye-view – tell us about the intelligibility of political economy and social conflict? If Jameson is correct, if the study of 'capital itself' is 'now our true ontology', then how can we shift from the way we imagine the absolute mapping of the universe and our knowledge of it to a cartography of capital as world-system?[6] If the image of world-knowledge as seamless continuum, so compellingly choreographed by the Eames, is hard to square with the complex and contested nature of scientific representations, an understanding of our social world that takes its cue from the related technologies of GPS and Google maps, while of unimpeachable military and commercial expediency, will prove a remarkably unreliable guide. The map will hinder the mapping, as we come to be captivated by fetishes of scale and precision that smooth over the world's contradictions; views which, to paraphrase Hito Steyerl, allow the vertical zoom to distract us from – or to punitively distort – a condition of 'free fall', in which neither our aesthetic devices nor our political strategies can comfort themselves with a 'single unified horizon'. As she observes:

The view from above is a perfect metonymy for a more

general verticalization of class relations in the context of an intensified class war from above – seen through the lenses and on the screens of military, entertainment, and information industries. It is a proxy perspective that projects delusions of stability, safety and extreme mastery onto a backdrop of expanded 3-D sovereignty. But if the new views from above recreate societies as free-falling urban abysses and splintered terrains of occupation, surveilled aerially and policed biopolitically, they may also – as linear perspective did – carry the seeds of their own demise within them.[7]

Surrealist Map of the World, published in *Variétés*, 1929

Before gleaning for such seeds, we should also consider how this politics of verticality is enmeshed with those of globality, with a planetary paradigm that seeks to hold at bay the potential disorientation that the scalar expansion diagrammed by *The Powers of Ten* could be seen as heralding. If 1968 was the year of the slogan 'the whole world is watching', it also signalled, in the activities of the Californian entrepreneur Stewart Brand and his *Whole Earth Catalogue*, the moment when this could be presented as a spiritual, cybernetic tautology: the whole world is watching... the world. Where the likes of Henri Lefebvre signalled '68 as the breaching of spatial difference into the 'homogeneous-broken' space of the logistical state,[8] the *Whole Earth Catalogue*'s only apparently eclectic synthesis of ecologism, cultural liberationism, technophilia and New Age found in the 'blue planet' what Anselm Franke has dubbed the 'last universalistic icon': a symbol of undifferentiated unity – beyond class, race, gender and antagonism – that doubled as the emblem of a 'boundless containment'[9] which continues to structure our present, relentlessly hunting down (unrepresentable) negativity, blandly voracious promise of integration and cosmic naturalisation of capital.

The visual regime of which Brand's earthscape proved a forerunner reproduces its planetary views through complexes of military and commercial satellites that together compose 'theory machines' which, while incarnating the logics of relativity nonetheless ceaselessly produces the effect of wholeness. Images of the 'whole earth' are today 'composites of massive quantities of remotely sensed data collected by satellite-borne sensors', not 'photographs' as such. As Laura Kurgan notes in her technically meticulous and illuminating exploration of our cartographic moment, the current ubiquity of 'mapping' 'disorients under the banner of orientation'[10] – and it is all the more ironic that a regime so inherently decentring should plug the holes in its knowledge, should dampen it its anxieties about (in Nietzsche's words) 'rolling from the centre towards x', with icons of the globe, the ultimate simulacrum of location. Brand's catalogue began with the distribution of badges that read 'Why haven't we seen a photograph of the whole Earth yet?' Today we might wonder, when will we *stop* seeing *so many* images of the whole earth, so many views of mastery that dissimulate our domination?

What is cognitive mapping?

The title of this book, *Cartographies of the Absolute*, is taken from a phrase in the preface to *The Geopolitical Aesthetic*, where Jameson employs it, in the singular, with reference to what he calls 'the aesthetic of cognitive mapping'. In a combative conference presentation in the mid-eighties, in the midst of Reaganite neo-liberalism and at a low-point of Left energies in the North (and not only), Jameson called for the emergence of such an aesthetic – a call intertwined with the broader effort to counter a widespread repudiation of the Marxist dialectic as a compass for cultural critique. The phrasing is important here: he didn't announce its existence, detecting its presence in a corpus of works, but stressed instead the political need for its elaboration in both theory and practice.

Such an aesthetic called for the imperative elaboration of a cultural and representational practice adequate to the highly ambitious (and, Jameson suggests, ultimately impossible) task of depicting social space and class relations in our epoch of late capitalism or postmodernity. Behind this call lay the claim – splicing the original formulation of 'cognitive mapping' by the urban planner Kevin Lynch with Althusser's definition of ideology as the subject's imaginary representation of their relation to the Real – that an inability to cognitively map the gears and contours of the world system is as debilitating for political action as being unable mentally to map a city would prove for a city dweller.[11] The absence of a practice of orientation that would be able to connect the abstractions of capital to the sense-data of everyday perception is identified as an impediment to any socialist project.[12]

Works emerging under the banner of this aesthetic would enable individuals and collectivities to render their place in a capitalist world-system intelligible: 'to enable a situational representation on the part of the individual subject to that vaster and properly unrepresentable totality which is the ensemble of society's structures as a whole'.[13] While such artworks and narratives would not be merely didactic or pedagogical, they would of necessity *also* be didactic or pedagogical, recasting what political teaching, instruction or even propaganda might mean in our historical moment.[14] What is at stake is the figurability or representability of our present and its shaping effect on political action. In a strong interpretation, the mapping of capitalism is a precondition for identifying any 'levers', nerve-centres or weak links in the political anatomy of contemporary domination.

The idea of cognitive mapping is embedded in an argument about historical change and the correlation between culture and political economy: each epoch develops cultural forms and modes of expression that allow it, however partially and ideologically, to represent its world – to 'totalise' it. Following seminal studies by Ernest Mandel and Giovanni Arrighi, Jameson posits three key phases in the patterns of correlation between historical forms of capitalism and modes of cultural representation. The three historical 'bases' are classical or market capitalism, monopoly capitalism (imperialism), and the contemporary period, the postmodern. Representation is not particularly difficult in the 'classical' age of capitalism. The 'totality' that determines the life of an individual can be plausibly delineated in terms of the political-economic space of city and nation, the space of the great realist and naturalist narratives. Representation, understood as an oriented relationship between individual and collective, locality and world, is unsettled with capital's colonial projection. The forces that determine the life of a clerk in late Victorian London, for example, stretch far beyond his lived experience or the arc of his perception (we will return in a moment to the way in which Jameson's periodisation relies on a view from the 'core' of the capitalist world-system). His 'truth', as Jameson puts it, is connected to the entire colonial system of the British Empire: a space so far-flung and complex – but, most importantly, so spatially segregated from his own – that he cannot possibly 'synthesise' it beyond the screen of jingoistic cliché. To adopt a psychoanalytic vocabulary, repression shades into foreclosure, and the imperialist world-system insists at the level of the political and economic unconscious.

> Such spatial disjunction has as its immediate consequence the inability to grasp the way the system functions as a whole. Unlike the classical stage of national of market capitalism, then, pieces of the puzzle are missing; it can never be fully reconstructed; no enlargement of personal experience (in the knowledge of other social classes, for example), no intensity of self-examination (in the form of whatever social guilt), no scientific deductions on the basis of the internal evidence of First World data, can ever be enough to include this radical otherness of colonial life, colonial suffering and exploitation, let along the structural connections between that and this, between daily life in the metropolis and the absent space of the colony.[15]

Whence the imperial end of 'immanence': though the inhabitants of the imperial metropolis may still delude themselves that it is possible, by dint of various investigative and formal stratagems, to uncover the truths of their social world 'from within' – expanding experiential and cognitive horizons – this is no longer the case. The lived experience of 'European nihilism', of a hollowing out or loss of meaning, has its disavowed origins in the colony, which in turn provides the 'other dimension' which – again silently – presents artistic modernism with (the content of) its (formal) 'problem', insofar as 'the structure of imperialism also makes its mark on [modernism's] inner forms and struc-tures'.[16] This materialist hermeneutic is what then allows Jameson to read the surging forth of experiences of infinity in the narratives of E.M. Forster or Virginia Woolf as indices of a formal struggle with a new configuration of totality, and thus a new kind of absence. In these writers, 'common-sense perception is disrupted by the emergence here and there of a dawning sense of the non-perceptual spatial-totality' of imperialism.[17]

It is in Jameson's attempt to tackle the imperial genealogy of cognitive mapping that we perhaps get the clearest sense of how representation, visibility and the aesthetic are articulated. The predicament of imperial modernism, so to speak, underscores how '*representational* effects' are also 'objective effects'; the spatial disjunction, and its ideological expression, is constitutive of the political economy of imperialism. It is in the *aesthetic* realm – whether in the formal innovations of 'high' art or in the containment of otherness performed by the racial imaginaries of popular art (e.g. adventure stories) – that we can register 'the most obvious consequences' of problems of representation that transcend literature and the arts. It is there that 'the mapping of the new imperial world system becomes impossible, since the colonized other who is its essential other component or opposite number has become invisible'.[18] In other words, a kind of political and economic invisibility undergirds a representational order which is in its turn both registered and transfigured at the aesthetic level. Conversely, we could argue, to *propose* an aesthetic of cognitive mapping under conditions of late capitalism could be taken as an attempt to force into being a certain kind of political visibility and thus to counter the objective, material effects of a dominant regime of representation.

Needless to say, cultural producers, for the most part, do not literally attempt to generate maps of the new interconnected global reality, or even to address it frontally. Rather, it is the task of the critic to tease out the symptoms of, at one and the same time, the consolidation of a planetary nexus of capitalist power and the multifarious struggles to imagine it – we could even say that such symptomatic reading, and dialectical criticism with it, gain in salience precisely with the actualisation of that 'world market' which is both capitalism's goal and its presupposition. Jameson points to the way in which, with the consolidation of the age of empire, various writers independently forged what he terms 'monadic relativism'. In Gide, Conrad, Pessoa, Henry

James and Proust one can see, to varying extents, how 'each consciousness is a closed world, so that a representation of the social totality now must take the (impossible) form of a coexistence of those sealed subjective worlds and their peculiar interaction, which is in reality a passage of ships in the night, a centrifugal movement of lines and planes that can never intersect.'[19] Our third and 'late' phase presents even greater challenges, or full-blown *blockages*, for representation and orientation.

As already noted, Jameson's notion of cognitive mapping builds on the US urban planner Kevin Lynch's book from 1960, *The Image of the City*. In that slim volume, Lynch was preoccupied with how urban inhabitants comprehend and navigate their built environment. As an urbanist, his concern lay in what sorts of cities, buildings, landmarks, and transportation systems afforded people the richest possible urban experience. Lynch argued that a well-planned city (or one that has evolved in an optimal way) should be 'legible' to its inhabitants, or even to a transient visitor. It should possess a certain '*imageability*'. In his investigation, Lynch looked primarily at Boston, Jersey City, and Los Angeles, interviewing and surveying residents to understand not only what they thought of their cities, but how they navigated them: how they pictured them in their minds as they made their way around, or how they would draw their urban environs from memory.

Arguably, the language of cartography and planning allows the political and aesthetic problems of representation or 'figuration' to be given a more concrete cast, a rooting in everyday life. Conversely, we should also be sensitive to the deeply ideological character of textual metaphors projected onto urban space, which, as Lefebvre repeatedly noted, are features of the modern *abstraction* of space. Beyond the contemplation of the 'image' of the city, mapping is above all a practical task involving an individual's successful, or unsuccessful, negotiation of urban space. Jameson writes that:

> Lynch taught us that the alienated city is above all a space in which people are unable to map (in their minds) either their own positions or the urban totality in which they find themselves. [...] Disalienation in the traditional city, then, involves the practical reconquest of a sense of place and the construction or reconstruction of an articulated ensemble which can be retained in memory, and which the individual subject can map and remap along the moments of mobile, alternative trajectories.[20]

Whence the demand of an aesthetic of cognitive mapping that would both reveal and instigate a certain 'self-consciousness about the social totality': 'The conception of cognitive mapping proposed here therefore involves an extrapolation of Lynch's spatial analysis to the realm of social structure, that is to say, in our historical moment, to the totality of class relations on a global (or should I say multinational) scale'.[21] As Jameson would later confess, he had, in a typical gesture, 'transcoded' the political and epistemological problem of class consciousness raised by the Hungarian Marxist philosopher Georg Lukács in the 1920s, to the context of sprawl and dispossession in the urban spaces of the 'postmodern' United States.[22]

Though Jameson's dialectical conception of the relation between social and aesthetic form makes his understanding of disorientation particularly potent, it is one that has some interesting precursors. In particular, it resonates with another programmatic text written amid political doldrums, C. Wright Mills's *The Sociological Imagination*, published in 1959, distilled an attempt to define something like a politics of inquiry and research that could dislocate technocratic one-dimensionality. It is not by chance that broadly aesthetic and projective terms – mapping, imagination – drive investigations aimed at thinking politically in anti-political times, nor that such texts continue to speak to present efforts to link political intervention and the comprehension of power's fulcrums, structures and devices.

Mills's bitter salvo feels far less dated than many of the prophetic declarations of his contemporaries ('the end of ideology', for one): 'Ours is a time of uneasiness and indifference – not yet formulated in such ways as to permit the work of reason and the play of sensibility. Instead of troubles – defined in terms of values and threats – there is often the misery of vague uneasiness; instead of explicit issues there is often merely the beat feeling that all is somehow not right'.[23] Among the unrelenting themes of *The Sociological Imagination*, drawing together its ethos of intellectual craftsmanship and its political ideal of 'collective self-control over the structural mechanics of history',[24] is an image of the social sciences as concerned with biography, history, and the intersections of these in the social structure. At first glance, this might seem anodyne enough, but, as the no-holds-barred attacks on structural 'grand theory' and the 'abstracted empiricism' of research bureaus suggest, Mills thought that this classical imperative of social thought was imperilled, and the political upshot was extremely grave.

The disparity between a public need for social knowledge and academic practice was what led Mills to sound harsh notes of reprobation against 'the social scientists of the rich societies', whose unwillingness to confront social problems was 'surely the greatest human default being committed by privileged men in our times'.[25] Instead, the vocation of the imaginative social thinker was to span the hiatus between individual anxieties and collective transformations, in so doing acquitting a task that was simultaneously intellectual and political – one which the shift from intellectual insurgency to administrative practicality threatened (and threatens) to render impossible. As Mills writes:

The 'basic problem' ... and its answer, usually require

attention both to the uneasiness arising from the 'depth' of biography, and to indifference arising from the very structure of an historical society. By our choice and statement of problems, we must first translate indifference into issues, uneasiness into trouble, and second, we must admit both troubles and issues in the statement of our problem. ... Any adequate 'answer' to a problem, in turn, will contain a view of the strategic points of intervention – of the 'levers' by which the structure may be maintained or changed; and an assessment of those who are in a position to intervene but are not doing so.[26]

What are we to make of such theoretical demands today, in a moment when the Cold War conformism that Mills was struggling against seems distant? It is worth recalling that Mills regarded his own epoch as a threshold and was in fact among the first to make theoretical use of the idea of the 'post-modern', to qualify what he called The Fourth Epoch, a period 'in which for the first time the varieties of social worlds it contains are in serious, rapid, and obvious interplay'.[27] Mills's idea of the sociological imagination can thus be seen to have endured in mutant form in the acrid debate around postmodernism.

In 1941, Mills wrote to a friend: 'All new things are "up in the air". If you stay too close to the "earth", you can never fly over new regions. Theory is an airplane, not a pair of heavy boots; it is of the division of reconnaissance and spying'.[28] Reconnaissance, spying, cartography, 'situational representation' – Mills and Jameson can be seen to share in an aesthetics of theory which, in its para-military and urbanist references, speaks to us of the entanglement between a totalising vision (its absence, or present impossibility) and a strategic imperative: finding and eventually controlling the 'levers'; diminishing powerlessness.

Other worlds

The 'worlding' of our planet and species, to use an expression of Heidegger, means that conceptions of the world as a unity, as a whole, are part of everyday life – increasingly so, as they come to be incorporated into the technologies that permeate the navigation of social space and the communications that largely constitute it. However much we operate with devices that mimic the *scientia dei*, this vision of global social space is subjective and partial – based on the vagaries of past experience, where we've been, what we've read, what we've seen, what we've heard, what we've been able to do with what's been done to us (which is to say on much that we are contingently or necessarily unconscious of). 'Cognitive maps' vary and recombine along axes of class, race, gender, sexuality and more; they affected by the vicissitudes of praxis, by different uses of the city, by ideologies, by those comprehensive attitudes toward reality which have taken the loaded name of 'world-views'. Some will be made invisible to others who are segregated and excluded. In ways that often barely contain conflict, the 'oneness' of space is saturated with difference and disconnection.

Even if we retain the orientation towards totality, we cannot evade the challenge of those critics who see the perspective of worlding as nothing but a late product of an imperial and colonial imaginary, which homogenises difference by locating it on a temporal line and projecting that line onto territories of extraction and subjugation. Though these questions largely transcend our investigation, it is worth noting that, as it emerges in Jameson's own understanding of the experience of modernity and the succession of literary genres, the problem of cognitive mapping is a problem posed in and from 'the West', as centre of capital accumulation as well as ideological lodestar for the imperialist imagination. As we already hinted at, it is indeed in the age of empire, as it overlaps and intertwines with the genesis of modernism and its aesthetic abstractions, that the nexus of cognition and cartography truly comes into its own.

Jameson argues that in the West, the consequence of the radical separation between the public and the private, 'between the poetic and the political', is 'the deep cultural conviction that the lived experience of our private existences is somehow incommensurable with the abstractions of economic science and political dynamics'.[29] Modernism's abstraction – manifest in its conceptions of space, time and agency, as well as in the formal inventions that it created to respond to or intensify the rifts in subjectivity – has to be understood in terms of its 'absent cause': the realisation, at the level of the 'political unconscious', that the causes of 'our' social life are elsewhere, in the processes of extraction, dispossession and subjugation that constitute imperialism and colonialism. The novels of Virginia Woolf, for example, are not *about* imperialism, but imperialism inhabits them, namely by shaping their form – like a strange attractor whose existence can only be registered in the deformations it elicits.[30] Considering this imperial genesis of cognitive mapping complicates its identification with the phenomena of postmodernity, expanding its geographical and temporal range, and revealing it as a complex product of an imperialist capitalist world-system spanning the late nineteenth, twentieth and twenty-first centuries.

The hypothesis that the forms of aesthetic experience are mediated by the geographies and rhythms of historical capitalism, and that we cannot understand the mutations of narrative without thinking through the disjunction between experience and abstraction, everyday life and the forces of capital in a fundamentally unequal world, lie behind a text by Jameson, written in the wake of his 'Cognitive Mapping' essay, which was the target of intense criticism from Aijaz Ahmad and a series of postcolonial critics: 'Third-World Literature in the Era of Multinational Capital'. We won't enter into the debate (qualified defenses of Jameson have been provided by Neil Lazarus, Neil Larsen and Mashava Prasad, among others[31]) but what's interesting for our purposes is that the US Marxist critic wanted to stress the importance of the political and epistemological *difference* between the first and third worlds, and their respective forms or genres of social and literary experience – not ecumenically vindicating the equal value of 'non-canonical' texts, but their antagonistic singularity. This was, perhaps inevitably, viewed by critics as a reinstatement of an us/them, present/past, centre/periphery mechanism; to the extent that he presupposed that American imperialism generated these dichotomies, Jameson may indeed have argued that they were true dichotomies, products of a really distorted world. But this was not for Jameson a *historical* difference, a difference between the advanced and the backward, since, to use a term from Fabian, these worlds are *coeval*.

The problem of cognitive mapping is over-determined – in ways that our book has only alluded to, working as it does principally with materials from the heartlands of capitalism – by this geopolitical, colonial and racial history. The disjunction between experience and abstraction that characterises metropolitan modernism in the age of empire can thus be contrasted with the 'national allegory' whereby in Third-World Literature 'the story of the private individual destiny is always an allegory of the embattled situation of the public third-world culture and society', giving rise to a 'very different ratio of the political to the personal'.[32] Rather than a demotion to the instrumental narrowness of a nationalist aesthetic, which Ahmad chastises Jameson for, the hypothesis is that third-world literature is invariably politicised, appearing not as a circuitous attempt to resolve the unrepresentability of capitalist domination, but as an allegory of anti-imperial and decolonising struggles.

The privileges of domination are accompanied by a poverty of experience and a deficit of knowledge: 'The view from the top is epistemologically crippling, and reduces its subjects to the illusions of a host of fragmented subjectivities, to the poverty of individual experience of isolated monads, to dying individual bodies without collective pasts or futures bereft of any possibility of grasping the social totality'.[33] In passage such as this, the 'we' of the subject of cognitive mapping is an unstable one – caught between the ignorance of the imperial (American) citizen and the striving for class consciousness of the anti-imperialist and anti-capitalist intellectual, whose unfulfillable epistemic imperative was perhaps best encapsulated by Sartre in a dense cinematic metaphor from his 'A Plea for the Intellectual'. For Sartre, the intellectual had to take the 'objective perspective of the dominated', which is that of:

> a *tilt shot* angled from below, in which [the elites and their allies] appear not as cultural elites but as enormous statues whose pedestals press down with all their weight on the classes which reproduce the life of society. Here there is no mutual recognition, courtesy or non-violence (as between bourgeois who look into each other's eyes at the same height), but a panorama of violence endured, labour alienated, and elementary needs denied. If the intellectual can adopt this simple and radical perspective, he would see himself *as he really is*, from below.[34]

Such a political torsion in perspective can also take artistic and cartographic form. Consider the 1929 Surrealist Map of the World, which lays out a joyously distorted planisphere in which the Atlantic, imperial North is compressed into inexistence, disappearing (Paris excluded) the White Centre, while, in a gesture in which some have discerned the primitivist impulse of surrealism, drawing the outlines of a hypertrophic Alaska and an engrossed Papua New Guinea. Soviet Russia looms enormous, in a gesture made all the more politically ambiguous by surrealism's conflicted communist allegiances. Though its primary impetus might have been 'belittling' imperial Europe and the capitalist

USA, its drive is perhaps more properly seen – as David Roediger suggests in a comparison with Haifa Zangana's *Destruction of a Map* (1978) – 'not only on challenging the specifics of imperialist, capitalist, and technocratic mapping but also on blowing the cover of exactitude and science that the idea of mapping as reproduction gives to the acceptance of a world of misery'.[35] It is this world – of black skins and white maps – which was also challenged in the map published in the Belgian surrealist review *Les lèvres nues* in 1956, in which the toponymy of the French hexagon had been reoccupied, counter-colonised by Algerian place-names.[36] Adding counterfactual inversion to distortion and substitution in the aesthetic and political arsenal of anti-colonialism, we could also consider those narratives in which white 'First World' domination is turned upside down – Terry Bisson's splendid *Fire on the Mountain* (1988) or Abdourahman A. Waberi *In the United States of Africa* (2006).

It remains to be ascertained to what degree the very desire for cognitive mapping is haunted by the fantasy of a 'perfect ratio' between the personal and the social, an aesthetic and political romanticism in which a disoriented subject of the capitalist core would project the possibility of true political knowledge and experience into the lives and struggles of subalterns. The Brazilian critic Roberto Schwarz has voiced an important caution in this respect, which suggests that we should resist the

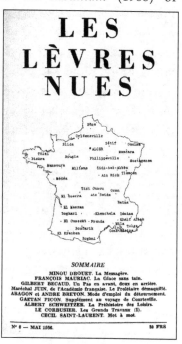

Cover illustration, *Les Lèvres nues #9*, 1956

temptation to treat cognitive mapping as a problem of the 'core', as if the latter were simply *more* capitalist and thus more prone to the disjunction between the personal and the political-economic, experience and abstraction:

> Once reality has migrated into abstract economic functions, it can no longer be read in human faces. Observation of life in a former colony, where social divisions remain stark, might then seem more rewarding. But such concreteness is suspect too since the abstractions of the world market are never far away and belie the fullness of spontaneous perception at every moment.[37]

We might then consider the disjunction between perception and abstraction to be a problem that is not resolved by the supposedly more direct, more *visible* exploitation at the periphery, but rather one that is inflected by the unevenness of capitalism and its geographically-differentiated formations, giving rise to differential instantiations and partial resolutions of a common problem of cognitive mapping.[38] The shearing pressure of capitalist unevenness gives rise to 'cracks' in form, where, in Franco Moretti's elegant formulation, 'the world goes in the strange direction dictated by an outside power; the worldview tries to make sense of it, and is thrown off balance all the time'.[39]

Mapping capitalism

The motivation behind this book is a simple one. We have been drawn to visual and narrative works that provide, in one way or another, glimpses into, or distant refractions of, the functioning of a global political economy; works that address the place of individuals and collectives within this 'sublime' system. It is written in the context of a noticeable increase, one could even say an inflationary boom, in tales and artefacts that, consciously or otherwise, seem to answer the call for an aesthetic of cognitive mapping. This book tries to thread its way through many of the works that we have found particularly cogent, and a few that have struck as revealingly disappointing. As such, it might occasionally read as a survey, at other times as an essay on contemporary aesthetics, or politics, or their intersection. We have conceived of it – in part compelled by the constraints of long-distance collaboration – as something like a collection of investigations, commentaries and arguments on, from and about works that have stoked our own cartographic desire. This compendium or panorama is tied together both by the undeniable regularities in contemporary representations of capital – common trends, themes and genres – as well as by an attempt to capture some of the critical fault lines in a variegated, if oftentimes repetitive, field of cultural production.

The works we have considered are also rather scattered – from the genre-transcending horror film *Wolfen* to the conspiratorial graphs of Mark Lombardi, from the cover art of various editions of Guy Debord's *The Society of the Spectacle* to the 'landscape theory' (*fûkeiron*) proposed by militant artists in the late sixties and early seventies in Japan, and from the video work of Melanie Gilligan to the cartography of William Bunge. We were drawn to them by the vagaries of taste and the contingencies of reception, but also by the wish to test a preoccupation with the mapping contemporary capital against a diversity of themes, methods and aesthetic strategies. All the works we consider share in an effort, more or less explicit, to depict and present a visual and narrative proposition about the social forces that shape their present. Even or especially when they home in on specific locales – be it David Simon's Baltimore, the industrial parks of the American South West in 'new topographics' photography or Lake Victoria in Hubert Sauper's documentary *Darwin's Nightmare* – they do so in a ways that register the reverberations of global capital through the specificity of their media and genres. In this respect, the mapping or figuring of capital is not a question of accuracy or resemblance, in which aesthetic form would be a mere instrument for knowledge, but constitutes a kind of force-field in which our conceptions of both modes of production and aesthetic regimes are put to the test.

While, as this introduction amply testifies, we have been influenced by the manner in which Jameson has insistently posed the problem of representing capital, what follows is not an application of the aesthetics of cognitive mapping to the recent past. First, while much of our focus is on the contemporary, we also reflect on many works that appeared long before Jameson called for the emergence of this aesthetic – for example, linking the construction of a 'complex seeing' in the contemporary visual arts to the dialectical montages of the 1920s.[40] Secondly, Jameson's theory of cognitive mapping is, in Colin MacCabe's words, one of the 'least articulated' of Jameson's categories.[41] Beyond the call for the emergence of the aesthetic and a few mentions sprinkled throughout his books, it is never presented as such as a coherent aesthetic, technique or theory. Its ephemeral status is of course also an index of its ubiquity, and a goad to its systematisation.

Cognitive mapping is not just a synonym for class consciousness, it is also intimately linked to the idea of dialectical criticism, the problem of Marxism and form, the Sartrean idea of totalisation. Though many of these themes from the Western Marxist critical canon will resonate in what follows, we are not seeking to systematise the unsystematisable. Jameson's formulation can still function as a cue for thinking about the present precisely because it does not provide a method, or advance a concept; rather, it poses a *problem* which is at once political, economic, aesthetic and existential. This problematic understanding of cognitive mapping also requires that, following Neil Smith's pointed criticisms of the convergent turns to space and culture in the 1980s, we remain sensitive to the how spatial metaphors can serve as a 'powerful mask', and work to 'fill in the conceptual abyss between metaphorical and material space'.[42]

One of the reasons we have latched on to the phrase 'cartographies of the absolute' is because of how it encapsulates the problem of visualising or narrating capitalism today. As the science or craft of map-making, cartography connotes a technical endeavour, judged by its accuracy. And so we experience it in our everyday, especially through the saturation of our lifeworld by the imperative of navigation (or, more sinisterly, of *targeting*). The 'absolute' is a theological and then a philosophical category, gesturing towards that which defies representation, which, contrasted to our mortal perception, is infinite and unencompassed. 'Cartographies of the absolute' is a wilfully paradoxical expression, but one that directs us towards the way in which picturing our social and economic world is a predicament at once technical and, so to speak, philosophical. Capitalism, after all, is a religion of everyday life, an actually-existing metaphysics.

Cartography is one of the privileged forms taken by contemporary critical art. In a manner that both mirrors and inflects a broader cultural and visual predicament, saturated with SatNavs, GoogleMaps and GIS, critical representations of society increasingly appear as mediated, both literally or metaphorically, by maps. In the fine arts, the past few years have seen significant collective exhibitions like *Uneven Geographies: Art and Globalisation*, curated by T.J. Demos and Alex Farquharson at Nottingham Contemporary and *Whose Map Is It?* at INIVA in London, not to mention individual works at countless shows and biennials.[43] Indicative surveys and advocacies of a cartographic political aesthetics include titles like *The Map As Art, An Atlas of Radical Cartography, Else/Where Mapping: New Cartographies of Networks and Territories* and many more. The 'cartographic' turn in the arts responds with a genuine and at times militant curiosity to the mutations being wrought by global capitalism and the oppositional counter-moves that sometimes meet it. The most interesting artists and groups producing work in this register demonstrate a capacity to address the question of cartography in a formally reflexive way, thwarting fantasies of locational transparency while strategically deploying the visual repertoires of geographic representation. Maps themselves however, though they punctuate our own narrative, are not our primary concern. We have taken their prominence in contemporary art practice more as the index of a much vaster problem, analogically identified under the rubric of 'mapping', than as a panacea for political disorientation. Maps have become some of our dearest fetishes, and some of what we consider to be our relations may just be social relations between maps (or antisocial and antihuman ones, as in drone targeting). It is perhaps fitting then to end this introduction with a warning and even a negation of the problem of cognitive mapping from its foremost advocate: 'Since everyone knows what a map is, it would have been necessary to add that cognitive mapping cannot (at least in our time) involve anything so easy as a map; indeed, once you knew what "cognitive mapping" was driving at, you were to dismiss all figures of maps and mapping from your mind and try to imagine something else.'[44] Which is also why, if anything, it is the second noun in our title that should be stressed.

The absolute, in Jameson's resolutely Hegelian phrasing, is a stand in for the totality of class relations on a global scale. Hegelianism and class analysis, though not the pariahs they were in the roaring eighties and nineties, are still unwelcome in fashionable company, and 'totality', in the tin ears of many theorists, still echoes with totalitarianism at worst, or paranoid criticism at best. For many then totality *is* conspiracy – a category corrupted by the metaphysical desire for coherence and the hubris of intellectual mastery. Yet capitalism as a totality is devoid of an easily grasped command-and-control-centre.[45] That is precisely why it poses an *aesthetic* problem, in the sense of demanding ways of representing the complex and dynamic relations intervening between the domains of production, consumption and distribution, and their strategic political mediations, ways of making the invisible visible. A social theory of capitalism as a totality, and the imaginations and aesthetics that strive toward it, could only be marked by an excess of coherence – as its opponents see it – to the extent that it papered over the incoherence (or contradictoriness, difference, unevenness) in its object, and refused to acknowledge its own theoretical activity – with all of its highly artificial stylistic, political, and method-ological devices. After all, among the first products of a genuine striving for orientation is disorientation, as proximal coordinates come to be troubled by wider, and at times overwhelming vistas.

Part I

The Aesthetics of the Economy

Euro-scepticism and Little Englander nationalism could hardly survive if people understood whose sugar flowed through English blood and rotted English teeth.
Stuart Hall

What Does the Spectacle Look Like?

When, in 1971, the French publishing house Champ Libre decided to republish one of the great efforts at representing contemporary capital, Guy Debord's *The Society of the Spectacle* (1967), Debord decided that he wanted nothing for the cover other than a geographic map of the world in its entirety. Not happy with the suggestions of Champ Libre's designer, he eventually settled on a world map from the turn of the century whose colours represented the commercial relations between the nations of the world and the course they were expected to take in the future – a distant descendant of Charles Joseph Minard's formidable nineteenth-century maps of commodity flows.[46] This choice elucidates a few things about Debord's theory of contemporary capitalism. First, the global character of the society of the spectacle. The different colours suggest that while the spectacle

Cover illustrations for Guy Debord, *The Society of the Spectacle*

'covers the entire globe', as Debord put it, it is not completely homogenous.[47] The fact that the map is of commercial relations rather than, say, political blocs, focuses our attention on production and circulation rather than geopolitical antagonism. Moreover, the choice of a map from the close of the nineteenth century, specifically one that anticipated contemporary patterns of international trade, suggests that the spectacle is intimately coupled to the world-economy and particularly its development since the age of empire.

The cover of the iconic English edition of *Society of the Spectacle*, republished by Black & Red in 1977 without official authorisation or approval from Debord, features a black and white image of a cinema audience, all donning 3-D glasses. This image casts the theory of the spectacle as an ocular-centric discourse and suggests that life under its spell resembles the experience of sitting passively in a darkened cinema, living vicariously through the actions of the characters on screen, with the added indignity of wearing silly glasses.[48] It directs struggle and critique to the world of leisure and consumption rather than production. Being a subject in the society of the spectacle is portrayed as analogous to being a spectator at a theatre production taking place on a traditional proscenium stage: one sits in one's chair observing the action, powerless to intervene in unfolding events. It pushes the reader – before even getting to the preface – to make a connection between Debord's conception of the spectacle and Plato's myth of the cave. The implication is that the technology modern society can enlist to keep subjects transfixed before its illusions is significantly more sophisticated than Plato's shadow puppets: a qualitative rather than quantitative difference. Furthermore, it seems to hint towards a close correlation between the concept of the spectacle and the growth of the media, and identifies the cinema – escapist Hollywood cinema in particular – as the temple of spectacle *par excellence*.

Both these choices of cover art present problems. Initially, the

Black & Red cover is the more misleading. For Debord, unlike a film or a 'show' (the plainer translation of the French *le spectacle*), the spectacle is not 'itself perceptible to the naked eye – even if that eye is assisted by the ear.'[49] More precisely, the 'spectacle is not a collection of images; rather, it is a social relationship between people that is mediated by images.'[50] To continue with the analogy of cave and cinema, when the spectator stumbles out of the theatre, stretches her legs and interacts with her companions, she is by no means escaping the confines of the spectacle. Trespassing into the projection room would not improve matters much.

The spectacle is continually reconstituted in the relationships people create in their everyday lives, which are obviously channelled by the media but also mediated by teachers, psychologists, politicians and the multifarious array of state and capitalist institutions. The mass media in general, claims Debord, is simply the 'most stultifying superficial manifestation of the spectacle'.[51] Debord is at least partially at fault for encouraging a misinterpretation centred on the equation of media-imposed passivity and spectacle. Giving short thrift to any notion of active or emancipated spectatorship, Debord considered the latter to be the general condition of those living in the society of the spectacle. His disdain for the spectator endured until his death in 1994, leading him to christen the inhabitants of those societies in which modern conditions of production prevail with the derisive title of 'Homo Spectator' as late as 1992.[52]

Debord's choice of cover art for the Champ Libre edition does not have as many obvious problems as the unauthorised 1977 translation, yet it leaves more questions unanswered, and is considerably vaguer in its intimation about the sort of theory advanced in the actual text – though it should be noted that the Livre de Poche image of an even more generic globe map, recently refunctioned as the wrapping for an insurrectionary projectile by Claire Fontaine, in *La Société du spectacle brickbat*

(2006), is even more so. The Champ Libre atlas image helps illustrate Debord's axiom that 'The spectacle has its roots in the fertile field of the economy'.[53] It figures his claim that the 'spectacle cannot be understood either as a deliberate distortion of the visual world or as a product of the technology of the mass dissemination of images. It is far better viewed as a *Weltanschauung* that has been actualized, translated into the material realm – a world view transformed into a material force.'[54] Debord elsewhere placed the origins of the spectacle firmly within the twentieth century, and the map can thus be read as a representation of the spectacle during its gestation phase. Yet it gives no hint as to why Debord chose to label this epoch the society of the spectacle. If the focus on Debord's book is 'capitalism today', as he claimed in his correspondence, how does 'spectacle' become the central term for defining this moment of capitalist accumulation, and how does this old map represent contemporary capitalism? Does it perhaps represent the very fantasies of globality, the imaginaries of globality that constitute the spectacle as the apotheosis of ideology itself?

For Debord, *The Society of the Spectacle* showed the essence of the spectacle as 'the autocratic reign of the market economy which had acceded to an irresponsible sovereignty, and the totality of new techniques of government which accompanied this reign'.[55] We start here with Debord not to embrace the concept of the society of the spectacle as the most cogent tool with which to prise open the contemporary, but because Debord's wrangling over his book's cover art nicely frames one of the main concerns of Part I: how has that realm of human affairs called 'the economy' been fixed as an object of inquiry and of technical or aesthetic representation? Debord's covers were striving to capture something of a relation that lords it over the totality of human experience and permeates the most insignificant of gestures. The practical, graphic problem of trying to signify or indicate the spectacle hints towards the broader tension between the global map and the social whole.

Debord's 1973 film of *The Society of the Spectacle* further complicates this short-circuit between capitalist totality and its emblems. Among the remediated images assembled by Debord we encounter cartographic ones – such as the profoundly ironic orbital map sporting the legend 'Rivoluzione della Terra' (approx. 49 min) – but also photographs and film footage of the earth that had only become available after the book's 1967 publication. The book's famous first lines – 'In societies where modern conditions of production prevail, all of life presents itself as an immense accumulation of spectacles' – are read over footage of astronauts manoeuvring in space (2 min 30 sec), a type of image that recurs at least twice later in the film, one matching quite closely the famous 'Earthrise' shot celebrated in the *Whole Earth Catalogue* (9 min 20 sec). The 'whole earth' can be seen as a crowning moment in the history of spectacular accumulation, planetary video-feed drowning out the negativity required for any political experience of totality.[56]

Chapter 1

Capitalism and Panorama

Prophecy now involves a geographical rather than a historical projection; it is space not time that hides consequences from us.

John Berger

Vision and value

In the context of a widespread preoccupation with the aesthetics of politics and the politicisation of art, less attention has been accorded to that area of practical and theoretical effort which we could temporarily class under the rubric of *the aesthetics of the economy* (we say temporarily, since a rigorous exploration of such an aesthetics soon enough challenges the separation between politics and economics). The latter comes to the fore with special urgency in moments of *crisis*, when our cognitive and political deficit, faced with the unravelling of a system whose intelligibility was always partial but is now suspended, can be registered at the aesthetic level – very broadly construed to include both artificially constructed representations and the individual and collective organs of perception.

As an initial methodological proviso, it is worth noting that representations *of* the economy and *in* the economy cannot be compartmentalised without losing the complexity of the question of representation itself. Susan Buck-Morss's essay 'Envisioning Capital' provides some orientation in this regard. Importantly, Buck-Morss presents the 'making' or 'fixing' of the economy as a fundamentally representational problem, to the extent that this process involves establishing agency and efficacy for an abstraction – 'picturing' economic relations and transactions as a unity, a totality, or even, to quote Marx, as an 'automatic subject'. Among other protocols, this mapping practice involves projecting a virtual external point from which to grasp and navigate a situation in which one finds oneself multiply embedded. Such an attempt at economic cognitive mapping is thus a kind of transcendence laboriously extorted from immanence, a painstakingly constructed dis-embedding.

In this story, the eighteenth-century invention and stabilisation of diagrams and images of the economy marks a kind of epistemic and political shift with significant repercussions for the very idea of representation. The economic representations which, in intimate conjunction with theoretical developments in political economy, allow one to envision capital, can, for instance, short-circuit or circumvent the problems of a linear, sequential discourse, as in the French physiocrat François Quesnay's reflections on his *tableau économique*: 'the zigzag, if properly understood, cuts out a whole number of details, and brings before your eyes certain closely interwoven ideas which the intellect alone would have a great deal of difficulty in grasping, unravelling and reconciling by the method of discourse'.[57] The tableau thus allows for a kind of totalising snapshot of temporal and material movements, which a sequential diagram of production would be incapable of figuring.

Quesnay was trained as a physician, and in light of this fact we could also think of the disciplinary sources of these representations: for instance in the passage from blood circulation, to the circulation of humans in cities, to circulations of money and resources.[58] The diagrams are not only diagrams of flow but also of origination (for the physiocrats, in the 'fertile' relation between landowners and farmers). It is crucial then also to think of the metaphorical reservoirs from which these representations draw, for instance the relationship to mechanical and organic models of the economy, with their varying presuppositions about the latter's integrity, composition, operation, degradation; and also to link these economic representations to their political counterparts, thinking of the passage, for instance, from the visibility of Quesnay's table, overseen by legal despotism, to the charting of the effects of the division of labour over time in William Playfair's *Commercial and Politics Atlas* of 1786, the first major work to use statistical graphs (Playfair is credited with inventing bar, line and pie charts).

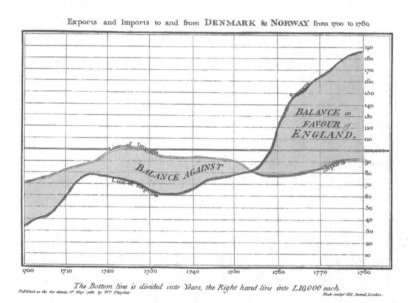

Exports and Imports to and from DENMARK & NORWAY from 1700 to 1780

The Bottom line is divided into Years, the Right hand line into L10,000 each.

William Playfair, *Time Series of Exports and Imports of Denmark and Norway*, from his *Commercial and Political Atlas*, 1786

Writing on the origins of the economy as an autonomous and self-defined domain, Timothy Mitchell underscores the efficacy and influence of 'mechanical analogies for the functioning of economic processes':

> At the same time, professional economists continued to imagine mechanical analogies for the functioning of economic processes. Irving Fisher's 1892 doctoral dissertation, which Paul Samuelson called 'the best of all doctoral dissertations in

economics', developed a mechanical model of an economic market consisting of a network of cisterns, levers, pipes, rods, sliding pivots and stoppers, through which the flow of water represented the working of the principle of utility. In 1892 he built a working model of this contraption which he used in his classes at Yale for years, until it wore out, and in 1925 he replaced it with an improved model. Fisher argued that the model provided not just a picture of the market but an instrument of investigation, and that the effect of complex variations in the market could be studied by altering the positions of the various stoppers, levers and pivots.[59]

These activities of modelling, diagramming, and envisioning are thus representational in what is perhaps a counter-intuitive sense, since they break with a model of representation as mirror, photograph, or correlation between signifier and signified, index and referent. As representations of practically-abstract processes and relations, they are also representations of invisibilities.

What is it that we see in fact, when we 'see' the economy? In Buck-Morss's account of Adam Smith's vision, only the results ('invisible except in its commodity effects'), from which, by induction, we infer a process (the division of labour, the real protagonist in Smith, whose distributional effects are spoken of in the providentialist, theological image of the invisible hand): 'We see only the material evidence of the fertile process of the division of labor: the astounding multiplication of objects produced for sale. Commodities pile up'.[60] Parenthetically, we can recall here a famous dramatic flourish from Marx's *Capital*:

Accompanied by Mr. Moneybags and by the possessor of labour-power, we therefore take leave for a time of this noisy sphere, where everything takes place on the surface and in view of all men, and follow them both into the hidden abode of production, on whose threshold there stares us in the face

'No admittance except on business'. Here we shall see, not only how capital produces, but how capital is produced. We shall at last force the secret of profit making.[61]

Much of the modernist corrective to the aesthetics inhering in the Marxist representation of capital – be it in Brecht's critique of photographic realism or Louis Althusser's speculations on the realism of the abstract – will of course strive increasingly to separate representation from sight. For, as Marx's own work makes plain, when we walk into the factory we don't see capital 'itself' any more than we see it in the market.

These novel representations of a causally determinant but invisible system are also formative of certain modes of subjectivity and patterns of desire. This, for instance, is how Buck-Morss correlates abstraction, representation and agency in the classical political economy of Smith:

> Looking up from my work at this landscape of things, I cannot see the whole of its terrain. It extends beyond my ability to feel. And this blindness leaves me free to drop my sight to the short horizon of my own self-interest. Indeed, blindness is the state of proper action. Within that horizon, however, desire is free and knows no bounds. This desire expresses itself as a pursuit for things. The pleasure of mutual sympathy, when I find my companion entering into my situation as I into his, is replaced by the pleasure of empathy with the commodity, when I find myself adapting my behavior to its own – which is to say, I mimic its expansiveness.[62]

The shift between different regimes of economic practice can also be traced in terms of forms of envisioning, which is also to say forms of abstracting – in the sense of selecting, extracting, and shaping material for cognition and action. Indeed, Buck-Morss details an increasing formalisation and stylisation in the movement from classical political economy to neoclassical economics, which is both inscribed in and impelled by a different representational regime. We can then in a sense 'read off' the politics of neoclassical economics from its relation to visual display:

> Neoclassical economics is microeconomics. Minimalism is characteristic of its visual display. In the crossing of the supply-demand curve, none of the substantive problems of political economy are resolved, while the social whole simply disappears from sight. Once this happens, critical reflection on the exogenous conditions of a 'given' market situation becomes impossible, and the philosophy of political economy becomes so theoretically impoverished that it can be said to come to an end.[63]

Among the productive insights in this inquiry into the envisioning, graphing and diagramming of capital is its focus on money as 'the measurement of economic activity, the universal representation of all commodities.'[64] One may even see money's hegemony as leading, especially with its detachment from a standard or base (in gold, namely), to a general 'ungrounding' of representation, from floating currencies to floating signifiers – a theme evident in the concern with credit-money in the philosophical writings of Lyotard and Deleuze & Guattari in the days of the 'Nixon Shock'. Alongside the greater abstraction and volatility of money, we can follow Buck-Morss in noting how the formalisation and mathematisation of the graph – supreme tool and emblem of neoclassical economics – entails that representation no longer needs to *refer*, in the sense of being physically mappable onto the outside world. As she puts it, the graph is 'not a picture of the social body as a whole, but statistical correlations that show patterns as a sign of nature's plan'.[65]

Where her approach is perhaps less productive is in the contention that Marx's contribution is in making visible the embodied suffering generated by capital's voracious abstractions. *Das Kapital*'s 'critical eloquence', she writes,

> is derived from the fact that we are plunged beneath the surface of commodity exchange to the actual level of human suffering – here thousands of factory workers –that was the lived truth of really existing capitalism during the era of its industrialization. Marx insisted that the human effects of the economy be made visible and palpable, and this remains his contribution to political economy no matter how often his theories – of crisis, of value, of increasing misery – may be disproved.[66]

This formulation could almost be reversed. It is not just that Marx's visualisations of mortified labour are expressly drawn from factory inspections and their meliorist, pragmatic aims, but that there were more detailed, incisive and poignant contemporary accounts of the misery wreaked by capitalism – not least Engels's own *Condition of the Working Class in England*. Though without doubt conditions comparable to, or worse than, those depicted in the mid-nineteenth century by Marx are still constitutive of contemporary accumulation, it is not the historically and geographically specific descriptions of human suffering, but the dialectical exposition of its founding dynamics that renders Marx's approach unique. What is at stake in this representation of capitalism is, to borrow Donald Mackenzie's expression, an 'engine, not a camera'. If Marx is still relevant then to the question of capitalism and its representation, it is to the degree that his theories – of crisis, of value, of increasing misery in the shadow of towering wealth – remain analytically and critically incisive even when his (borrowed and dramatised) descriptions of the cruelly concrete effects of abstract domination become anachronistic.

Ventriloquism

Though our concern here is primarily visual, when issues of opacity and invisibility are at stake it is not possible to ignore that the impasses of an economic aesthetics sometimes escape the tyranny of sight over cognition, that representational dramas may play themselves out through other senses. The notion that capital – as an infinitely ramified system of exploitation, an abstract, intangible but overpowering logic, a process without a subject or a subject without a face – poses formidable obstacles to its representation has often been taken in a sublime or tragic key. *Vast*, beyond the powers of individual or collective cognition; *invisible*, in its fundamental forms; *overwhelming*, in its capacity to reshape space, time and matter – but unlike the sublime, or indeed the tragic, in its propensity to thwart any reaffirmation of the uniqueness and interiority of a subject. Not a shipwreck *with* a spectator, but a shipwreck *of* the spectator.[67]

Yet unrepresentability need not be approached solely in this iconoclastic, quasi-theological guise. A surfeit of representations – of personae, substitutes, indices and images – may turn the unrepresentability of capital into something more akin to a comedy of errors, a sinister masquerade. Those abstractions that in one register are as immaterial, mute and unrepresentable as the most arcane deities, reappear in another as loquacious, promiscuous, embodied.

In classical rhetoric, *prosopopoeia*, the 'personation of characters', as the Roman rhetorician Quintilian puts it in his *Institutes of Oratory*, was the figure that made it possible for another to speak through oneself – to ventriloquise the soliloquy of an enemy, for instance; it also made it 'allowable even to bring down the gods from heaven, evoke the dead, and give voices to cities and states' (think for instance of the 'father of the atom bomb', Robert Oppenheimer's infamous *détournement* of the Bhagavad Gita: 'Now I am become death, the destroyer of worlds'). Readers of *Capital* will be familiar with the extensive use of this figure in the whole representational choreography of commodity fetishism, which shows us how the most bloodless of formal abstractions are put into motion, irrespective of the psychology of buyers or sellers, by the representational relations between one commodity and another. And so we have passages such as the following, from Volume 1, Chapter 1:

> We see, then, all that our analysis of the value of commodities has already told us, is told us by the linen itself, so soon as it comes into communication with another commodity, the coat. Only it betrays its thoughts in that language with which alone it is familiar, the language of commodities. In order to tell us that its own value is created by labour in its abstract character of human labour, it says that the coat, in so far as it is worth as much as the linen, and therefore is value, consists of the same labour as the linen. In order to inform us that its sublime reality as value is not the same as its buckram body, it says that value has the appearance of a coat, and consequently that so far as the linen is value, it and the coat are as like as two peas.[68]

The personation, or representation, of the real abstraction of value in the relation between commodities (this is still at the level of the relative form of value, before the revolutionising representational and abstractive powers of money enter the stage) is not a mere rhetorical ploy. It involves displacing the locus of subjectivity from persons to value, variously identified in *Capital* as 'an automatic subject', 'the dominating subject', a 'self-moving substance'. In a world that truly is inverted (rather than just erroneously perceived), men and women too speak, or are spoken by, the language of commodities.[69]

Marx sounds a warning here that cuts across philosophy, method and politics:

To prevent possible misunderstanding, let me say this, I do not by any means depict the capitalists and the land owners in rosy colours. But individuals are dealt with here only in so far as they are the personifications of economic categories, the bearers [*Träger*] of particular class relations and interests. My stand point, from which the development of the economic formation of society is viewed as a process of natural history, can less than any other make the individual responsible for relations whose creature he remains, socially speaking, however much he may subjectively raise himself above them.[70]

The entire difficulty then lies in attending to the very real, socially determining sense in which subjects are, in many of the most crucial aspects of their social existence, puppets of value, subjected by abstractions, while averting the kind of reactionary anti-humanism that would treat this 'real mystification' as a simple social fact, devoid of the ironies or reversibilities of representation. This point is nicely brought home by Slavoj Žižek in a discussion of how Hegelian spirit is not, as customarily perceived, a mode of idealist prosopopoeia. As he writes, we cannot conceive of 'objective spirit' as a meta-subject who runs history:

The moment we do this, we miss the point of Hegel's 'objective spirit', which is precisely spirit in its objective form, experienced by individuals as an external imposition, constraint even. There is no collective or spiritual super-Subject that would be the author of 'objective spirit', whose 'objectivization' this spirit would have been. There is, for Hegel, no collective Subject, no Subject-Spirit beyond and above individual humans. Therein resides the paradox of 'objective spirit': it is independent of individuals, encountered by them as given, pre-existing them, as the presupposition of their activity; yet it is, nonetheless, spirit, that is, something that exists only insofar as individuals relate their activity to it, only as *their* (pre)-supposition.[71]

So, a materialist prosopopoeia could be regarded as one among the rhetorical devices and figures to tackle the representability of those abstractions which, albeit invisible and intangible, and existing as complex processes and relations, not things, nevertheless determine, in generally overpowering ways, the actions of individuals and collectives.

In this light, it is noteworthy that variants of prosopopoeia often appear when an impasse in the ability to represent the causalities of economic domination and the logic of crisis is reached. American post-73 crisis cinema provides us with two memorable examples, the soliloquies through which in Sidney Lumet's *Network* (1976) and Alan Pakula's *Rollover* (1981), Ned Beatty and Hume Cronyn respectively channel the automatic, unstoppable abstract force of capital, expressed, in an imagery of delirium, precisely as something that defies representation.[72] That the speeches are voiced by capitalists, or to be more precise *managers* of capital, corporate valets of financial abstraction, takes us back to Marx's own distinction between capital and its human agents:

> As the conscious bearer [*Träger*] of this movement, the possessor of money becomes a capitalist ... The objective content of the circulation ... – the valorization of value – is his subjective purpose, and it is only in so far as the appropriation of ever more wealth in the abstract is the sole driving force behind his operation that he functions as a capitalist, i.e. as capital personified and endowed with consciousness and a will.[73]

Cinematic ventriloquisms of capital not haunted by crisis in the same way – to remain with film, the uplifting paeans to enterprise and industriousness at the end of the 1950s boardroom dramas *Executive Suite* (dir. Robert Wise, 1954) and *Patterns* (dir. Fielder Cook, 1956), or indeed the various monologues by Michael Douglas/Gordon Gekko in *Wall Street* (dir. Oliver Stone, 1987) and its sequel (2010) – often try to contain this impersonal dynamic of personification in more recognisably individual forms, whether heroic or villainous. In Scorsese's *Wolf of Wall Street* (2014) there is a very knowing subversion of the monologue: every time the protagonist is about to explain something about the structures of finance he interrupts himself, signalling that what drives his debauched accumulation is something other than the mere imperatives of the market; that its structures are indifferent to him, that perhaps ultimately that we don't want to know, and in the end couldn't even process the nature of the market in its key but abstract determinants, so we might as well go back to the spectacle of fraudulent selling and obscene expenditure. While in *Wolf of Wall Street*, a personal *id*, albeit one commensurate to that moment in the market's history, is at stake, in the other films the speaker assumes their dependency on this abstract driving force, and subjectifies himself accordingly. An instrument of an indifferent Other, namely the imperative of accumulation, such a subject would take the clinical figure of the pervert, enjoying the strange mix of activity and passivity, of freedom and irresponsibility that comes from being the *conscious* bearer of an unconscious process.[74] But Beatty and Cronyn's speeches present a far more unstable, and indeed in a sense seemingly unliveable fantasy. They tell us of being conduits for a power so encompassing as to make a mockery of any agency, even that of the shrewdest, most rational investor.

The fact that here it is the voice that 'represents', that stands in and articulates a fantasy of capital, of its inhuman agency, is significant. The unsettling impact of these monologues is borne at least in part by the voice's singularly ambivalent position

Sidney Lumet, *Network*, 1976

between matter and immateriality, body and spirit, external authority and inner conscience. Mladen Dolar has some insightful indications about this strange ontology of the voice, particularly suited to conveying the disorienting ubiquity and insidious dominion of financial capital in its crisis-generating mode:

> What language and the body have in common is the voice, but the voice is part neither of language nor of the body. The voice stems from the body, but is not its part, and it upholds language without belonging to it, yet, in this paradoxical topology, this is the only point they share. ... The voice cuts both ways: as an authority over the Other and as an exposure to the Other, an appeal, a plea, an attempt to bend the Other. It cuts directly into the interior, so much so that the very status of the exterior becomes uncertain, and it directly discloses the interior, so much so that the very supposition of an interior depends on the voice. So both hearing and emitting a voice present an excess, a surplus of authority on the one hand and a surplus of exposure on the other.[75]

The power and vulnerability of the voice is exquisitely captured by Beatty's booming, nearly hypnotic monologue in *Network*, where, modulating his peroration from authoritarian master to professor to utopian soothsayer, he verbally bludgeons 'The Mad Prophet of the Airways', Howard Beale, into submission to the logic of capital.

This shift from the customary patterns of commodity fetishism to what we could christen capitalist shamanism – a ventriloquism of impersonal structures that registers an ambient experience of powerlessness before the abstraction, complexity, and global scope of an economic spirit – crops up in the ordinary language of finance as well. Consider this exchange, taken from an interview carried out by the economic sociologist Karen Knorr-Cetina with a Swiss investment banker, who insensibly moves from Smithian dogma to zoomorphic delirium:

LG: You know it's an invisible hand, the market is always right, it's a life form that has being in its own right. You know, in a sort of Gestalt sort of way (…) it has form and meaning.

KK: It has form and meaning which is independent of you? You can't control it, is that the point?

LG: Right. Exactly, exactly!

KK: Most of the time it's quite dispersed, or does it gel for you?

LG: A-h, that's why I say it has life, it has life in and of itself, you know, sometimes it all comes together, and sometimes it's all just sort of, dispersed, and arbitrary, and random, and directionless and lacking cohesiveness.

KK: But you see it as a third thing? Or do you mean the other person?

LG: As a greater being.

KK: ( )

LG: No, I don't mean the other person; I mean the being as a whole. And the being is the foreign exchange market – and we are a sum of our parts, or it is a sum of its parts.

(...)

KK: I want to come back to the market, what the market is for you. Does it have a particular shape?

LG: No, it changes 'shape' all the time.

KK: And what is shape referring to (...) for you?

LG: Well, the shape is the price action. Like this (pointing at screen) tells me – short term trading. You know, try and buy here, sell here, buy here, sell here, buy here, sell here.[76]

This sort of figuration is not confined to the 'masters of the universe', but can be found across the class spectrum, for example, in workers' recognition of the supposed inevitability of a process no one, not even politicians or captains of industry, is able to thwart.[77] The despondent rendering of the logic of capital as a force of nature by those made redundant, however, is rarely articulated with the demented intensity of those who live themselves as its conduits.

This predicament – being spoken by the speech of capital – finds a kind of apotheosis in the figure of the Oracle in artist Melanie Gilligan's film series *Crisis in the Credit System* (2008),[78] a financial analyst operating for 'Delphi Capital Management' who is only capable of processing the sheer complexity of information required for forecasting by entering into an unconscious, hypnotic state, one which itself is thrown into a psychotic crisis of sorts as the abstract financial information comes to implode under the scale of its own magnitude and connectivity, and by the psychic pressure of political events. As he breaks down the Oracle utters these jagged indices of crisis:

highest unemployment for decades, falling standard of living, Alan Greenspan, there is no bottom in sight, crisis expression of underlying problems, debt, borrowing, no production, looting what's left of our resources... when necessities are only ours through the market... unemployment, bankruptcy... food riots...

It is tempting here anachronistically to adapt Quintilian's first century warning about proposopoeia as one that addresses the aesthetic and political difficulties of representing capital, finance and crisis today: 'great power of eloquence is necessary for such efforts, for what is naturally fictitious and incredible must either make a stronger impression from being beyond the real or be regarded as nugatory from being unreal'.[79]

What is true has no windows

In light of our brief survey of cognitive mapping and the sociological imagination in the introduction, it should be of no surprise that one of the most resonant present challenges to the regulative and ethico-political ideal of totality in social theory should come with its own 'aesthetics', its own arsenal of metaphors. Bruno Latour – approached here as an influential advocate of an all-too ubiquitous theoretical attitude – has recently proposed that we put the totalising theories generated by 'sociologies of the social' in their circumscribed and specific place, as fragile and monadic *panoramas*. We want to explore Latour's mobilisation of this term, how it encapsulates his dismissal of critical theory, and the manner in which its presence in the practices and writings of some recent artists engaged in social and political research might return us instead to the troubles and anxieties pinpointed by Mills and Jameson, showing in the end that the theoretical desire for totality is not incompatible with a painstaking attention to traces, objects and devices.

Actor-Network Theory's affinity for metaphors drawn from cartography ('mapping' controversies, sketching a 'topography of the social'), as well as logistics, forensics and accounting, is in keeping with a shift in social theory's imaginary which has also accompanied the 'network' as a talisman of modern managerialism. It is also exquisitely self-aware, hardly the working of an economic unconscious. ANT's choice of metaphor for its supposedly hegemonic rival, the 'sociology of the social', or the social theory of totality, is more intriguing and indicative. The cover of Latour's *Reassembling the Social* sports a coloured lithograph depicting the construction of a rather late panorama, a 'Taking of Antananarivo' from the *Exposition de Madagascar* in the 1900 Paris Universal Exhibition. Visually, we are presented with an impeccably 'critical' move. Despite the currency of the term, 'panorama' is a modern neologism, dating from the early 1790s, when it was coined to describe massive 360-degree oil paintings, exhibited in cylindrical buildings and viewed from platforms that hid the devices of light and architecture which made the immersion into the image possible.[80] It also covers a whole set of spectacular apparatuses, from Daguerre's diorama to the Kaiser-panorama, from the diaphanorama to the stereorama, which constitute 'nineteenth-century examples of the image as an autonomous luminous screen of attraction, whose apparitional appeal is an effect of both its uncertain spatial location and its detachment from a broader visual field'.[81] Thus, where Latour's lithograph shows all of the 'work-net' that goes into the production of the panorama-effect – the painters, the scaffolding, the workers, the heaters, the coat-racks, and so on – the projected viewer of the panorama would have wandered, with the help of studiously designed features, in a 'continuous boundaryless field'.[82]

The panorama also makes an appearance in Latour's collaboration with the photographer Emile Hermant in *Paris: Invisible City*, a book and online project that fleshes out the aesthetics of ANT as it wrestles with the problems and pitfalls of illustrating theory. Weaving together representations, textual and visual, of sites and modes of representation, and following the pathways through which the social come to be stabilised, *Paris: Invisible City* can be fruitfully compared to some recent photographic attempts at social mapping, though one wonders to what extent the methodological repudiation of totality imposes a skewed frame onto Hermant's photowork. Tellingly, and programmatically – though as ever with a heavy dose of Latourian irony – the book begins with a partially obsolescent 'panorama' of *Tout-Paris* in the *grand magasin la Samaritaine*, a 360 porcelain relief on the perimeter of the building's roof, which no longer quite matches up with the capital's skyline.[83]

By exploring and photographing some of the locations and conduits of the production and circulation of the representations of 'Paris' (deposits for street signs, meteorological stations, metro command and control centres), Latour and Hermant assemble a set of partial totalisations, channelling the conviction that the city is 'moulded by an accumulation of series of views, one after the other, *juxtaposed but never summed up*'.[84] They thus intend both to account for and to undermine the spherical projections and scalar hierarchies that supposedly structure our (aesthetic) common sense about the social and the city. In identifying totalisation with circumscribed and 'blind' sites (dioramas, panoramas, etc.), Latour enlists this photographic investigation in a political polemic, or rather an attack against the politicisation of 'sociologies of the social', one that of course does not refrain from marshalling an explicitly political rhetoric, as evident in this mission statement:

Paris: Invisible City doubles as a photographic education of those 'Romantics', who always dream of an assembly that, with neither schedules nor lists, signs nor intermediaries, transparently reveals Society in its immediate solar presence. By dreaming of a full, entire reality, common sense simply dreams of a diorama enclosed in a narrow room. For four thousand years we haven't had the good fortune of living in a Swiss canton, gathered in the town square to decide on current affairs, hands raised. It's been a long time that Society hasn't seen itself entirely in a single glance.[85]

But these same 'Romantics', friends of political transparency and social totalisation (Latour's critical arsenal here unimaginatively repurposes that of anti-utopian and anti-socialist discourse), are also ones who allegedly 'scorn the poor actors overwhelmed by the environment'. The latter, we are confidently told, *pace* Mills and his 'trouble', 'are never particularly overwhelmed, let's rather say they know they are numerous, populous, mixed, and that they ceaselessly sum up in a single word whatever it is that binds them in action'.[86]

As a metaphorical device, that is a real, if mostly obsolescent device enlisted as a metaphor, Latour's panorama fills a precise function: it permits him to 'regionalise' (or perhaps more literally, belittle) the pretensions of social theory to 'see it whole', in the name of the right of actors to frame their own worlds and the duty of researchers to pay all the 'transaction costs' involved in moving from one frame to another, one actor to the next. Latour is perfectly cognisant of the Millsian desire to see it whole, as evidenced by his citational use of the kind of generic question which would lead to the conjunction of the sociological imagination and a desire for politics: 'There is something invisible that weighs on all of us that is more solid than steel and yet so incredible labile'; 'Why are we all held by forces that are not of our own making?'.[87] But, in a strange re-edition of a Weberian injunction, he wants to cut the very knot indicated by Mills and Jameson, the one that ties together (individual and collective) subjective disorientation, theoretical elaboration and political action. One of Latour's curiously disembodied examples is worth citing here:

A worker, who labors all day on the floor of a sweatshop, discovers quite quickly that his fate has been settled by invisible agents who are hidden behind the office walls at the other end of the shop. ... So, it is perfectly true to say that any given interaction seems to overflow, with elements which are already in the situation coming from some other time, some other place, and generated by some other agency. ... Although there is indeed, in every interaction, a dotted line that leads to some virtual, total, and always pre-existing entity, this is just the track that should not be followed, at least for now: virtual and shadowy it is, virtual and shadowy it should remain. Where political action has to proceed forward, sociologists should fear to tread. Yes, interactions are made to exist by other actors, but, no, those sites do not form a context around them.[88]

It is particularly revealing that, despite the supposed primacy of the actor, and Latour's rather opportunistic appropriation of critiques of the silencing of marginal and minoritarian (or prole-tarian) actors, he is advising here that the workers' drive to see it whole be thwarted. The pretext here seems to be that, *contra* Mills, this 'theoretical' drive is not that of the actors themselves. What's more, sociology and politics should be compartmen-talised, not allowed to devolve into hybridity (a curious differen-tiation indeed from the theorist who once instructed us that we have never been modern...). When Latour writes that 'It is little use to respect the actors' achievement if in the end we deny them one of their most important privileges, namely that they are the ones defining relative scale',[89] we could easily retort, and the examples are legion, that most (human, exploited, oppressed) actors rarely if ever control the relative scales within which they work and live.

Considering the centrality of capitalism to the development of the 'sociology of the social', it's little mystery that this should be one of Latour's bugbears. In *The Pasteurization of France*, he had declared that 'Like God, capitalism does not exist. ... Capitalism is still marginal even today. Soon people will realize that it is universal only in the imaginations of its enemies and advocates'.[90] This theme is extended in *Reassembling the Social*: 'From the floor of the sweatshop is there any canal that goes to a "capitalist mode of production" or to an "empire"? ... Capitalism is certainly the dominant mode of production but no one imagines that there is some *homunculus* CEO in command, despite the fact that many events look like they obey some implacable strategy'.[91] Precisely, no one – and certainly not theorists like Mills or Jameson – imagines that capitalism as a totality possesses an easily grasped command-and-control-centre.[92] That, as we've already suggested, is precisely why it poses an *aesthetic* problem, in the sense of demanding ways of representing the complex and dynamic relations intervening between the domains of production, consumption and distribution, of making the invisible visible.

Sliding from the register of manual labour to that of financial mediations, in *Reassembling the Social*, Latour writes that,

> capitalism has no plausible enemy since it is 'everywhere', but a given *trading room* in Wall Street has many competitors in Shanghai, Frankfurt, and London ... that may shift the balance from an obscene profit to a dramatic loss. Yes, Wall Street is connected to many places and in this sense, but in this sense only, it is 'bigger', more powerful, overarching. However, it is not wider, larger, less local, less interactive, less an inter-subjective place than the shopping center in Moulins, France or the noisy and smelly market stands in Bouaké, Ivory Coast. Don't focus on capitalism, but don't stay stuck on the screen of the trading room either: follow the connections, 'follow the actors themselves'.[93]

Though it may be possible to gain precious insights into the metric and mathematical machinations of contemporary finance armed with such injunctions,[94] they should be disjoined from the high-handed and sterile dismissal of social-theoretic accounts of capitalism. If we don't 'focus' on capitalism 'itself', phenomena like the crisis that began in 2008 will be artificially banished from the purview of our inquiry. That a theory of crisis, for instance, could be dismissed due to its inevitable incapacity to trace *all* the 'canals', seems to move beyond a methodological polemic to a lobotomy of the relation between social research and political action, and to a muzzling of those 'actors', rising in number, who seek such explanations.

It is beyond doubt that it often costs little to make generic gestures towards capitalism, or other totalising horizons; to treat individual agents and objects as mere husks for some Spirit or other. And the methodological requirement that one locate the sites for the production of globality, or of scale, is surely both an important investigative prescription and an antidote to a metaphysical treatment of totalities. But Latour's way of local-ising the global, in the name of a methodological ethics of flattening, proves to misunderstand both staging and totality. Speaking of modernist masters of the panorama like Hegel and Marx, he writes:

> They design a picture which has no gap in it, giving the spectator the powerful impression of being fully immersed in the real world without any artificial mediations or costly flows of information leading from or to the outside. Whereas oligoptica are constantly revealing the fragility of their connections and their lack of control on what is left in between their networks, panoramas give the impression of complete control over what is being surveyed, even though they are partially blind and nothing enters or leaves their walls except interested or baffled spectators. ... Most of the time, it's this excess of coherence that gives the illusion away.[95]

But the modern panorama (perhaps there is no other kind) is not the static, mastered totality that Latour wishes to stage. As the cases of Mills and Jameson suggest, it is only those who believe that theories of the totality conform to a Stalinist caricature of 'dialectical materialism' who would tax them with an 'excess of coherence'. A social theory of capitalism as a totality, and the imaginations and aesthetics that strive toward it, could only be marked by such an excess if it neglected the incoherence, the trouble in its object, refusing to acknowledge its own theoretical activity – with all of its highly artificial stylistic, political, and methodological machinations. If anything, great dialectical writing would constitute precisely the kind of panorama that would, like the lithograph on the cover of Latour's book, present both the totality and its constituent devices, as well as the attendant gaps and dislocations.[96]

It was of one of the more heterodox of the twentieth-century's dialectical thinkers who noted that, somewhat in the way of a Leibnizian monad, the panorama's truth could be drawn precisely from its closure. In trying to understand the physical and fantasy spaces of an emergent nineteenth-century commodity culture, Walter Benjamin pointed to the panorama as a space in which the blindness of the interior was a pre-condition of perspective, but also where fiction was a condition of truth: 'The interest of the panorama is in seeing the true city – the city indoors. What stands within the windowless house is the true. Moreover, the arcade, too, is a windowless house. ... What is true has no windows; nowhere does the true look out to the universe'.[97] In *The Arcades Project*, he quotes Baudelaire, 'These things, because they are false, are infinitely closer to the truth'.[98] In this sense, it would be in plunging into the closed, 'false' perceptual worlds generated by capitalism that we could draw the necessary sustenance for thinking against it.

We can also note, following Jonathan Crary, that the panoramas of the nineteenth century did not in the end elicit a totalising perception that would nourish the seamless illusion of mastery, of vision wedded to knowledge. Though, on one level, the panorama 'provided an imaginary unity and coherence to an external world that, in the context of urbanization, was increasingly incoherent', it 'was in another sense a derealization and devaluation of the individual's viewpoint'. In fact, 'the panorama image is consumable only as fragments, as parts that must be cognitively reassembled into an imagined whole. A structure that seems magically to overcome the fragmentation of experience in fact introduces partiality and incompleteness as constitutive elements of visual experience'.[99]

Purposeful immersion

It is in the intersections between the will to a totalising vision, cognitive and perceptual fragmentation, and the opacities and blind spots generated by political and economic change, that the most appealing invocations or practices of the panorama in the contemporary arts are to be sought. Repurposing aesthetic creation as social and political research, various attempts to 'see it whole' have confronted the complexity of that 'it' – be it contemporary capitalism and/or the political machinations of an imperial security state. Among artists taking up this challenge, Mark Lombardi and Allan Sekula are of particular note for their turn to the very concept of 'panorama' as a resource to grasp the aesthetic and cognitive challenges of tracing or representing totalising political and economic processes.

Lombardi began his career labouring as an archivist and librarian during the day and struggling as an abstract painter with a consuming interest in political and economic scandals by night. Inspired in part by the information design of Nigel Holmes and Edward Tufte, as well as panorama painting, in the mid-nineties he began work on a series of large-scale pencil drawings of networks of finance, collusion and covert activity – what he called 'narrative structures' – which trace the connections between different private actors, banks, corporations, and government agencies. The deadpan titles of some of these delicate diagrams gives an inkling as to their content and character: *George W. Bush, Harken Energy and Jackson Stephens (Fifth Version)* (1999); *Banca Nazionale del Lavoro, Reagan, Bush, Thatcher and the Arming of Iraq, 1979-90 (Fourth Version)* (1998); *Inner Sanctum: The Pope and his Bankers Michele Sindona and Roberto Calvi ca. 1959-82 (Fifth Version)* (1988). From one angle, Lombardi's art would seem to verify Latour's oft-stated suspicions about critical theory and critical art descending into forms of conspiratorial thought, in which the network is not a careful method for the tracing of associations, but a paranoid represen-

Allan Sekula, six photographs from *Fish Story*, 1989-1995

tation of a total and unverifiable Power. Indeed, Lombardi has been criticised by other practitioners of art as political research (or political research as art) for producing indisputably beautiful images whose cognitive consistency is nevertheless as tenuous as the pencil-drawn lines between the named 'nodes' of collusion.[100]

As the painter Greg Stone claims, reflecting on Lombardi's drawings, 'We didn't know what we were looking at when we read about it (the political and economic scandals, etc.) – it had to be articulated visually'.[101] An enormous amount of research went into the drawings, yet their pedagogic capabilities – narrowly conceived in terms of their ability to inform the viewer about a given scandal – are severely limited. As Robert Hobbs notes, 'Instead of simply solving crimes, Lombardi's work often intensifies their mystery'.[102] Lombardi's rhizomes eschew any hierarchy of responsibility, and instead depict networks of sometimes only loose association, never coming together in a simple solution, some kind of cognitive or political epiphany. His 'structures' are painstakingly neat, their immediate visual effect is one of ordered complexity; but cognitively, and politically, they are nothing if not messy: 'his brilliantly detailed drawings actually make things harder to understand, not easier. Looking at the endless miasma of names, institutions and locations, his charts are more about obfuscation than revelation … Lombardi's drawings are like a pointillist work, best viewed from afar. From a distance you can see that a system has been revealed, but the closer you get to it the more invisible it becomes.'[103] If studiously explored, they could at best orient and punctuate an investigation, driving the researcher back to the archives to discover the precise texture of the links and transactions between different actors – whose types are minimally indicated by Lombardi with simple, broken or crenellated lines.

Pausing in front of these vast sheets, whether for seconds or hours, but unable herself to plunge into the thickets of research into the 'deep state', it is difficult to imagine what the uninitiated visitor to a museum or gallery might 'learn' from Lombardi's work. Even if endowed with a decent knowledge of the BCCI scandal or the networks in which Roberto Calvi or George Bush (I and II) operated, it would take a considerable investment of intellectual labour to make any 'sense' of the drawings, to specify their structure and project a coherent narrative onto them. No doubt, this was something that Lombardi was aware of when elaborating his practice. In that respect, the drawings are intentionally opaque. In later works, for instance, the viewer isn't even provided with a legend to explain the difference between a solid line, a dotted line, and the squiggles that intervene in some of the lines of connection. Lombardi's obsessive passion for inquiry is writ large, but it is also evident that he judged that the results of this research could not be presented with the kind of direct communicational economy endorsed by Tufte. Thus, as much as Lombardi's work is about the actual conspiracies revealed by his drawings, it is also about the very gap – the perhaps unbridgeable gap – between lay viewers and the activities of, and collusion between, the 'overworld' and the 'underworld'.[104]

Among Lombardi's papers are two unpublished manuscripts, one on the 'parapolitical' links between the US government and the drug trade, entitled *On Higher Grounds*; the other a history of the panorama as art form.[105] Lombardi, who had worked in minimalist and conceptual registers, began to produce his drawings as research aids for personal investigations into covert dimensions of US state power. The diagrams – which tellingly shifted from a timeline approach to spherical configurations – eventually attained autonomy, becoming a distant contemporary equivalent of the kind of enclosed and encompassing history paintings that were a privileged genre for many of the panoramas studied in Lombardi's other, art-historical manuscript. Lombardi's narrative structures thus reiterated that fertile tension between totalisation and fragmentation, clarity and opacity, overview and oversight, which, following Crary, we can note in nineteenth-century panoramas themselves. Rather than fantasies of an all-knowing eye, or indeed conspiracy *theories*, they become records of research at the same time as aesthetic goads to inquiry.

The fact that panorama, as colloquially used, derives from those obsolescent but formative devices of modernity that so beguiled Benjamin, is indicative of the force that artificial constructions of perception have both on our everyday life and on our experience (or lack thereof) of our position in a broader social order or historical dynamic. But modernity, as the photographer and critic Allan Sekula has detailed in *Fish Story* – his critical montage of photographs, long essays, and observations on the mutations of maritime capitalism – is also a passage from panorama to detail, from a mercantile ideology of the sea as an object of strategic overview to an increasingly Taylorised and militarised 'forgotten space', in which the difficulty in producing an aesthetic 'realism' concerning capitalism's more abstract dimensions is redoubled by the rendering invisible, and powerless, of maritime labour. While Sekula's photographs resist, with their attention to the slowness and materiality of labour at sea, the immaterialisation of global capitalism into a smooth space of flows, his essays track the withering away of the historical and geographical overview and the intrusive specialisation of the logistics of perception, the emergence not just of detail, but of targeting and of what we'll consider in Part III under the heading of the 'instrumental image'.

This can also be thought as a passage from one panorama, the sort that contributed to the unfolding of maritime power in the seventeenth-century, to another 'panorama', best exemplified perhaps in those control towers in container ports where the immensely profitable modularisation of maritime logistics is monitored through organisational and calculative activities on screens – veritable oligopticons of the sea. It is also a shift between different worlds of capital, namely, into a world that 'submits the totality to the same pecuniary accounting proce-dures with which it had grasped the fragments'.[106] If considered in terms of the aesthetic and economic transformations of the sea, modernity, that well-known Latourian nemesis, 'dissolved the edifying unity of the classical maritime panorama'.[107] But this process is not one of seamless integration: 'under conditions of social crisis ... the bottle of representation can burst, and the sea again exceeds the limits imposed upon it by a de-radicalized and stereotypical romanticism'.[108] And in order to burst (the dominant order of) representation via (acts of) representation, one needs to immerse oneself in the 'social', in a connectedness that counters the smoothness of financial networks with the abjected practical inertias of material flows:

> in an age that denies the very existence of society, to insist on the scandal of the world's increasingly grotesque 'connect-edness', the hidden merciless grinding away beneath the slick superficial liquidity of markets, is akin to putting oneself in the position of the ocean swimmer, timing one's strokes to the swell, turning one's submerged ear with every breath to the deep rumble of stones rolling on the bottom far below. To insist on the social is simply to practice purposeful immersion.[109]

It could also be argued that the end of the seventeenth-century panorama, of that kind of visual-mercantile dominion, gives way to a *proliferation* of panoramas, first as an attempt to encompass the world in a closed space, then directly to control, shape and measure it. But rather than this making possible a liberation from totalisation, what we are everywhere confronted with is a molecular or capillary form of totalisation-by-assemblage or totalisation-by-control. Against ambient asseverations against 'seeing it whole', Sekula's practice, in its 'impure', reflexive and polyvalent approach, its systematic montage of media and formats, shows that it is indeed possible to do considerable justice to the sociological imagination in both social theory and artistic practice. Sekula also criticises a view of frictionless transactions, seeing it in fact as a contemporary fetishisation of finance and the immaterial,[110] and he undoes through his photographic practice the idea of a commanding overview of the totality[111] – but he does so from the standpoint of a painstaking critique of the ways in which de-totalisation and de-nationalisation have been rolled out on the neoliberal scene, not as an *ontologies* but as *strategies*, ones that can and should inspire opposition, in political and artistic registers alike.

Dark geography

How do we depict what is literally out of sight? What does it mean to detail the sites in which representations of our world are produced when these are 'black sites', whose invisibility is violently guarded? For the past several years, geographer, artist and writer Trevor Paglen has been creating a body of work investigating the contours of the US security apparatus. This work – which comprises photo series, installations, critical travelogues and political commentary – is an incursion into the more secretive reaches of the 'dark world', the covert geography of empire through which the US state conducts its classified military and intelligence activities. His exploration of this world and its accompanying juridical vacuum doesn't just lead Paglen to remote desert locations in which the national security state has hived itself off from the everyday lives of most citizens and denizens. These are of course included, but beyond the sweltering expanses of the Nevada desert and the carceral dungeons on the outskirts of Kabul, Paglen's investigation takes him to sites like the geography department at the University of California, Berkeley (where he carried out his own doctoral research), corporate parks in northern Virginia and hotel conferences rooms in New Mexico. What transpires from this interlinked series of inquiries, is the war on terror's 'relational geography' – a geography that permits us to pose questions such as: 'How do facts on the ground in Afghanistan sculpt the future of the United States?'[112]

Paglen's photo series, *The Other Night Sky*, captures classified reconnaissance satellites by taking long exposures of the nocturnal heavens, while in *Limit Telephotography* he employs photographic equipment designed for capturing astronomical imagery to 'access' secret military installations at great distances. Vastness and indeterminacy connect both series, and one has to take the artist's word that one is in fact looking at a spy satellite and not merely an ordinary communications satellite, at a secret military installation and not merely a remote airport hanger. The banality of appearances – to which we'll return in the discussion of logistical landscapes in Part III – is one of the abiding cognitive and political leitmotivs of this work. In *I Could Tell You but Then You Would Have to Be Destroyed by Me* (2007), Paglen presents a collection of patches connected to various 'black world' projects – incongruous hieroglyphs of covert action, featuring, for example, an image of a topless woman riding a killer whale with the words 'Rodeo Gal' stitched onto the patch, worn by flight crews involved in testing a classified cruise missile prototype. The distance in this work is not as literal as in Paglen's photography, but the viewer is yet again compelled to put a great trust in the veracity of the artist's revelations. Here too a layer of mystery cloaks the images, intensified by the thrilling notion that one is perhaps viewing sensitive, classified information. In intimating, through its artefacts and traces, the reality of an unimaginably vast and largely inaccessible universe of secrecy and domination, the knowledge of which seems as essential for any understanding of contemporary power, just as it remains restricted in its totality for anyone without the highest levels of security clearance, these works engage our epistemological drive. As Gail Day and Steve Edwards write, Paglen's 'photographs are just one element in a process of tracking and location. They are traces, put into the public domain, of power structures that otherwise remain invisible. If Paglen does not provide us with an actual map or diagram, his work nonetheless offers cognitive maps that reveal hidden facilities of the secret state'.[113] Paglen's attention to geographic materiality, to the production of space that accompanies the proliferation of secrecy, arguably allows him to attain a degree of definition which is lacking in the purely diagrammatic trajectories of Lombardi.

Trevor Paglen, *KEYHOLE IMPROVED CRYSTAL from Glacier Point (Optical Reconnaissance Satellite; USA 224)*, 2011

Be it geographically or economically, the secret state delineated by Paglen is immense – its 'sublimity', to borrow from Kant, is *both* mathematical and dynamic. In the United States approximately 4 million people have security clearances to work on black world classified projects, in contrast to the 1.8 million civilians employed by the federal government in the so-called 'white' world.[114] In terms of sheer quantity of pages, more of the recent documented history of the US is classified than not. While the number of classified documents can only be roughly estimated in the billions, precise and jaw-dropping figures do exist: in 2001, for instance, the US Information Security Oversight Office reported a \$5.5 billion expenditure to protect secret documents.[115] While Wikileaks has provided us with a vast moving archive of the covert communicational networks through which US imperialism threads itself, and the Snowden revelations with a sense of the stupefying scale of transactions mined by the security state, the geographical blueprint of secrecy is more difficult to quantify[116] – the immense classified spaces of the US South West, dispossessed from their indigenous inhabitants, shading over into a very heterogeneous series of sites within and without the United States, from business parks in which CIA shell companies are allegedly located to the torture dungeons to which the victims of extraordinary rendition are dispatched.[117]

Paglen identifies the Manhattan Project as the founding act of the black world, in its enormous expenditure, mobilisation of manpower, and generation of huge covert sites employed unprecedented magnitudes of materiel and human capital: 'Building secret weapons during a time of war was nothing new. Building *industrialized* secret weapons, employing hundreds of thousands of workers, the world's top scientists, dedicated factories, and multibillion-dollar budgets hidden from Congress – that was unprecedented. It would become a standard operating procedure'.[118] If the quest to build the world's first atomic bomb set the coordinates of the black world, it became a legitimate part of the US state with the National Security Act of 1947, which, among other things, spawned the Central Intelligence Agency and the National Security Council, and merged the various branches of the military into the Department of Defense. A key event in this history is the CIA Act of 1949, which remains the statutory basis for the black or classified budget. Remarkably, the bill was voted into legislation without congress even being able to read it in its entirety. It had been vetted by the Committee on Armed Services, which removed portions of the bill that were 'of a highly confidential nature'. As Paglen emphasizes: *'The bill itself was secret'*.[119]

Trevor Paglen, *Code Names: Classified Military and Intelligence Programs (2001-2007)*, 2009

Blank Spots on the Map depicts the black world as a space of power whose influence is global and systemic. In her reflections on the Pentagon Papers, Hannah Arendt wrote that 'secrecy – what diplomatically is called discretion as well as the *arcana imperii*, the mysteries of government – and deception, the deliberate falsehood and the outright lie used as legitimate means to achieve political ends, have been with us since the beginning of recorded history'.[120] While this is undoubtedly the case, what is novel about the current period is not only the fact that secrecy has been generalised – to borrow an idea from Guy Debord's *Comments on the Society of the Spectacle* – but that the black world has swelled in size as a driving component of the military-industrial complex. This does not just impact the art of government, but has insidious effects on society as a whole. Paglen captures this well when, echoing earlier arguments about the permanent arms economy, military Keynesianism, and the inextricable relationship between militarism, imperialism and late capitalism, he concludes that the 'black world is much more than an archipelago of secret bases. It is a secret *basis* underlying much of the American economy'.[121] The dark geography of the repressive apparatus largely overlaps with the dark geography of capital itself.

In its full span, Paglen's work brings into relief the epistemological boundaries that stand in the way of any investigation into the dark geography of the 'war on terror'. This is dramatized in an illuminating passage in *Blank Spots on the Map*, where Paglen goes through the Department of Defense's public budget from the 2008 fiscal year. As fat as a phonebook, the budget contains line items for sundry projects. Many programmes include descriptions, but alongside banal expenses like latrines and postage, we find entries like Chalk Eagle, allocated $352 million for 2009 but unaccompanied by any programme description. Beyond this lie another class of programmes, with names like Cobra Ball and Forest Green, that don't even have their budgets listed, while at the extreme end we find (or rather don't) programmes whose names or expenses are not revealed and are only listed as 'Special Program' or 'Special Activities'. By adding up all the line items and comparing the result – $64 billion – with the overall Department of Defense budget – just under $80 billion – one can roughly figure out how much was spent on these completely secret projects. This $16 billion is only a part of the overall black budget, however; Paglen claims that it was around $34 billion for the 2009 fiscal year.

Yet again attending to the overlap between militarism and political economy, Paglen acknowledges his literal inability to 'follow the money', along with the inevitable incompleteness of any investigation into the black world: 'I must confess that when I began this project, I was seduced by blank spots on maps, by the promise of hidden knowledge that they seemed to contain. It was easy to imagine that if I could just find one more code name, if I only knew what the HAVE PANTHER project was ... somehow the world itself would change for the better'.[122] As he concludes, however, this is not enough. Detection and discovery fall short. Simply revealing even some of the details of these classified projects is a complex and time-consuming task – getting the state to acknowledge their existence is even more difficult. While exposure makes for important political (and aesthetic) work, it has to be linked to systemic concerns if is not going to be reduced to a mere cataloguing of the black world – an activity which, like that of the satellite-spotters whom Paglen enlists to such effect in his work, has its own downside, with its libidinal investment in infinite registering, itemising, classifying, in the desperate attempt to leave no hole in knowledge. The power of this kind of work is to be sought in the interplay between, on the one hand, the strategies through which visual and documentary form is given to the refractory geography of covertness, and, on the other, the awareness of limits that are simultaneously political and cognitive. Paglen is able to shed a refracted light on many of the dark corners of this world, but the map that emerges is inevitably incomplete. Their contours can be grasped, but the blank spots are not completely filled in. In fact, we should perhaps not speak of a map at all.[123] The scalar, material and subjective complexities of the geographies explored in works like *The Other Night Sky* or *Blank Spots on the Map*, and the intricacy of their visual and textual mediations, mean that the black world which emerges in relief through these inquiries far exceeds the limited capacities of cartography proper.

Conspiracy as totality

By a single crime know a nation.
Virgil, *Aeneid*

Um… It just all ties together.
Alex Jones

Towards the end of his original presentation of cognitive mapping, Jameson makes what seems to be a disparaging remark about the ubiquity of the theme of paranoia in contemporary cultural production: 'Conspiracy, one is tempted to say, is the poor person's cognitive mapping in the postmodern age; it is a *degraded* figure of the total logic of late capital, a *desperate* attempt to represent the latter's system, whose *failure* is marked by its slippage into sheer theme and content'.[124] With this statement Jameson seems to chime with the mainstream of what can be called 'conspiracy-theory theory'. Belittled by Richard Hofstadter in 1964 in one of the groundbreaking essays in the field as a 'political pathology', conspiracy theory is widely regarded as, at best, a misguided and inadequate attempt to understand the functioning of power in an increasingly complex global society.[125] Awash in symbolic misery and bereft of any conceptual apparatus to understand the antagonisms, fluctuations, and developments in global politics and the economy, people turn to conspiracy theory as an immensely oversimplified narrativisation of amorphous or anonymous global power dynamics. An inability cogently to map or understand the complexities of global capitalism is supplemented by paranoid visions of nefarious elites and cabals bent on world domination. The panorama generated by conspiracy theory appears to fall into the traps of the hubristic attempt to 'see it whole', generating an all-too-perfect and complete vision of political economy without including the necessary work of dislocation, the panorama's 'derealization and devaluation of the individual's viewpoint' – which could be regarded as a prelude to a not entirely ideological 'mapping'.

Shortly after his famous intervention at the *Marxism and the Interpretation of Culture* conference, Jameson published *The Geopolitical Aesthetic*, the first chapter of which – 'Totality as Conspiracy' – is a bravura exploration of the desire called cognitive mapping in the 'conspiratorial texts' of a series of North American 1970s and early eighties films including *Three Days of the Condor, All the President's Men, Parallax View,* and *Videodrome.* These films, Jameson claims, can be understood as an attempt 'to think a system so vast that it cannot be encompassed by the natural and historically developed categories of perception with which human beings normally orient themselves'. This is an inevitably impossible task, but in the intent to map 'lies the beginning of wisdom'.[126] To summarise rather crudely Jameson's engrossing dialectical investigation: the conspiracy narrative allows these films – partly by way of allegory – to depict global, postmodern capitalism and the place of the individual in this massively complex system, and simultaneously to reveal the limitations which our conceptions of agency and our 'social organs' of perception impose on our capacity to orient ourselves in this phase of capitalism.

Two decades on, conspiracy theory has become increasingly prevalent and conspiratorial narratives seem to have lost none of their appeal, becoming all the more visible in both the cinema and the fine arts, as both theme and content. Endless examples can be sampled from Hollywood, but we could also point to cases like Peter Greenaway's recent film on Rembrandt's *Night Watch* (2007) – an instance of 'the conspiracy theory of art history' – or Robert Boyd's *Conspiracy Theory* (2008), a dual-projection video installation set to Kylie Minogue's 'I Believe in You', featuring a montage of images and audio samples about event conspiracies, systemic conspiracies, and super conspiracies, to use Michael

Barkun's terminology. In the conspiracy-theory theory jargon, event conspiracies seek to explain a single event (say, the JFK assassination); systemic conspiracies account for a series of events by uncovering a single, evil organisation behind them (Masons, Jews, Catholics, etc.); while super conspiracies are a combination of event and systemic conspiracies, in which conspiratorial groups are linked to various series of events over a considerable time span (Illuminati, the New World Order, reptilian humanoids, and the like).[127]

What kind of consequences might an acknowledgement of parapolitical concerns have for a conception of an aesthetic of cognitive mapping, in which the conspiratorial network does not stand in for or allegorise the logic of capital but is rather seen as a literal embodiment of unparalleled power? Papers, books, files and photographs are strewn about wildly. Folders overflow with scraps of paper. Layers upon layers of photographs and documents are pinned to a bulletin board. Early in Tom Tykwer's *The International* (2009) we catch a glimpse of the office of the protagonist, Louis Salinger, an Interpol agent played by Clive Owen. The film is loosely based on the scandal surrounding the Bank of Credit and Commerce International (BCCI): 'the banking swindle of the century, the largest single drug-money operation ever recorded, and the most pervasive money-laundering operation ever undertaken'.[128] Before folding in 1991, the bank was involved in laundering money to the mujahideen in Afghanistan, Manuel Noriega in Panama, Saddam Hussein in Iraq, and elements of intelligence services throughout the world, including the US, UK, Pakistan, and Saudi Arabia. In the film, Owen's character is investigating a bank – dubbed the International Bank of Business and Credit (IBBC) – he suspects of being involved in money laundering, illegal arms deals and other shady activities including the assassination of political enemies, competitors and whistleblowers. At this point in the film, the audience doesn't know what to think about Salinger. Is he a courageous rebel, investigating a criminal conspiracy that involves some of the world's most powerful bankers and corporations or is he a paranoid and delusional conspiracy theorist? In a tiresomely ubiquitous visual trope, the messiness of the office, the apparent absence of order or hierarchy, is intended to mirror Salinger's psychic state. Where Salinger perceives an intricate web of connections and evidence of a murderous conspiracy, the viewer just sees an unintelligible mess of documents, news clippings and police reports. The delirium of cognitive mapping, perhaps.

This image of a researcher sifting through piles of material, finding meaningful connections where others see coincidences is a persistent trope in conspiracy films (*Parallax View*, *JFK*, *Conspiracy Theory*), and in some of the more problematic examples of conspiracy-theory theory this desperate attempt to 'conjure order' and place events in a narrative is also regarded as a primary characteristic of the conspiratorial imagination. Alasdair Spark, for instance, argues that conspiracy theories 'seek totality and impose order'. Spark claims that Noam Chomsky's technique of sifting through 'a capacious box of the day's intake of tripe – newspapers, weeklies, monthlies, learned journals, flimsy mimeo-ed mailers' resembles conspiracy theory in its 'exhaustive plotting of a mass of detail' and its 'deep mining of the world's detail for bits of evidence'.[129] One wonders how theory could be produced or research undertaken without one's work resembling conspiracy theory. Willman's argument rings true: those debunkers of conspiracy theory who claim it erroneously posits a perfectly-ordered universe full of causality and without coincidence posit their own 'equally ideological vision of historical causality'.[130] Willman refers to the position held by many critics of conspiracy theory as the 'contingency theory of history'. While the conspiracists sees mysterious forces and cabals dictating historical movement, according to contingency theory, history is driven by random chaos, chance, accident. Citing Žižek's *Sublime Object of Ideology*, Willman argues that these two conceptions of social reality are both ideological visions that shroud society's fundamental antagonisms. Conspiracy theory presupposes the fantasy of an ordered society that is prevented from being harmonious by the conspirators behind the scenes, rather than by any fundamental (class, gender or racial) antagonisms. 'The essence of conspiracy beliefs lies in attempts to delineate and explain evil', whose 'locus lies outside the true community'.[131] In this light, white supremacy or anti-Semitism aren't just political ideologies, they are, to fuse together August Babel and Jameson, the cognitive mapping of fools. Contingency theory, meanwhile, 'maintains the existing capitalist system by attributing any deviations from the social equilibrium to chance and accident rather than immanent social antagonisms or contradictions.'[132] Wars, financial crises, school shootings, and crime are all regarded as exceptions to an otherwise harmonious society (for which individuals are to take sole responsibility). Contingency theory 'as a form of historical causality represents a renunciation of any attempt to grasp the operations of the social totality'.[133] For contingency theory, any form of cognitive mapping (or 'sociology of the social') is both impossible and pernicious, and conspiracy theory misunderstands the world as much as Marxism, precisely inasmuch as it tries to totalise the plural, fragmented, dispersed character of reality.

Sissela Bok has argued that increases in secrecy in government and business have a direct connection to the rise of conspiracy theory: as secrecy multiplies so does the fear of conspiracy.[134] This process seems to work the other way as well: as conspiracy theory has become all the more prevalent over the past two decades, many researchers are scared of dealing with the black world for fear of being taken for cranks. Paglen claims early in *Blank Spots on the Map* that one of the reasons that research into the black world is nearly non-existent is its susceptibility to the charge of conspiracy theory: many associate the very notion of a 'dark geography' with paranoid visions of New World Order helicopters, holding facilities for extraterrestrials at Area 51, and anxious visions of obscure elites manipulating history from the shadows – made all the more repugnant by their association with the Protocols of the Elders of Zion and other such racist grand narratives. Paglen's refusal to use his nuanced and rigorous research as the basis for speculation, his capacity to indicate the gaps in knowledge and their materiality without filling them in, can also be considered in view of these traps and pitfalls.

Tom Tykwer, *The International*, 2009

Returning to Twyker's film, while in the vast majority of works in the conspiracy thriller subgenre, the evil bank/corporation/cabal is depicted as an aberration, *The International* is rather unique in portraying the rot as thoroughly systemic. Corruption and criminality are revealed as features of contemporary capital and there is no sense that the whole might be immune to reproach or open to reform. The only way Salinger is able to get results is by not only dispensing with worries about jurisdiction and protocol, but by 'going rogue'. Even another of the ostensible good guys – an Italian arms manufacturer whose boss was assassinated by the bank – resorts to mafia-style hits. At one point, Salinger is able to

corner two members of the bank; their insistence on the insur-
mountability of Owen's task and their defence of their own
behaviour is revealing. First, the bank's ex-Stasi *consigliere* insists
that the reason Owen's efforts have been officially ignored or
actively stymied is because everyone has a vested interest in the
bank's success:

> The system guarantees the IBBC's safety because everyone is
> involved ... Hezbollah, CIA, Columbian drug cartels, Russian
> organized crime, the governments of Iran, Germany, China,
> [Britain]. Every multinational corporation. Everyone. They all
> need banks like the IBBC so that they can operate in the black
> and grey latitudes. And this is why your investigative efforts
> have either been ignored, or undermined, and why you and I
> will be quietly disposed of before any case against the bank
> can reach a court of law. ... If you really want to stop the IBBC
> you won't be able to do it within the boundaries of your
> system of justice.

Salinger appears ultimately persuaded by this panorama of
unbounded collusion, thus framing an act of vigilantism against
this particular capitalist as the only possible solution, the only way
fleetingly to satisfy an urge for justice – in the midst of a system
both unreformable and unremovable. When Salinger corners the
head banker at the point of a gun, the latter – in a distant echo of
Hume Cronyn's council of despair in *Rollover* – argues that he is
just a vessel, a contingent bearer of the capitalist imperatives and
as such utterly dispensable. Begging for his life in the film's (anti-
)climax, he exclaims: 'Executing me won't change anything.
There will be a hundred other bankers to take my place. All
you'll do is satisfy your blood lust and you know it.'[135] Such
'realism' makes the film's denouement particularly frustrating.
The final credits prove the bankers right, featuring as they do, in
a gesture of claustrophobic closure, a series of news stories about

the bank's continued successes. This ending works as a direct counterpoint of the naïve, bordering on delusional conclusion of the largely awful *The East* (dir. Zal Batmanglij, 2013), in which the closing credits reveal how the protagonist and a host of precocious corporate intelligence agents are able to give late capitalism a kinder and gentler face by informing the media of their former corporate clients' misdeeds.

In the despair of its conclusions, the narrative of *The International* is much closer to that of the *roman noir* than to the traditional detective novel. As the French noir master Jean-Patrick Manchette remarked, in the classic detective story 'crime disturbs the order of the law, which it is crucial must be restored by the discovery of the guilty party and his *elimination* from the social field'. In the *roman noir*, instead, the very order of the law is corrupted: 'evil dominates historically. Evil's domination is social and political. Social and political power is exercised by bastards. More precisely, by unscrupulous capitalists, allies of or identical to gangsters brought together in organizations, having in their pay politicians, journalists, and other ideologues, as well as justice, the police, and other henchmen'. Resonating with the plotting of *The International*, Manchette observes that the hero in the *roman noir* is struggling against the crime he is tasked with solving, stepped in an evil milieu, but disconnected from the class struggle. As such, as a lone man struggling against pervasive evil, he is only ever capable of righting a few wrongs, 'but he will never right the general wrong of this world; he knows this, and this is the source of his bitterness'.[136]

Jameson has asserted that 'successful spatial representation today need not be some uplifting socialist-realist drama of revolutionary triumph but may be equally inscribed in a narrative of defeat, which sometimes, even more effectively, causes the whole architectonic of postmodern global space to rise up in ghostly profile behind itself, as some ultimate dialectical barrier or invisible limit'.[137] In both *The International* and

Lombardi's drawings, as well as the tragic orientation of *The Wire* (discussed in Part II), it is a double sense of failure – the failure of reform and the failure to transgress certain established episte-mological limits – that emerges as a unifying theme. What's more, in both cases heroic, rogue individuals are set up against truly collective conspiracies, framing the impotence of the individual without allowing any glimpse of a viable reformist (let alone revolutionary) subject.

Chapter 2

Seeing Socialism

Crisis and transparency

In 1920, Georg Lukács posed the problem of class consciousness in terms of the aesthetics of capitalist crisis – that is to say, in terms of the political and epistemological conditions for seeing an essential if contradictory unity behind the disjoined appearances of capitalism. For the Lukács of *History and Class Consciousness*, the invisibility of capitalism *as such was* something of an axiom: 'It is true that society as such is highly unified and that it evolves in a unified manner. But in a world where the reified relations of capitalism have the appearance of a natural environment it looks as if there is not a unity but a diversity of mutually independent objects and forces'.[138] Whence the 'empiricism' of bourgeois consciousness. The unity of capitalism is accordingly a veiled, opaque unity, recalling Marx's contrast between capitalist and pre-capitalist modes of production, his only use of that vexed notion of transparency, to which we'll return. The formulation is from *Capital, Vol. 1:* 'Those ancient social organisms of production are, as compared with bourgeois society, extremely simple and transparent'.[139]

Now, one of Marx's key insights, in Lukács's eyes, was that 'one of the elementary rules of class warfare was to advance beyond what was immediately given ... to look beyond the divisive symptoms of the economic process to the unity of the total social system underlying it' or, to put it in Marx's own words, the workers 'ought not to forget that they are fighting with effects, but not with the causes of those effects'[140] (when, for instance, they are engaged on the trade-union front). It is in this sense that the impasses of class consciousness and revolutionary action are *aesthetic* problems, specific to capital's regime of (in)visibility, concerning which crisis provides potential opportunities. As Lukács observes:

> In the age of capitalism it is not possible for the total system to become directly visible in external phenomena. For instance, the economic basis of a world crisis is undoubtedly unified and its coherence can be understood. But its actual appearance in time and space will take the form of a disparate succession of events in different countries at different times and even in different branches of industry in a number of countries.[141]

But while in 'so-called periods of normality ... the gap between appearance and ultimate reality was too great for that unity [in the economic process] to have any practical consequences for proletarian action. In periods of crisis the position is quite different. The unity of the economic process now moves within reach'.[142] At this level, crisis is a rupture, but paradoxically it is a *synthetic rupture*, potentially rendering visible the unity between seemingly disparate domains and determinations.

This articulation between class consciousness and crisis – on which we can project the dyads of transparency/opacity, visibility/invisibility, and unity/multiplicity – is worth keeping in mind when we reflect on the crucial role played in critiques and deconstructions of Marxism and communism precisely by the problem not just of its 'aesthetics of politics', but its *aesthetics of the economy*. The critique of the critique of political economy, and the striving towards a society of associated producers that motivates it, that is crystallised in the stigmatised notion of 'transparency' is at the heart of so-called post-Marxism. It also featured prominently in Cold War critiques of communism, portrayed as a millenarian political theology heralding a society purged of conflict and difference, as well as in neoliberal refutations of centralised planning, depicted as a doomed fantasy based on the premise of a complete intelligibility of economic information. In a 1987 intervention concerning psychoanalysis and Marxism, Ernesto Laclau proposed that there existed a tension within Marxism, graspable in terms of its interiority or exteriority to the Enlightenment project. On the one hand, Marxism breaks with the Enlightenment in 'the affirmation of the central character of negativity – struggle and antagonism – in the structure of any collective identity', and, most significantly for our purposes, in 'the affirmation of the opaqueness of the social – the ideological nature of collective representations – which establishes a permanent gap between the real and the manifest senses of individual and social group actions'. On the other:

> Marxism is not only a discourse of negativity and the opaqueness of the social, it is also an attempt – perfectly compatible with the Enlightenment – to limit and master them. The negativity and opaqueness of the social only exist in 'human prehistory', which will be definitely surpassed by communism conceived as homogeneous and transparent society. It is from this mastery of totality that the moment of negativity loses its constitutive and foundational character. ... It would be absurd to deny that this dimension of mastery/transparency/rationalism is present in Marxism.[143]

And so it might be. But it would also be absurd to ignore the concrete historical and polemical context in which this 'aesthetic' dimension of Marxist knowledge and praxis was played out, in other words that of class consciousness *in and of crisis*.

Though regressive utopian myths of untrammelled visibility, as well as depoliticising fantasies of machinic administration, may be channelled more or less unconsciously by communist politics, the notions of social transparency that it generates – in particular as regards the transparency of planning as against the unintelligible anarchy of capitalism – have to be treated as *deter-*

minate and not *generic* negations of capitalism in crisis. The cognitive, economic or artistic figurations of a transparency of the social must therefore always be thought in counterpoint to the opacity of capitalism – the very opacity that is not only celebrated but operationalised in the 'aesthetics' of classical and neoclassical, as well as neoliberal, political economy.

Dialectical cinema, divisive symptoms

This was a problem that dogged some of Lukács's communist contemporaries, most importantly perhaps Eisenstein and Brecht. Eisenstein's abortive project to film *Das Kapital*, what he somewhat churlishly called a 'new work on a libretto by Karl Marx', was envisaged as an attempt not to narrate or depict the structure and dynamic of Marx's argument, but to appropriate its *method* for cinema – in particular to take the everyday experience of crisis as an occasion for a filmic dialectic of the abstract and the concrete, incorporating an affective dimension of pathos and shock specific to film.

Against 'abstract formal experiment', Eisenstein sketched sequences that advance a theoretical movement: 'Somewhere in the West. A factory where it is possible to pinch parts and tools. No search of workers made. Instead, the exit gate is a magnetic check point. No comment needed'.[144] The method had a didactic aim: to instruct the worker in the practice of thinking dialectically. Not to present capitalism as a stable, intelligible system, but to develop the cognitive organs to think through and against its crisis-prone and contradictory structure; to provide what Eisenstein called a 'visual instruction in the dialectical method', an instrument of 'dialectical decoding'. 'The most important tasks in a cultural revolution', writes Eisenstein in his notes, 'are not only dialectical demonstrations but instruction in the dialectical method, as well.'[145] To approximate the dialectic in film, it was thus necessary to break with a model of representation founded on 'thematic imagery' (though it is worth noting, in contrast to Vertov, that Eisenstein still relied on symbolism, as in this annotation: 'A balalaika and a Menshevik "resemble" each other not physically but abstractly').[146]

The method of this film is thus one that, so to speak, descends from the concrete to the abstract, and ascends from the abstract to the concrete, mediating the conjunction of apparent clarity and real opacity of banal everyday life with the complex, conceptual unity of capital:

> The first, preliminary **structural** draft of CAPITAL would mean taking a banal development of a perfectly unrelated event. Say, 'A day in a man's life', or something perhaps even more banal. And the elements of this chain serve as points of departure for the forming of associations through which alone the play of concepts becomes possible. The idea of this banal intrigue was arrived at in a truly constructive manner. ... The maximum abstractness of an expanding idea appears particularly bold when presented as an offshoot from extreme concreteness – the banality of life. ... Joyce may be helpful for my purpose: from a bowl of soup to the British vessels sunk by England.[147]

The chain of associations moves the particular to the universal: 'Completely idiotic (all right in the first stages of a working hypothesis): in the third part (for instance), association moves from the pepper with which she seasons food. Pepper. Cayenne. Devil's Island. Dreyfus. French chauvinism. *Figaro* in Krupp's hands.'[148] To achieve this one has to think of montage as unifying – in a dialectical class vision – a multiplicity of seemingly disparate events, what Lukács had called *divisive symptoms*: 'The "ancient" cinema was shooting one event from many points of view. The new one assembles **one point** of view from many events'.[149]

To know catastrophe

Brecht articulated crisis and representation, the representation of crisis and the crisis of representation, in an even more forthright manner. As in Lukács, we encounter a specific aesthetic valorisation of crisis as a moment of complex revelation. As the German playwright wrote apropos the crime novel:

> We gain our knowledge of life in a catastrophic form. It is from catastrophes that we have to infer the manner in which our social formation functions. Through reflection, we must deduce the 'inside story' of crises, depressions, revolutions, and wars. We already sense from reading the newspapers (but also bills, letters of dismissal, call-up papers and so forth) that somebody must have done something for the evident catastrophe to have taken place. So what then has been done and by whom? Behind the reported events, we suspect other occurrences about which we are not told. These are the real occurrences. If we knew these incidents, we would understand. Only History can inform us about these real occurrences – insofar as the protagonists have not succeeded in keeping them completely secret. History is written after catastrophes. The basic situation, in which intellectuals feel that they are objects and not subjects of History, forms the thought, which they can display for enjoyment in the crime story. Existence depends upon unknown factors. 'Something must have happened', 'something is brewing', 'a situation has arisen' – this is what they feel, and the mind goes out on patrol. But enlightenment only comes, if at all, after the catastrophe. The death has taken place. What had been fermenting beforehand? What had happened? Why has a solution arisen? All this can now be deduced.[150]

But, just as reflection on industrial photography instructs that a naïve realism is disarmed before the complexity of capital, as the latter 'slips into the functional',[151] so the dramatisation and figuration of its contradictory, mutating logic imposes formidable tasks upon the artist, and upon our unreflected conceptions of agency, character, and plot:

> Simply to comprehend the new areas of subject-matter imposes a new dramatic and theatrical form. Can we speak of money in the form of iambics? 'The Mark, first quoted yesterday at 50 dollars, now beyond 100, soon may rise, etc.' – how about that? Petroleum resists the five-act form; today's catastrophes do not progress in a straight line but in cyclical crises; the 'heroes' change with the different phases, are interchangeable, etc.; the graph of people's actions is complicated by abortive actions; fate is no longer a single coherent power; rather there are fields of force which can be seen radiating in opposite directions; the power of groups themselves comprise movements not only against one another but within themselves, etc., etc.[152]

As his collaborator Elisabeth Hauptmann noted, recalling Brecht's work on a play on the Chicago wheat stock exchange:

> We gathered the technical materials. I myself made inquiries of several specialists as well as of the exchange in Breslau and Vienna, and at the end Brecht himself began to study political economy. He asserted that the machinations of the money market were quite impenetrable – he would have to find out how matters really stood, so far as the theories of money were concerned. Before, however, making what for him were important discoveries in that field, he recognized that the current dramatic forms were not suited to reflecting such modern processes as the world distribution of wheat or the life-story of our times – in a word, all human actions of consequence. 'These questions', Brecht said, 'are not dramatic in

our sense of the word, and if they are transported into literature, are no longer true, and drama is no longer drama.
When we become aware that our world no longer fits into
drama, then drama no longer fits into our world.'[153]

This predicament, when 'drama no longer fits into our world',
when the intelligibility and legibility of crisis is threatened by a
crisis in the intelligibility and legibility of the world, has should
be regarded as the spur and context for attempts, in the arts and
in social practice more broadly, to experiment with what a 'transparent society' might mean.

The aesthetics of the plan and the limits of transition

Many of the utopian schemes that emerged in the wake of 1917,
in the crucible of civil war and war communism, combined the
euphoria of world-transformation with a cult of a unified and
regimented bio-machinic order which can only be understood in
view of the catastrophic retardation and grievous condition of
the Soviet economy, which was undergoing an unprecedented
de-industrialisation – as novel's like Gladkov's socialist-realist
classic *Cement* (1925) memorably detail.[154] The quasi-religious
character of invocations of Taylor and Ford, the attempt to
fashion a new man out of the devastated human material of the
postwar years is well-documented, finding dystopian expression
in texts like Zamyatin's *We*. But attention to less 'mythical'
productions, in the domains of urbanism, architecture and
cinema, can allow us to reflect on what an aesthetics of planning
and transparency might mean, when it seeks to generate,
through a 'cultural revolution', something which we could
provisionally term *socialist cognitive mapping* (or *communist
cartography*). This can in turn provide a way of criticising, in an
aesthetic register, the one-dimensional and ahistorical character
of the accusation of transparency, levelled at Marxism,
communism and socialism alike.

Conceived of in terms of planning, rather than as a messianic social vision, 'transparency' ties together the questions of class consciousness, economic control and political direction in a manner that permits us to explore the aesthetics of the economy as a crucial node for any reflection on the meaning of a transition out of capitalism. Ironically, the most effective statement we have come across about planning envisioned as a politically vital form of socialist cognitive mapping, is to be found in a fifty-year old text by Perry Anderson, then a young editor of the *New Left Review*, about Swedish social democracy. Anderson foregrounds the status of the plan as instrument, field and object of a cultural and political transformation. 'In its ultimate significance', he writes, 'the plan is not a rationalisation of resources, it is a revelation of values' – or, we could say, a mechanism for making the social essence transpire through its forms of appearance. By contrast to the impossibility *within* capitalism of a situational representation of one's being and activity, the plan

decodes the vast, interlocking, impenetrable, inspissated economy and ascribes a lucid meaning to every one of the myriad cryptic gestures which compose it. It renders the entire work-force transparent to itself as engaged in one task, so that each member of it can see how his own task complements and completes that of all the others and is in turn carried beyond itself by them. ... Everything possible should be done to maximise the transparency of social construction, and the local community has a crucial role to play here: the national plan should be routed wherever possible via a complex of local plans which realise in the most vivid and immediate way the interdependence of work in the community (profits from local concerns to go directly to the financing of local flats, schools, concert-halls, etc.). ... Transparency is one of the crucial defining characteristics of socialism: a community in which all the multiple mediations between our public and private existence are visible, where each social event can be seen right back to its source, and legible human intentions read everywhere on the face of the world.[155]

Now, if we approach the aesthetics of the plan as it emerges in some of the foremost political and artistic debates thrown up by Russian Revolution, the superficiality of the usual criticisms of communism as a messianism – hallucinating a society without contradiction, antagonism, and so on – becomes patent. Attention to such post-revolutionary controversies also allows us to identify the thorny and at times tragic problems thrown up by the attempt to create an aesthetics of the plan that would at one and the same time serve as a form of pedagogy ('production propaganda', as Lenin might have it) and as an experimentation in form.

By analogy with Lukács's own antinomies of bourgeois thought, we could outline here something like three antinomies of communist aesthetics: (1) the combination of a radical subordination of the proletarian as labourer to an exaltation of the proletarian as future administrator of communism; (2) the tension between, on the one hand, a humanism that strives, to repeat Anderson's phrase, to make it so that 'legible human intentions [are] read everywhere on the face of the world' and, on the other, an anti- or post-humanist biomechanical horizon of social change; (3) the aestheticisation of the economic plan in the context of a worldwide capitalist economy.

The first problem is at the heart of Robert Linhart's arresting study of the conjunctural and contradictory character of Lenin's thought and politics post-1917, *Lenin, the Peasants and Taylor* – a study unique in its combination of a real appreciation of the Bolshevik leader with a welcome rejection of the comforting apologias of Leninism. In a chapter entitled 'The railways: the emergence of the Soviet ideology of the labour-process', Linhart recounts how, in the context of the famine, the authoritarian Taylorist turn in the organisation of work was driven through in the sector that represented the vital hinge between production, services and administration, and whose disorganisation was exacerbated by the very autonomous workers' organisation that had previously made it into a hub of anti-Tsarist agitating. Workers' opposition now appeared as a kind of economic blackmail, all the more menacing in that it took place within the all-round crisis of the civil war. The Bolsheviks, Linhart notes, were 'almost instinctively attentive to everything that concerns communication, flow, circuits'.[156] The Bolshevik's state could not but strive, to borrow from Lefebvre's *De l'état*, to become a *logistical state*.

In the throes of revolution, the railways appeared as the nerve-fibres and life-blood of a 'state in movement'; militarised centralisation, planning and labour discipline were raised to the standing of imperatives – as evidenced, among others, by Trotsky's 'Order No. 1042', viewed by Linhart as a milestone in state planning.[157] After all, 'if there is an activity that must, by nature, function as a single mechanism, one that is perfectly regulated, standardised and unified throughout the country, it's the railway system'.[158] The seemingly inevitable Taylorisation of the railways both forges and deforms the USSR, especially in furthering the split, thematised by Linhart, between the proletarian as political *subject* and the proletarian as *object* of an iron discipline. Among the critical sites of the necessary fixation on logistics (namely, on railways and electrification) are the films of Dziga Vertov, which strive to realise an unprecedented totalising vision – not so much a seeing *of* totality as a sighted totality, the eye-machine.. Such a vision would combine the Taylorist transmutation of labour into 'a regular, uninterrupted flow of communication', with collective subjective mastery over this flow, as the 'transparency of the productive process'[159] comes to be provided to each worker in the guise of an all-penetrating perception.

Vertov's films are the locus of a kind of physiological pedagogy, a refunctioning of the proletarian nervous system aimed at educating the eye of the spectator, decoding the world through an inhuman kino-eye that can nevertheless permit workers to see the totality that they themselves form. As the Soviet director wrote in *Kinopravda & Radiopravda* (1925):

> The textile worker ought to see the worker in a factory making a machine essential to the textile worker. The worker at the machine tool plant ought to see the miner who gives his factory its essential fuel, coal. The coal miner ought to see the peasant who produces the bread essential for him. Workers ought to see one another so that a close, indissoluble bond can be established among them.[160]

Normal propaganda and pedagogy, based on the whims and character of writers and instructors, are insufficient. 'How, therefore, can the workers see one another? Kino-eye pursues precisely this goal of establishing a visual bond between the workers of the whole world.'[161] Note that, to touch on our second antinomy, this proletarian humanism is predicated on a technical anti-humanism, on 'the emancipation of the camera, which is reduced to a state of pitiable slavery, of subordination to the imperfections and the shortsightedness of the human eye',[162] as 'the mechanical eye, the camera, reject[s] the human eye as crib sheet [and] gropes its way through the chaos of visual events'.[163]

But such a pedagogical emancipation through the machine is also predicated on an obfuscation of labour. This can be registered, for instance, in Vertov's *A Sixth Part of the World* (1926) – a visual poem to Gostorg, the foreign trade department of the Soviet Union – punctuated as it is by the call for 'you', 'sitting in the audience', 'the master of the soviet land', 'knee deep in grain', to assume 'your immense wealth' and contribute to the plan to accelerate the growth of the Soviet economy through

Dziga Vertov, *A Sixth Part of the World*, 1926

trade with capitalism. The state is all-present but in a sense invisible, while proletarian toil is decomposed into the ideal of, as Linhart puts it, 'a regular, uninterrupted flow of communication: productive activities are strictly interdependent – extraction, transport of fuel, transformation of wood, stone, iron'.[164]

The visual analysis breaks up and recomposes the labour-process but removes its proper logic and complexity, together with its agency, creating a socialist abstract labour subsumed by the flow and the plan. For Linhart, this matches Lenin's own attempt to square the circle in the state of political and economic emergency that dominated the late teens and twenties: the hope of a Taylorism that could be appropriated and transvalued by the masses. This is also what transpires from Vertov's attempt to give to each worker a vision of the whole, which for Linhart suffers from the same problem as Lenin: the collectivisation of labour is not essentially grounded on a redistribution of agency, of workers' control, but on the mutual, 'horizontal' publicity of work. It could be said that the class consciousness thus generated is more of a passive revelation than a progressive mutation in the articulation between the individual and the collective, the overall system and local situations. The transparency of the productive system puts 'the people' at the helm but workers as workers remain subordinated to the exigencies of the plan. Publicity and agency are disjoined, while 'the double play of the rational evidence of tasks and the habit of carrying them out without constraint would reduce the place and importance of decisions properly so-called'.[165]

An even harsher verdict was emitted by the Italian Marxist architectural theorist, Manfredo Tafuri, in his 1971 essay 'Realised Socialism and the Crisis of the Avant-gardes', which argued, not entirely fairly perhaps, that Vertov's *Kinopravda* and the works of El Lissitzky were 'attempts to manage one's own alienation'. The effort to create a kind of cognitive, nervous and erotic union of man and machine through cinema would thus reveal: 'the ultimate aim of the productive avant-garde. It is the collective, the class, which is now called upon to *become machine*, to identify with production. Productivism is indeed a product of the avant-garde: but it is the project of the conciliation between Capital and Labour, operated through the reduction of labour-power to an obedient and mute cog of the comprehensive machine'.[166] The further result is that in turning formal experimentation into a productive instrument, any of its anti-ideological, demystifying character is squandered. By 'attributing to the proletariat the historical task of reintegrating Man with himself and his social environment, the recuperation of a resacralised work understood as no longer alienated translates directly into the *ideology of organisation*, the Plan'.[167] This project would thereby dissipate Lenin's affirmation, however precarious, of the need *not* to erase the class within the plan, to retain an exteriority between the proletariat and the instruments of valorisation of fixed capital. This is what vanishes, it could be argued, in works like *A Sixth Part of the World*, which subordinates the construction of a kind of cinematic atlas of the Soviet economy, and of its indigenous peoples, to a peculiarly contradictory if eminently realist goal, that of maximising production for export to capitalist countries (and thus, one imagines, the exploitation of the Soviet proletariat, not to mention nature) – all in order to accelerate the building of a socialism whose one condition is the maximisation of 'constant capital', or, as the film relentlessly reminds us in the second person singular and plural, 'machines that build machines'.

All of the contradictions of socialist cognitive mapping, in its Soviet phase, are here: the exaltation of labour and its subsumption to the plan; humanism (anti-colonialism, mastery over collective fate, Vertov's characteristic attention to faces, expressions and moments of happiness) and anti-humanism (the subordination of the former to the flow of logistics and the accumulation of fixed capital); capitalist trade as a precondition for socialist construction. The problems of cognitive mapping in socialist transition thus turn out to be even more complex, if markedly different, than those thrown up by capitalism's distinctive modalities of opacity and invisibility.

Red iconoclasm, then and now

We have tried to suggest that an exploration of the aesthetics of the economy is of necessity torn between the absoluteness of capital – which can easily transmute into a fetish, or worse, a basilisk – and the horizon of that absolute's abolition, oftentimes, as in Lukács, glimpsed in moments of crisis. Transparency has been one of the most laden and polemical of terms in efforts to think the political economy of representation – which is why we've intimated that rethinking it in terms of the transition from capitalism might helpfully shift the problem away from one of metaphysics. Iconoclasm has been another. Whether the horizon of full representability, of the egalitarian presence of producers to one another, is in the end separable from a rejection of the icons of authority and the idols of the market, is a difficult question indeed. Yet the critique of communist iconoclasm has taken directions that differ in interesting respects from the attack against the Marxist metaphysics of presence, which are worth considering briefly.

In the context of what some have taken to calling the contemporary 'image wars' – many of them intensely mediated and manipulated corollaries to contemporary geopolitical and 'religious' conflicts – a discourse has surfaced linking the age-old theological aesthetics of image-breaking, banning and concealing with the fate of critical thought. Among the most distinctive aspects of the theoretical framing provided by Bruno Latour and Peter Weibel to their 2002 exhibition catalogue *Iconoclash* was indeed the declaration that time has come to pacify the wars of and against images that threaten to tear any foreseeable democratic compact, and that do so one must simultaneously bring the age of critique to a close.[168] For Weibel, new aesthetic practices emerging after the 'crisis of representation' and the supposed 'end of art' signal that 'iconoclasm as axiom of modern art comes to an end', and we can indeed bid farewell to the idea of modernism. For his co-curator Bruno Latour, who some time ago famously declared that we have never been modern, the aim of *Iconoclash* was to investigate the uses of images in Western culture in order to grasp and to neutralise the origins of hatred, nihilism, fanaticism and critique. Along with the work of their erstwhile collaborator, the German pop-philosopher Peter Sloterdijk, Latour and Weibel's texts testify to a widespread trend – very ably anatomised by Benjamin Noys in *The Persistence of the Negative* – to have done with the negativity and destructiveness haunting the politics and aesthetics of the twentieth century, and to affirm in its stead an ethics or even a therapy of images and statements that takes irreducible complexity, difference, and multiplicity as what is given.

For Latour, to step beyond iconoclasm is also to produce an 'archaeology of fanaticism'. The return of this term of intellectual opprobrium is very symptomatic. One of the notable features of this stigmatising idea, and a source of its abiding attraction to liberals and conservatives steeled against sundry extremisms, was indeed its applicability to both 'barbarians' and 'rationalists', to those who persist in their inassimilable particularity as well as to those who affirm an uncompromising universality.[169] Backwards intolerance and excessive reason alike have fallen under the accusation of fanaticism, and the equation of critical negativity with religious zealotry has a long and distinguished pedigree in the counter-revolutionary writings of the late eighteenth and nineteenth century, exemplarily so in the work of the conservative thinker Edmund Burke. Echoing Burke's juxta-position of the carefully tended and differentiating customs of England to the geometrical levellings of the French revolution-aries, Latour homes in on the need to defend fragile mediations against abrupt reduction and negation. These are the stakes of what he calls an economy of images, or, for short, 'civilisation' (in which, contrary to Burke, the sublime and its terrors play no part). Here it may be worth recalling how the British philosopher allegorised the evils of equality in the destruction of aristocratic buildings and their transformation into revolutionary nitre, recalling the Lyonnais radicals who spoke of the 'beautiful effect of a perfect equality' achieved in mixing destroyed monuments with dust.[170]

An ecumenical approach to the myriad images that populate our worlds, and to the elaborate devices that keep them in existence would thus operate as an antidote against the destructive legacies of iconoclastic monotheism, carried over or secularised into the 'political religions' of the twentieth century (and in turn into the religious politics of the twenty-first). This new instantiation of the early Enlightenment's struggle between tolerance and fanaticism, now boosted by science studies, anthropology, and art history, would thus serve to have done with the iconoclasm of the radical or revolutionary Enlightenment in its Kantian, Hegelian and Marxian guises. Tellingly, the notion of mediation is here removed from its association with notions of negation and totality, with the former, negation, relayed by a fundamentally additive ontology and the latter, totality, dispersed by iterations of the idea of network.

Egalitarianism in general, and communism in particular have long been associated with iconoclasm, in the specific sense of the demolition or profanation of the symbols and edifices of power. The 'age of extremes' is bookended by the drawing and quartering of the Tsar's massive monuments, as immortalised in Eisenstein's *October*, and the felling of legions of Lenins in 1989 and after – a theme nicely investigated in Laura Mulvey and Mark Lewis's documentary *Disgraced Monuments* (1994) or Buck-Morss's *Dreamworld and Catastrophe*. But to counter the reiteration of anti-fanatical discourse by Latour and his ilk, which takes place at the level of a repudiation of the totalising negativity of 'critique', it is worth turning our attention to the question of iconoclasm conceived not as an act of desecrating vandalism, but as a matter of the aesthetics and politics of theory – more specifically, as the crucial hinge between the theory of capital's reproduction and that of communism's production.

The Marxian critique of political economy has been deemed, alongside Freudian psychoanalysis, to be a modern inheritor of the Hebraic ban on graven images, the war on pagan illusions (and thus also to share a complex affinity with Kant's iconoclastic theory of the sublime – such that we could conceive of both capital and communism as both dynamically and mathematically sublime, if in different ways). In *Les Iconoclastes*, Jean-Joseph Goux argued that Marx's attack on transcendent illusions had effectively shifted Feuerbach's humanist critique, aimed at the subject's imaginary projection of his capacities onto divine idols, to an investigation into the symbolic alienation which sees human powers invested in and inverted by money as the general equivalent. Both Marx and Freud, 'translate the iconic enigma of the hieroglyph into a new language, the abstract language of the concept'.[171] While saluting the suspicion of appearances in Marx, Goux chastises him for the utopian turn taken by his iconoclasm, embodied in the drive, already present in Thomas More, to abolish – in the guise of money – the very idea of a symbolic third, of mediation.[172]

As Goux observes, 'the utopian republic is a society without money and without concepts'. Having identified a critical dimension of Marxian theory, namely its standing as a theory of the constituent role of invisible real abstractions in capitalism – that is of capitalism as a kind of actually-existing metaphysics – Goux then shifts into the familiar discussion of Marxism as a theory haunted by social transparency, the end of mediation, or, to sum it all up, totalitarianism. The result of Goux's take on Marx's iconoclasm is thus to separate two dimensions, theoretical and political, of Marx's work – an iconoclastic *deconstruction* of illusions from an iconoclastic *destruction* of mediations. And the upshot is that the iconoclastic critique of illusions seems to underwrite the eternity of mediation, the eternity of the money-form as that 'intermediary', which 'delegates value, sundering use and exchange, opening up substitution and representation, inhibiting the community of life'.

Important in its own regard as an attempt to articulate the isomorphies between monetary, linguistic and philosophical abstractions – though ultimately failing to consider the specificity of the real and determinate abstractions of capital – Goux's discussion of iconoclasm indicates an interesting avenue for considering the 'aesthetic' dimensions of contemporary connections between capital and communism. For it is perhaps increasingly the case that those theories which underscore the character of capital as abstract domination are also those which regard communism as a movement of negation that cannot be crystallised into any images or mediations. Thus we read, in a recent article on communisation:

> We don't know, we cannot know, and therefore we do not seek to concretely describe, what communism will be like. We only know how it will be in the negative, through the abolition of capitalist social forms. Communism is a world without money, without value, without the state, without social classes, without domination and without hierarchy, …
> If we cannot foresee and decide how the concrete forms of communism will be, the reason is that social relations do not arise fully fledged from a unique brain, however brilliant, but can only be the result of a massive and generalised social practice. It is this practice that we call communisation. Communisation is not an aim, it is not a project. It is nothing else than a path. But in communism the goal is the path, the means is the end.[173]

Communism as *a world without*, without the very forms that structure what we've come to inhabit as a social world, is thus perhaps resonant with that messianic quotation from the Zohar, invoked by Goux: 'The messianic world will be a world without images, in which it will no longer be possible to compare an image and what it represents'.

If by iconoclasm we intend a theory founded on a critical suspicion of appearances, especially inasmuch that the latter involve the treatment of relations as things, then the critique of political economy fits the bill. It is a materialist theory whose building blocks are to be found in the categories of the idealist dialectic, whose object (capital) is a relational reality nowhere to be encountered 'in the flesh' – as memorably encapsulated in a vignette from Alfred Sohn-Rethel's pioneering *Intellectual and Manual Labour*:

Money is an abstract thing, a paradox in itself - a thing that performs its socially synthetic function without any human understanding. And yet no animal can ever grasp the meaning of money; it is accessible only to man. Take your dog with you to the butcher and watch how much he understands of the goings on when you purchase your meal. It is a great deal and even includes a keen sense of property which will make him snap at stranger's hand daring to come near the meat his master has obtained and which he will be allowed to carry home in his mouth. But when you have to tell him 'Wait, doggy, I haven't paid yet!' his understanding is at an end. The pieces of metal or paper which he watches you hand over, and which carry your scent, he knows, of course; he has seen them before. But their function as money lies outside the animal range.[174]

Accordingly, as Althusser noted in his remarkable essay on Cremonini, that painter of the real abstract, of the capital-relation: 'The structure which controls the concrete existence of men, i.e. which informs the lived ideology of the relations between men and objects and between objects and men, this structure, as a structure, can never be depicted by its presence, in person, positively, in relief, but only by traces and effects, negatively, by indices of absence, in intaglio (*en creux*)'.[175] Or, in the terms of *Reading Capital*, the preoccupation of theory is with 'a necessary invisible connection between the field of the visible and the field of the invisible'.[176]

Similarly, the definition of communism as a movement undoing those social relations which find their form in the real abstractions of capitalism is also marked by a negative icono-clasm. And yet we should be wary of an excessively clear link between a theory of mediation based on real abstractions and a theory of emancipation based on the end of mediations. Communism is not the end of social forms altogether, but rather the end of those equivalential forms specific to capitalism, in the direction of social mediations that would, inasmuch as they regulate the relationship between differences and singularities without a common measure, of necessity require formidable complexity – a complexity which, bearing on the capacity to control economic life 'from below', is one of the interesting meanings that could be ascribed to the notion of transparency, as Perry Anderson's aforementioned discussion of Swedish Social Democracy suggests.

What is more, we should also be suspicious of an iconoclasm about mediations that mistakes the destruction of capital's forms of appearance for the undoing of its mediations. In this sense the profanation of money and gold, from Lenin's plan to turn gold into communist urinals, to the cash flushed down the toilet of Haneke's *Seventh Continent* (1989), from More's abolition of money to its current epigones, may turn out to be a strategy to dispose of abstract things while not grasping the real abstractions that animate them, destroying money as representation without traversing capital as totality.

The aesthetic temptation, which is also a political one, is to treat the struggle against capital's abstract domination – the domination over human beings of capital as an automatic subject, of social forms that are as invisible as they are ubiquitous – as a struggle for concrete community, a movement from the supersensible to the sensible. But communism is not a mere negation of abstraction, form and invisibility, it is their refunctioning – to borrow a notion from Brecht. In this sense it is a determinate negation of a society traversed, in the form of the commodity, by sensuously supersensible

Michael Haneke, *The Seventh Continent*, 1989

things. The point though is not to abrogate this aesthetic ambivalence of real abstractions, for some abstract, nostalgic desire for 'true life'. It is to experiment with forms of social organisation which, necessarily combining the sensuous and the supersensible, will not do so through forms of equivalence founded on the abstract commensurability of labour, time and life. It is perhaps in this light that we can turn back to that enigmatic junction of communism, iconoclasm and abstraction that made El Lissitzky and Malevich propose what to do with red squares (the iconoclasm of communism) and black squares (the iconoclasm of capital): 'Let the overthrow of the old world of arts be marked out on the palms of your hands. Wear the black square as a mark of the world economy. Draw the red square in your workshops as a mark of the revolution in the arts. Clear the areas in the wide world of the whole chaos that prevails in it'.

Part II

Cities and Crises

Villages shoot up and cities where this class digs for ore, /
Dead & unpeopled in a flash when it moves away. So quick /
A boom was never seen before, nor so quick a bust.
Brecht, *The Manifesto*[177]

Prologue

Slums and Flows

The following three chapters range over narratives and images that have sought to capture the traces of capital's intangible machinations by scanning the integument of the US city, the 'urban fabric', and observing its financial colonisation – registered in soaring real estate values, the mystifying icon of the skyscraper, or, more literally, in the occupation of key locations by the infrastructure of high-frequency trading and algorithmic finance.[178] As a frame through which to begin to think how to approach the contemporary city as a space innervated by seemingly abstract logics as well as viscerally concrete conflicts, we propose the map reproduced on this book's cover, drawn by William Bunge for his remarkable 1971 book *Fitzgerald: Geography of a Revolution*.[179]

Though Bunge is amply deserving of rediscovery, he is of particular relevance to us and to the inquiries in Part II for several reasons. *Fitzgerald* is a signal example of counter-mapping as a collective political practice: Bunge formed the Detroit Geographical Expedition and Institute in the wake of the insurrection of 1967 as a reconnaissance and reclamation of urban space, as well as a pedagogical project, which would have Detroit's black proletariat and subproletariat as its agent.[180] *Fitzgerald* is also a combative counter to the tendency of much thinking about the abstractions of capitalist space to collude in the occlusion or erasure of the politics of everyday life and the placed character of conflict: note Bunge's choice to focus in meticulous if idiosyncratic depth and detail – historical, spatial, graphic, biographical, and even poetic – on a square mile of what by the early 1970s was a mainly black residential neighbourhood in the mobile, concentric space between black slum and white suburb. This is a combative instance of cognitive mapping from below, the 'tilt-shot' of which Sartre wrote in the passage cited in our introduction. In Bunge's words: 'While Fitzgerald cannot escape the world, at least it can maintain the dignity of seeing its imprisonment within it through its own eyes'.[181]

Yet, though Bunge criticises cartographers for making a hash of both the abstract and the real by not properly distinguishing them, his map and diagram of racialised rent extraction in Detroit, and the narrative accompanying it, is a model of how the tools (including mathematical ones) of abstraction can bring home the most painful but also somehow invisible of dynamics.[182] Bunge employs a tested tool of agricultural geography, von Thünen's 1826 model – which explains how land closer to the centre of a settlement can demand proportionately higher rents – transposing it, through the substitution of the 'crop' from agricultural to human, to the economic morphology of Detroit.[183] The result is a radical challenge to a spatial prejudice, namely that the blighted 'inner city' is materially poorer, and that it is sustained by the supposedly generous taxes from outer, affluent rings. Factoring in to his equation the total rent per neighbourhood, number of renters, unit rent and ownership cost per household, as well as transport costs and distance from downtown, Bunge can demonstrate, transposing the results onto the space of his map, that:

Paradoxically, slums command the highest rents per land unit. The wealthy cannot afford to live in the slums. They cannot afford the rent, for although as individuals they pay much higher rent, per acre of land they pay much lower. Similarly, though the affluent may travel by expensive chauffeur, they cannot afford the collective transportation costs that slum dwellers pay per unit of impacted slum land. The rent per individual and transportation costs per individual is lower in the slums than elsewhere in the city.

Slum dwellers, with their low incomes, are compelled to live there. Because of the number of people crammed into the hovels, the rent *per acre* is highest while *per individual* the rent is the lowest.[184]

In an arrangement that combines the cold efficiency of economic compulsion with the mechanisms of racial privilege (as mapped in some of the other graphics from Bunge and the Expedition, such as the stark 'Where Commuters Run Over Black Children on the Pointes-Downtown Track'), what Bunge shows is precisely the unequal exchange structuring the city as a space of the racialised exploitation and segregation of the poor, whose injury is compounded by the insulting common sense that they are a 'burden' on the affluent taxpayer.[185] Or, in Bunge's pungent metaphors: 'The affluent suburbs own Detroit's heart. All told, money is sucked out of the people of Fitzgerald by the affluent white suburbanites in Grosse Pointe like lamprey eels suck the juices out of Michigan Lake trout'.[186]

Chapter 3

Werewolf Hunger
(New York City, 1970s)

All usurpers have shared this aim: to make us forget that *they have only just arrived.*
Guy Debord

Though their impact on the rural and exurban has been notoriously devastating, modern capitalist crises have often been figured as exquisitely urban affairs – slum populations and vacant, rusting, rotting fixed capital, side by side. From 'ruin porn' to miserabilist class melodrama, one could lay out a whole typology of the aesthetics of urban crisis. In this chapter, we take our cue instead from a work which, precisely in the manner that it inhabits *too many* genres, displaces our stereotypes and fantasies about cities abandoned by the life-blood of capital, dramatising the uncanny negativity of capitalism without the moralistic voyeurism which often accompanies narratives of sin and blight.

Hesitant to apply the hackneyed and thoroughly recuperated label 'cult film'[187] (besides, it isn't nearly popular enough to earn the title), it may be said that *Wolfen* is a film awaiting a cult. Entangled in a plot symptomatically torn between political history, capitalist practice and mythologies of the land, *Wolfen* is set during a critical moment in the collapse of radical politics and the emergence of a feral neoliberalism, against a backdrop of urban dereliction and redevelopment. When the film was made New York was a city in crisis, both fiscal and existential. In 1975, bankruptcy loomed, and changing demographics, rising crime, and the dismantling of the 'social democratic polity'[188] that had developed after the Second World War cast a pall of anxious uncertainty over the city's future. *Wolfen* is a weird amalgam of werewolf movie, police procedural, and serial-killer thriller whose plot touches on a wide variety of then (and still) urgent political concerns, ranging from corporate surveillance and terrorism, to dereliction and gentrification. Its generic and thematic eclecticism – making it a failure as a political thriller or a horror film strictly construed – is also what allows it be much truer to the experience of crisis as both a grimly material fact and a phenomenon of the political and economic unconscious.

Michael Wadleigh, *Wolfen*'s director, is best known for directing the Oscar-winning documentary *Woodstock* (1970), after being involved with *cinéma vérité* in the mid-sixties. The first film he worked on was about Gus Hall, head of the Communist Party USA. He was also involved in two films of interviews with Martin Luther King, visited the occupied Sorbonne, and claims all his films are at their core political.[189] *Wolfen* is adapted from Whitley Strieber's novel *The Wolfen* (1978), which shares a similar arc and characters with the film, but none of the political content or subtext. *Wolfen*, which struggled at the box office, was Wadleigh's first and last Hollywood film.[190] He has lamented that it 'gets sold as a horror film and not a serious political film'.[191] Considering certain inconsistent and illogical – yet not exactly experimental – aspects of the plot, and the frequency with which

Michael Wadleigh, *Wolfen*, 1981

characters' limbs are severed, not to mention the narrowness of ordinary understanding of political film-making, this may not be entirely surprising.

Many of the film's themes are introduced in its opening sequence, which begins with a pan of the downtown New York City skyline at dawn, before cutting to a Native American man standing high atop one of the towers of the Brooklyn Bridge, swinging a *bola*. It quickly cuts to the skeletal remains of a church in the ruins of the South Bronx, followed by a series of views of the devastated neighbourhood and the demolition of a tenement. We are then immersed in a heat-vision point-of-view shot from inside the church (throughout the film the perpetrators' perspective is shown in what the director and cinematographer called 'Alienvision', thermodynamic renderings of Steadicam shots that would later be popularized in the film *Predator* (1987)). We witness a ground-breaking ceremony at a demolition site making way for Van der Veer Towers, a complex of high-end condominiums, the ceremonial shovel wielded by the *crème de la crème* of New York's power elite, the old-monied real estate developer Christopher Van der Veer. Next it is nearly 5 AM and Van der Veer and his wife are heading home to their penthouse in the financial district in a limousine, their activities electronically tracked by a private security firm. The tycoon directs the driver to stop at Battery Park on the southern tip of Manhattan on the way – perhaps 'to visit his ancestors', quips a member of the surveillance detail. As the limo crosses the Brooklyn Bridge, a ghostly figure darts across the traffic lanes; it's the Native American from the earlier shot, who throws a bottle at the limousine, striking the back window to no great effect. (Was he waiting there for Van der Veer? We don't know.) When they arrive at the desolate park, the couple flirts and canoodles while checking out a replica of the first windmill built in North America, protected by their driver, who doubles as a bodyguard. A shot of the full moon serves as a transition to a thermal view of the Statue of Liberty, as Van der Veers and their bodyguard are stalked by the same creatures from the abandoned church in the Bronx. They wordlessly dispose of the bodyguard in a gruesome fashion, before savaging the billionaire couple.

This opening sequence frames in broad strokes the story that follows in terms of the conflict between the European colonisation of the North American continent and its victims. The narrative is built on the layers of violence and dispossession embedded beneath the New York City skyline and sets the story within a larger history of the New York region. Van der Veer's wife reads a plaque at the windmill that reveals Van der Veer's ancestors built a wind-powered machine on that precise spot in 1625, a year before Peter Minuit 'bought' the island of Mannahatta ('island of many hills') from a group of Lenape in 1626, according to settler lore. The windmill is flanked by demonically menacing Dutch gothic weathervanes. The attitude of the colonists towards the use and ownership of the natural environment can, at least superficially, be contrasted with that of the indigenous population, and the windmill seen as a metonym for the violence of the settler's 'technological advantage'. Inserted within this colonial frame is a jump forward three and a half centuries to another conflict over land use and real estate: the urban renewal then underway in the South Bronx, where the 'worst slum in America' is being cleared by Van der Veer for a luxury development, complete with a marina.[192] Between these waves of dispossession there is both sedimentation, or haunting, and a kind of short-circuit.

The NYPD, at this point unaware of any link between Van der Veer and Native Americans or the South Bronx, are baffled at the precision and brutality of the killings – the attacker(s) struck before the couple's Haitian, ex-Baby Doc bodyguard could get a shot off, and the victims' brains were taken. Van der Veer's corporate interests around the globe immediately steer the investigation towards international terrorism. The police and Van der

Veer's private security firm suspect a political assassination, the final spasm of the urban guerrillas of the 1970s. Initially suspicions fall on Van der Veer's niece, a trust-funded militant of the Weather Underground, but despite her militant posturing during questioning she is deemed irrelevant, shifting the state-corporate investigation towards a terrorist organization named *Götterdämmerung* – 'twilight of the gods' – perhaps a knowing nod to the nihilist or Nietzschean turn taken by some of the second and third generation armed struggle outfits in Europe

Not entirely convinced by the direction the investigation is taking, the film's protagonists – a dishevelled cop (Dewey), an expert on the psychology of terrorism (Neff), a charismatic city coroner (Whittington), and an eccentric zoologist (Ferguson) – launch one of their own. (We can register here a common, utopian feature of cognitive mapping fictions: the coming together of a disparate band of researchers, producing rogue knowledge against stifling and sinister bureaucracies.[193]) When bodies of missing persons showing the marks of the same inhuman *modus operandi* are discovered in the rubble of the South Bronx, in the vicinity of Van der Veer's development, the film's protagonists are left to make the connection between the city's most powerful forces and its most destitute terrains. Strange hairs are found on the bodies of the slaughtered junkies and derelicts, as well as on the millionaire couple. They are eventually identified as coming from *canis lupus*, or the grey wolf, suggesting a potentially lycanthropic murderer. When Dewey and his team put forward their theory, the police chief balks – 'That's a big jump form the South Bronx to Wall Street!' – and continues to focus the official investigation on *Götterdämmerung*. The zoologist Ferguson argues that wolves couldn't be involved, as they went more or less extinct with the Native Americans and the buffalo on the 'genocide express',[194] pushing Dewey towards Native American Movement-affil-iated[195] construction workers. Dewey trails Eddie Holt, the man from the bridge and a former NAM activist with a manslaughter conviction, and witnesses him shape-shifting in Coney Island – which seemingly amounts to little more than running around on a beach naked, lapping up sea water and howling at the moon.

Dewey and Whittington go to the South Bronx, suspecting the killers' den is located in the abandoned church. When Whittington is attacked and killed by a wolf-like creature, Dewey goes to talk to the Native Americans who reveal that the murders have all been perpetuated by a rare undiscovered breed of hyper-evolved wolf: the wolfen. The wolfen, they claim, lived in harmony with the Native Americans for thousands of years, as another Nation, but when the Native Americans were largely exterminated and the wolves culled, the smartest of the creatures went underground. Since then they live in the 'new wilderness' of America's cities, where they scavenge upon 'the sick, the abandoned, those who will not be missed'. This chimes with evidence that the coroner had found of derelicts being found with similar wounds and hair matches throughout urban America. The Native Americans stress that the wolfen only kill to eat or for territory, and Dewey comes to realise that they assassinated Van der Veer because his redevelopment plans for the Bronx would gentrify their hunting territory. Dewey visits the Van der Veer penthouse late a night and is surprised by the police chief and Neff, who inform him they've closed the case, arresting members of *Götterdämmerung* for the crimes (their 'terrorist motto' happened to be: 'The end of the world by wolves'). They leave the building and in front of Federal Hall National Memorial,[196] next to the New York Stock Exchange, they are surrounded by wolfen. Not appeased that *Götterdämmerung* is serving as a patsy, the wolfen attack, decapitating the police chief, while Dewey and Neff escape to the penthouse. The film ends with Dewey and Neff surrounded by growling wolfen. To assuage them, Dewey trashes a scaled model of Van der Veer Towers and refuses to tell the powers that be that the wolfen were behind the attack, instead blaming it on *Götterdämmerung*. As the sun rises, the wolves run back to their den in the church in the South Bronx.

Wolfen's engagement with the urban politics of New York City lies in its convoluted answer to the question: 'The South Bronx and Wall Street, what's the connection?' Posed a quarter of the way through the film, when the investigators find the same lupine hairs on corpses in these drastically different areas of the city, twenty kilometres apart, it is the question around which the narrative circulates. At the time, the South Bronx was infamous as the poorest section of New York City's poorest borough, globally recognised as a symbol of everything bad that could happen to a city.[197] By the early eighties it had become, according to South Bronx-born Marshall Berman, 'an international code word for our epoch's accumulated urban nightmares: drugs, gangs, arson, murder, terror, thousands of buildings abandoned, neighbourhoods transformed into garbage- and brick-strewn wilderness.'[198] As Mike Davis has observed in his discussion of ghetto geomorphology: 'Here urban dereliction has become the moral and natural historical equivalent of war. In 1940-41, the Heinkel and Junkers bombers of the Luftwaffe destroyed 350,000 dwelling units and unhoused a million Londoners. In the 1970s, an equally savage "blitz" of landlord disinvestment, bank redlining and federal "benign neglect" led to the destruction of 294,000 housing units in New York City alone.'[199] Part of *Wolfen*'s setting, a section of Charlotte Street famously visited by President Jimmy Carter in 1977, was so devastated that it was taken off official maps of the city in 1974.[200] What connection does this area have to do with the skyscrapers, banks, and financial firms that populate Wall Street, the financial centre of the global capital of capital?

As our rather lengthy synopsis suggests, the somewhat jumbled nature of the plot and the richness of its themes provide the viewer with ample room for both critical interpretation and wild theorising. It is almost irresistible, especially in light of the lavish location shooting, not to take the film as a document of its era. But perhaps the documentary element is to be sought at one remove, in the way that *Wolfen* registers a narrative and visual imagination that is both inspired and constrained by the political imagination of the day. Moreover, attending also to Wadleigh's express intentions, the film exists as an ambitious attempt to aesthetically frame and comment on the political and economic forces shaping (and failing to shape) post-crisis New York City, situating the relationship between the South Bronx and Wall Street within the long durée of North American colonisation.

A capitalist memento mori

When *Wolfen* was green-lit there was a widespread demand for films shot on location in New York, with the crisis city as the backdrop. In the late-sixties to mid-seventies film audiences saw the rise of what Miriam Greenberg calls the 'asphalt jungle' genre that depict New York as the embodiment of that nation's urban crisis.[201] Today, New York has been thoroughly rebranded as the safest big city in America – for capital and real estate investments, tourism, shopping and Sunday brunch – but for a time stretching approximately from the late sixties to the mid-eighties, the city was considered by many to be in a state of terminal decline. After remaining largely static for twenty-five years, between 1963 and 1973 reported murders went up by 95 percent, rapes by 120 percent, robberies by 82 percent and assaults by 90 percent.[202] This, coupled with rising homelessness, panhandling, vandalism and, in 1971, the widespread and systematic corruption revealed within the New York Police Department, gave an image of a city on the brink of self-immolation. The total number of yearly murders in the city would continue to rise, peaking in 1990 with 2,245. In the asphalt jungle films, the city is seen as a cesspit of crime, drugs, sexual perversion and poverty, in which its protagonists struggle to stay afloat. Despite often painting the city with a cynical brush, these films – Greenberg names *Mean Streets, Taxi Driver, Midnight Cowboy, Panic in Needle Park, Dog Day Afternoon,* and *French Connection,* among others – were dramatically sophisticated and managed to present their characters as involved in complex human struggles, at times shedding distorted light on their social milieu.

In the mid-seventies this genre would morph, or degenerate, into what Greenberg calls the 'New York exploitation film', with *Death Wish* (1974) leading the charge. The story of a mild-mannered architect, played by Charles Bronson, who becomes a vigilante after his wife and daughter are raped and murdered by street punks (including Jeff Goldblum in his screen debut as 'Freak #1'), *Death Wish* transposed the narrative form of the Western from the lawless desert to the asphalt jungle.[203] Other examples named by Greenberg include *The Warriors, Driller Killer, Fort Apache, The Bronx, C.H.U.D.* and the *Maniac Cop* trilogy. These films depict the city as an organic body that is terminally ill and rather than offer any suggestions, or even hope, for treatment or cures – or attempt to develop their characters and their relationships – Greenberg writes that they 'were all too happy to play up the worst New York stereotypes for thrills and laughs'.[204] The more gruesome sequences in the film led her to classify *Wolfen* as a New York exploitation film as well.[205] Ironically, this was the frustrated wish of the releasing studio, United Artists, which insisted on selling *Wolfen* as exploitation, displeased at having been saddled with far too weird and intellectual a product.[206]

Part of the appeal of the films set in New York in this era today – and one could name others, stretching from lower budget films like Paul Morrison's occasionally brilliant *Forty Deuce,* set largely in 42nd Street's Port Authority bus terminal and starring Kevin Bacon as a gay prostitute in an early role, to documentaries like *Wild Style, The Police Tapes, 80 Blocks from Tiffany's,* and *Flyin' Cut Sleeves,* to art films like Gordon Matta-

Clark's *City Slivers* – is the visceral thrill of seeing the city in a period where its deterioration seems coupled to a restless creativity, an era when the city as a whole was 'dark and apocalyptic and yet fecund', to quote the actor John Leguiziamo.[207] This notion of New York as a city on the brink is brought home hyperbolically in the bleak camp splendour of John Carpenter's *Escape from New York* (1981). The city is here imagined as a place where crime feels so out of control, where the authorities are so corrupt or inept, where class, racial and social conflicts are so intense that the possibility that in seven years time it will be literally abandoned to criminals and surrounded by a militarised *cordon sanitaire* makes for a vaguely plausible scenario. It seems that the transition of the much-vaunted cultural and financial capital of the nation and the world to an open-air penal colony did not seem laughably idiotic to the cultural imagination of the day.[208] Part of the premise of *Escape from New York* is that crime went up 400% in the eighties, prompting the authorities to turn Manhattan into Manhattan Maximum Security Prison. The bridges and tunnels surrounding the island have been blown up, mined or blocked and those sentenced there are exiled for life without possibility of parole. The first shot of the island from the prison's perimeter wall on Governor's Island, looking across the Upper Bay towards the World Trade Center and downtown Manhattan, is jarringly breathtaking. The city is bathed in darkness, lit only by the moonlight reflecting off the facades of the skyscrapers.[209]

Writing in a period when residential rents in Manhattan are at record levels and the city could have the least amount of murders since the NYPD starting keeping records in the early sixties,[210] it is difficult to imagine that just over thirty years ago popular culture could envision such a drastically different fate for the city. The seventies, however, were a transformative decade for the city, the nation, and the world system as a whole. New York stood, and still stands, as an iconic and highly influential example of the transformation to neoliberalism whose lessons would be learned and solutions applied in the US and beyond. Aspects of this transformation have undoubtedly, on their own terms, been enormously successful; largely erasing the memory that in the mid-seventies many thought the city was about to drop dead, to paraphrase the famous *Daily News* headline. But the dismayingly familiar narrative that New York had become a dangerous place and has merely been cleaned up, usually told through the prism of crime statistics, does little to elucidate the forces beyond the city's transformation and serves to further elide the memory of the city that existed before the crisis.

In 1975 New York nearly defaulted on its debts. It is often said that as the city became a dirtier and more violent place, those who could left the crumbling city for a better life in the suburbs – a house with a white-picketed fence and a garage where their kids had access to good schools – meaning tax revenues plummeted, starting a vicious cycle where cuts to city services made the city worse, encouraging even more people with money to leave. The reality was more complex and directly connected to various policy decisions and priorities at the city, state, and national level. The dominant narrative of the fiscal crisis places the blame on the city's comparatively generous welfare spending, which went from simply exceeding the revenues brought in, to pushing the city to the brink of insolvency when coupled with the national/global economic stagnation of the period. Following World War II, New York City saw the rise of what Joshua Freeman has called a 'social democratic polity'.[211] A politically-mobilised working class with high rates of union membership and comparatively powerful left-leaning political representation fought for and achieved an extensive public hospital system with over twenty hospitals, a growing City University system with free tuition and by 1969 'open admissions', rent control and large public housing stock, a cheap and extensive public transport system, civil rights legislation that was ahead of its time nationally, and a system of community boards that oversaw city government. The argument from the right and the city's business elite was that this system simply cost too much to maintain and was discouraging capital investment in New York. The racial overtones to this argument were shockingly blatant at the time. As a spokesman from the Municipal Assistance Corporation, a state-backed corporation formed to help restore the city's finances following 1975 put it: 'It's the fucking blacks and Puerto Ricans. They use too many city services and they don't pay any taxes. New York's in trouble because it's got too many fucking blacks and Puerto Ricans'.[212]

From this perspective, the decline of a welfarist class compact is seen as inevitable and the austerity measures necessary. Many on the left have made the argument that while it is undeniable that the form the New York fiscal crisis took was the result of a combination of recession and over-borrowing, the actual causes of the crisis were complex and multiple.[213] There was the global economic stagnation of 1974-75, which was the worst economic downturn since the Great Depression; the loss of manufacturing jobs from New York and the rest of the industrial northeast to the Sunbelt (some of which was actively encouraged by the city, for example by rezoning in the garment district); the urban ills that did in fact encourage middle and upper class taxpayers to leave the city for the suburbs; the office real estate boom that pushed up land prices yet failed to generate revenue because of tax breaks and exceptions; public bonds being used to finance private building projects and increasing reliance on short-term, high-interest debt; pork barrel contracts that saw contract, supplies and equipment budgets skyrocket between 1960-75; and finally federal allocations under Nixon and Ford shifting from urban centres and the northeast to the Sunbelt, Midwest and suburbs.[214]

Regardless of the causes, the response to this fiscal crisis gave the business elites in New York a chance to 'change longstanding municipal priorities'.[215] Nationally and internationally, big business in the 1970s refined its ability to act as a class (as the power of the left and labour unions was being eroded).[216] The international business elite in New York makes the city government not only subservient to local or even national economic interests, but global ones, vying with London, Tokyo and Shanghai for financial eminence. This elite had little interest in prolonging New York's fragile experiment with social democracy. As David Rockefeller concluded in a closed-door meeting in 1973, 'If we don't take action now, we will see our own demise. We will evolve into another social democracy' (one imagines the last two words pronounced with the kind of sneer now accorded 'failed state').[217] A 'crisis regime' was established in New York City and the aforementioned Municipal Assistance Corporation (MAC) demanded the city institute a wage freeze for city workers, lay off city employees, start charging tuition at City University, and raise subway and bus fares. To adapt Toni Negri's terminology, there was a passage from the planner-city to the crisis-city.[218] And then in September 1975 the Emergency Financial Control Board Priorities included capital infrastructure improvements that increased land values, low property and business taxes, tax breaks for office and luxury apartment construction, restricted spending on social programs and restrained spending on city worker wages and benefits.[219] Continuing problems led the federal government to intervene with a bailout including $2.3 billion in loans in November. As part of the deal, 40% of city worker pension funds were to be used to buy city bonds, tying the fate of the worker's pensions to the financial health of the city. The conditions of the bailout, as David Harvey writes, 'amounted to a coup by the financial institutions against the democratically elected government of New York City, and it was every bit as effective as the military coup that had earlier occurred in Chile.'[220]

The effect of all this on New York's poorest neighbourhoods

was devastating. Over the course of the seventies, the city lost about 10% of its population (1.3 million to so-called 'white flight', with 600,000 blacks and Latinos either moving out of their burnt out neighbourhoods to other parts of the city or the suburbs), while the metropolitan area as a whole lost about 20%.[221] These trends took a particularly extreme form in the Bronx. During this same period the South-Central Bronx lost an astounding 80% of its housing units and population, the equivalent of four square blocks a week.[222] In 1978, the vacancy rate in the South Bronx was increasing at ten times the pace of the city as a whole.[223] The 'master builder' Robert Moses had taken his 'meat cleaver' to the borough over the preceding decades – during which the Cross Bronx Expressway was built, displacing up to 60,000 residents directly and thousands more indirectly as entire neighbourhoods were destroyed – and it was victim to the policy of 'planned shrinkage' throughout the seventies, the goal of which was rapid population decline via the withdrawal of essential services, ranging from libraries and garbage removal to police and fire services.[224] As Greenberg writes, 'Applying Darwinian reasoning to the logic of capital, [the proponents of planned shrinkage] argued that just as corporations were eliminating unprofitable plants, the city should shift services and resources from poor neighbourhoods that were already "dying" to those that were better off and most likely to survive'[225] (an argument that continues to inform public policy at the time of writing, with the 'shrinkage' and bankruptcy of Detroit).

Again, the racial drivers of this policy were clear. The NY Housing and Development Administration chief Roger Starr put it bluntly: 'Stop Puerto Ricans and the rural blacks from living in the city. ... Our urban system is based on the theory of taking the peasant and turning him into an industrial worker. Now there are no industrial jobs. Why not keep him a peasant. Better a thriving city of five million than a Calcutta of seven million.'[226] This process, whose racist and classist coordinates are laid out in epidemiological detail in the Wallaces's *A Plague on Your Houses*, started a vicious circle as once tightly knit communities were scattered, causing overcrowding in adjacent areas, and neighbourhoods that already had serious problems saw escalating rates of crime, poverty, and disease. The abandoned buildings became havens for illegality and objects of arson, all the more difficult to douse as the city authorities closed down fire departments in these predominantly Black and Latino areas. As two *Village Voice* journalists reporting on this relentless wave of devaluation observed: 'There is simply no incentive for banks, insurance companies, or anyone else with money to invest in building or rebuilding dwellings at reasonable rents. In housing, the final stage of capitalism is arson.'[227] The director of a health clinic in the area called it a 'Necropoli: a city of death'.[228]

Wolfen begins as this neoliberal reshaping of the city is underway. In a similar, yet less exaggerated manner to *Escape from New York*, the New York of *Wolfen* feels eerily depopulated; not just the South Bronx, which is depicted as a complete wasteland, but the city as a whole, whose atmosphere is palpably drained and defeated. There are none of the visual clichés of New York film staples: swarming crowds, vibrant street life, honking taxis. Reading a grim terminus into the real trend of urban contraction, the streets are without exception empty or populated by a lone pedestrian or the occasional passing car. The only location that could be said to be bustling in the film is the morgue. You have the inevitable skyline shots, but they are invariably silent and still, lapidary. New York is more of a crumbling husk than an asphalt jungle.

This is no more pronounced than in the film's handling of the South Bronx. Shot in what looks like late autumn, with an overcast sky, the dull grey of the dusty concrete and brick wreckage is accentuated. There are only a few solitary people about – a man warming himself next to a fire in a garbage can, an old woman crossing the street with a walker – like the survivors of some catastrophe. When Dewey and Neff arrive at Charlotte Street to visit the site where the wolf hairs were found on the corpses of derelicts, their shock at the state of the neighbourhood is palpable. The destruction is so immense that it is nearly impossible to imagine that it had been a functioning city street; the impression is that the streets were built through the debris, with the only building standing the abandoned church constructed for the film. One of the undeniable attractions of *Wolfen* is the way it projects the ambiguous aesthetic of ruins onto the bullish capital of capital (resentful glee at its comeuppance no doubt an ingredient). These are images that have been seen elsewhere, for example in the Ray Mortenson's photos of the area taken between 1982 and 1984, and in documentaries from the area like *80 Blocks from Tiffany's* (1979), *Wild Style* (1983), and *Flyin' Cut Sleeves* (1993), but even after multiple viewings, the extent of the destruction of the city's landscape is startling. One wonders if there are hours of B-roll of Charlotte Street, and extra POV footage of wolfen wandering around the rubble of the South Bronx, mouldering away in crates in some warehouse in Los Angeles. The mere capture on film of this historical moment is one of the film's enduring attractions, and reinforces the perception that it is sometimes in its lateral representation in 'low' genres that the US city's mutations through the 'long downturn' and deindustrialisation can best be glimpsed – as evidenced in the L.A. of Carpenter's *Assault on Precinct 13* (1976) and *They Live* (1988), or the Pittsburgh of George Romero's *Martin* (1976).

In his classic essay from 1911, Georg Simmel writes: 'In the case of the ruin, the fact that life, with its wealth and its changes, once dwelled here constitutes an immediately perceived presence. The ruin creates the present form of a past life, not according to the contents or remnants of that life, but according to its past as such.'[229] The new form that is created by this 'brute, downward-dragging, corroding, crumbling power' is 'entirely meaningful, comprehensible, differentiated.'[230] Simmel sets up architecture as a battle between the creative spirit and nature. Ruins are the result of a sort of revenge of nature, whereby its forces retake the material shaped by humans. This is framed clearly in a series of ruin photographs by William Christenberry, in which the kudzu vine devours buildings throughout the south, but also can be seen throughout the 'genre' of 'ruin lust' imagery, as mold and lichen cover walls and trees push through roofs, so many 'ornaments of time'.[231] These images of nature conquering the urban environment more than risk lending it the semblance of a natural process, in which historical events, political struggles, economic interests, and policy decisions are irrevocably buried. They also occlude the deep class and racial rifts that condition the experience of ruination in the American metropolis.[232]

Michael Wadleigh, *Wolfen*, 1981

What is odd about the handling of this theme in *Wolfen* is that while the wolfen function as agents of nature, clawing urban space back from the settler-colonists, the ruins themselves feel so fresh that, unlike current photographs of Detroit's dereliction, nature (or 'the world without us') does not seem to have made its presence felt yet.[233] Time is without ornaments. Like the ruins of World War II, again, the ruins of the South Bronx bespeak the speed and 'humanity' of their origins: torching and demolition, not the slow creep of weeds and erosion of soil, decomposing long vacant buildings. Though the setting is framed by the narrative and the camera alike as a wilderness, where hapless derelicts and junkies are stalked by feral beasts, little about it feels 'natural'; which also undermines the film's temptation to elide colonised peoples and urbanised nature via the fantasy of predatory revenge.

The role played by the ruins in the narrative is ambivalent. One of the odd aspects of *Wolfen*'s engagement with the landscape of urban crisis is that the only available options for the hardest-hit neighbourhoods seems to be total abandonment or total gentrification; there is little to no consideration of those who might not have escaped during the period of planned shrinkage – in fact, none of the characters seem to find it particularly problematic that the wolfen are eating the city's most vulnerable inhabitants. In this sense, it would be relatively easy to charge *Wolfen* with decontextualising the decline of the city, celebrating and aestheticising the ruins while neglecting to consider the lives of city-dwellers, the same accusation levelled at 'ruin porn' in recent years.

The ideological subtext behind large swathes of the 'find-a-ruin' school of photography is not a critique of political economy or an interest in the social factors behind catastrophic disurbanisation. Yet in direct opposition to the pornography of the '"direct" representation of misery' that Allan Sekula excoriates – the sad alcoholic, the hungry child, the tired peasant – ruin porn is largely devoid of human beings. The author and photographer Camilo José Vergara, arguably a pioneer when it comes to US ruin photography,[234] writes that he would often wait for people to pass through the frame in his famous projects on 'American ruins' before snapping his pictures, in order to convey a sense of scale and show how people interact with the environment. Yet contemporary examples seem intentionally to consist purely of images of decaying buildings and their environs – constant capital reverting to catastrophic ornament in a resilient fantasy of 'the world without us'. In a way that nonetheless resonates with Rosler and Sekula's critique of a sentimental social realism, this tendency could be seen as shifting the 'blame' onto the cities themselves for not adjusting to the era of globalisation. The defeated city is not just the object of melancholy, it is also guilty of its choices: the choice to maintain welfare programs, the choice of unions not to accept lower paid jobs, the choice of black urban populations to elect corrupt politicians, etc. The more constructive readings of images of dereliction – questions about how cities built by Fordism can survive in a post-Fordist era and general questions about capitalism, real estate, and democracy – are easily occluded by the aestheticised rot.

Evan Calder Williams calls the film a 'documentary horror film' not only because it is shot on location in violence of the actual ruins of the South Bronx, but because it 'enacted such violence and left material remainders: the emptied husk of a church we see was built up by the film crew, burnt, and left to skeletally stand. As such, the film is the funereal, charred rubble-strewn present of a place with no future beyond the two possibilities modelled by the film: the sheen of gentrified renewal, or the reconquest by remnants of another past now adapted to flourish in the vacant wilds of a city too busy to notice.'[235]

Writing about Detroit in an essay in the architecture and design magazine *Metropolis* in 1995, Camilo José Vergara claimed, 'I propose that as a tonic for our imagination, as a call for renewal, as a place within our national memory, a dozen city blocks of pre-Depression skyscrapers be stabilized and left standing as ruins: an American Acropolis. We could transform the nearly 100 troubled buildings into a grand national historic park of play and wonder'. This claim, as one might expect, caused some uproar amongst many of Detroit's developers, politicians and residents.[236] This vision of posthumous urbanism is oddly realised in the conclusion of *Wolfen*, with the destruction of the model of Van Der Veer Towers; the film's sympathies seems to lie with the readymade ruin park over gentrification, hinting that the South Bronx will be left as a sort of 'social reserve', with the inability of the neoliberal city to care for its entire population making certain it is stocked with derelicts for the wolfen to hunt (and kept away from the financial and real estate oligarchy).

The myriad films released in the 1970s and 1980s depicting, documenting, exploiting or contributing to this dystopian image of a borough of one of the world's greatest cities, reduced to rubble, all incline – in the absence of some sense of the social causalities at stake – to implying that urban decline is an inevitable process and that violent depravity is its inexorable result. The city is an organic body that is terminally ill and will gradually depopulate and be taken over by street gangs and lunatics. Racist and classist imaginaries of august vintage clearly play their part here. The notion that the destruction of the South Bronx is, intentionally or otherwise, clearing the way for something else is never considered. A sort of cynical Malthusian necessity elides all attempts at cognitive mapping. In this sense, it is to its immense credit that *Wolfen* divines the strategy behind the abandonment of these neighbourhoods, the (re)development lurking behind the dereliction. In that sense, it is a rare beast, an exploitation film about exploitation. That it can only hallucinate and not properly imagine a counter-force is no reason for blame.

The second civil war and the twilight of the gods

The first civil war was fought over who should control the West. This civil war is to be fought over who should control the cites.
James Boggs, *Racism and the Class Struggle*

Midway through the riveting 1977 documentary *The Police Tapes*, in which filmmakers Alan and Susan Raymond spent several months with one of the first handheld video cameras and officers from the 44ᵗʰ Precinct in the South Bronx, Bronx Borough Commander Chief Tony Bouza launches into an eloquent and sympathetic explanation of the tensions between the civilians and the police, the causes of the era's urban violence and the ability of the police to stifle it. In a tirade that references everyone from B.F. Skinner and Stanley Kubrick to Aristotle ('poverty is the parent of revolution and crime'), Bouza argues that the problems of the ghetto, the frustration, rage and violence generated by poverty and inequality, and the failure of government to deal with them, have remained invisible to the majority of Americans and ponders whether his role of 'keeping the ghetto cool' is 'deflecting America's attention from discovering this cancer', and whether he'd be better off failing so the country would at last be obliged to confront the problem. His conclusion ends with a startling admission, in which while expressing his feelings of defeat and frustration, he claims his role is essentially 'to be the commander of an army of occupation of the ghetto'.

Walter Hill, *The Warriors*, 1979

In a suggestive footnote in his *The Geopolitical Aesthetic*, Jameson notes that many of the gang films of the late seventies and early eighties – he names only the New York films *Escape from New York*, *The Warriors*, and *Fort Apache, The Bronx* – can be read as 'visions of internal civil war.'[237] In each of these films, an armed and organised force threatens the state's monopoly of violence. This interpretation is particularly forceful in the case of *The Warriors* (1979), which starts with Cyrus, the head of one of the most powerful gangs in New York, the Gramercy Riffs, calling a gang summit in Van Cortlandt Park in the Bronx. Cyrus takes the stage and exhorts the members of the gangs to recognise their collective strength: 60,000 'soldiers' – gang members and their affiliates – who would outnumber the NYPD three to one if they were to unite into one gang and control the streets. The assembled delegates are receptive to the message, keen to continue the general truce and take over the city one borough at a time, until the leader of a gang called the Rogues shoots Cyrus and blames it on the Warriors, who then must fight their way all the way through the city to Coney Island.[238]

Jameson writes that these films 'shade into what is called, in Science-Fiction terminology, "near-future" representations and this is a distinctive genre in its own right, its form and structure sharply distinguished by the viewer from "realistic" verisimilitude or immanence.'[239] What is particularly interesting about *The Warriors*, however, is that despite being based loosely on Xenophon's *Anabasis*, being one of the campiest of the films mentioned above, and having the most bloodless, comic-book violence, aspects of its plot mirror real events in seventies South Bronx gang culture. In 1971, Cornell 'Black Benjie' Benjamin, the lead peacemaker of the South Bronx gang the Ghetto Brothers, was murdered trying to break up a fight between the gangs Seven Immortals, Black Spades, and the Mongols.[240] The Ghetto Brothers at this point no longer considered themselves a gang but spoke of themselves as a 'club' or 'organisation' whose purpose was to 'help blacks and Puerto Ricans live in a better environment'. Their jargon often mimed that of the black liberation and Nuyorican movements, as exemplified in this statement read by Benjy Melendez in 1971: 'We are being oppressed by the North American Yankee. We the Puerto Ricans should rise up and defend ourselves against these dogs who oppress us, and liberate our country from capitalism and imperialism.'[241] While they still had a Minister of War and access to weapons, rather than seeking retaliation over the murder of Benjamin, the Ghetto Brothers sought to organise a general truce and inter-gang alliance amongst the gangs in the area on December 7, 1971. Known as the Hoe Avenue Peace Meeting, over a hundred members of various gangs met at the Hoe Avenue Boys & Girls Club in Crotona Park in the Bronx.[242] These gangs would form a coalition called 'The Family', with a similar association coming together in Brooklyn. Besides keeping a general truce, the coalitions allowed the gangs to negotiate with the city for summer jobs and recreational programs for youth and federal antipoverty projects as a united front.[243] The official youth unemployment rate was at 60% (although advocates noted that in some neighbourhoods the rate was more like 80%) and the gangs, many of whose members had grown up in neighbourhoods central to the civil rights movement, began to realise that they could help get antipoverty funds into the area.[244] This was reflective of the rather sizeable amount of interaction between the gangs and the city bureaucracy, particularly the Youth Services Administration. With 10,000 gang members in the Bronx alone according to the police, the gangs also offered a pool of new recruits for the Young Lords and Black Panther parties: 'Gangbangers were natural recruits for revolutionary activity since they were accustomed to defying police and other authorities, and political organizing offered an appropriately masculine alternative to the self-defeating violence of gang conflict.'[245]

It might be tempting to read the wolfen as a lupine Bronx street gang, fighting for their turf, attacking as a pack – taking dubious and ever-ready metaphors of ferality literally. *Wolfen,* however, is unmistakeably set after the so-called 'Second Civil War', after drugs and COINTELPRO had decimated the black power and nationalist movements in the ghetto, at the brutal onset of a period of reaction where capital was re-colonising parts of the city, turning it into an ever more powerful engine for capital accumulation. By the time the crew of *Wolfen* got to Charlotte Street, the Turbans, the gang who patrolled the area, were long gone, their turf reduced to rubble.[246] There is no inkling of community resistance to the gentrification in the Bronx other than the wolfen; even the revolutionary Native Americans have (seemingly at least) abandoned their militancy and taken up day jobs. The name *Götterdämmerung* – 'twilight of the gods' – is particularly apt for the primary terror group suspected to be involved, encapsulating as it does as the incoherent terminus of the radical movements of the 1960s and 70s. The Wagnerian pomp of their title is replete with irony; any effectiveness they may have enjoyed is precluded by the power and resources of the security-industrial complex. In this historical moment left terrorism is a convenient scapegoat, or even a false flag, not a clear and present threat.

The wolfen in the film, however, do emerge as a sort of a radical subject, in the sense that they're the only collective able to challenge the elites' vision of the modern city. They manage to kill the most powerful man in New York, and in the end seem to convince the lead detective of the validity of their 'project'. Their mission achieved, the pack runs back to the South Bronx victorious. There are three different basic readings of all of this. First, if we take the action literally, it was indeed a species of hyper-evolved wolf that is behind the murders.[247] The second and third possibilities both rely on the 'supernatural': either the Native Americans shapeshift into wolfen or they are allied with them.[248] The director himself has said the film 'is about American Indians who are killing rich people.' He says, quite ambiguously, that this might be because they want Manhattan back, and his reading of the film's conclusion is that: 'The cop is upholding a society he begins to feel is unjust. … In the end he allows to let the murders or the terrorists get away with what they are doing because he no longer believes in the values of his society.' There are numerous problems with Wadleigh's take on his own film. First, most obviously, what the viewer sees throughout the film are wolves – not Native Americans. In fact, the zoologist Ferguson is killed while Dewey is watching Eddie Holt shape-shift on the shore. So either we have to believe that part of the film's premise is that Native American shape-shifting is indeed possible, or that somehow, because of their ancient wisdom or whatever, Native Americans, like the Na'vi in Cameron's *Avatar*, are able to conspire with or manipulate this band of ruthless predators. This interpretation is perhaps bolstered by the fact that the Native Americans work on the city's skyscrapers and bridges:[249] points that either or both connect (downtown) Manhattan with outer boroughs as well as provide an overview of the city as a whole from which to marshal their troops. The French poster features the eyes of the wolves over the city and the film's first and final shots are of Eddie Holt and his gang on top of the Brooklyn Bridge and Manhattan Bridge respectively, gazing at the skyline.

Whether it's just wolves, shapeshifting Native Americans, or a Native American and wolfen coalition, the film's 'green' message is trite. In a familiar, racialised fantasy, the wolfen serve as a utopian other on which we can project an image of organic wholeness in communion with mother earth. As the 'Old Indian' tells Holt: 'In their world, there can be no lies, no crimes. … In their eyes, you are the savage.' The werewolf as a metaphor is often linked to this boundary between culture and nature, the human and the savage, and here the Native Americans seem to fall on the side of the latter, albeit in a largely sympathetic fantasy.[250] Throughout the film, they stress the extent to which modern man has lost touch with nature. As Eddie Holt tells Dewey, 'You have your technology but you lost. You lost your senses.' In fact, the corporate security firm is often framed as the reverse image of the wolfen and Native Americans. Both keep watch over the city, both can sense fear or dishonesty in those they observe, but the firm can only do so with the help of technology, which allows them to do everything from tracking their targets all over the city to identifying when suspects are lying by detecting minor shifts in skin temperature and voice tone. The wolves, and perhaps by association the Native Americans, are able to do all of this based on their tremendously powerful senses and deep connection with their environment.[251] As the wolfen attack to prevent 'man' from encroaching on their lands, *Wolfen* could also be linked to a burgeoning list of eco-horror films in which nature takes revenge. While most of the urban crisis films, the danger or horror is thoroughly urban in its origin and connotations – street gangs, hoodlums, maniacs, Cannibalistic Humanoid Underground Dwellers – in *Wolfen* the horror comes from an ancient remainder forced underground by the forced development of the continent. As human expansion throughout the North American mainland decimated their populations, the wolfen moved into the cities.

Michael Wadleigh, *Wolfen*, 1981

From *Capital, Volume 1*'s declaration that 'Capital is dead labour, that, vampire-like, only lives by sucking living labour, and lives the more, the more labour it sucks,'[252] to Matt Taibbi's notorious description of Goldman Sachs as a 'great, blood-sucking vampire squid' – vampirism and capital have been joined in metaphor. The proletariat, associated with Frankenstein in Franco Moretti's seminal 1982 text 'The Dialectics of Fear', has more recently found transfigured form in the zombie craze of the past decade or so, which stretches back to the Romero films from the 1970s and 1980s. In Chapter 8 of *Capital* lycanthropes also make an appearance: 'In its blind unrestrainable passion, its were-wolf hunger for surplus-labour, capital oversteps not only the moral, but even the merely physical maximum bounds of the working day. It usurps the time for growth, development, and healthy maintenance of the body'.[253]

If we understand the capitalist (Van der Veer) as capital personified with its werewolf hunger, then here capital's werewolf hunger runs into actual werewolves; indifferently personified automatism comes up against an indomitable, clandestine collective. The horror of the gentrification of the South Bronx is transmuted into the horror of the creatures' predation. According to Franco Moretti: 'Fascinated by the horror of the monster, the public accepts the vices of its destroyer without a murmur. ... Whoever dares to fight the monster automatically becomes the representative of the species, of the whole of society. The monster, the utterly unknown, serves to reconstruct a universality, a social cohesion which in itself would no longer carry conviction'.[254] The death of the villain, an allegorical stand-in for all that is frightening in given historical moment, is sacrificial and guarantees the restoration of the status quo.[255] In this interpretation, horror expresses and then represses economic conflict and volatility. The genre is often conservative because the monster is commonly vanquished, making the return to the status quo seem like a cathartic victory.

Yet the wolfen do not create social cohesion contingent upon their terrifying threat. In fact, the wolfen appear less monstrous than the luxury development; the werewolf hunger of capital personified (Van der Veer) is more terrible than the actual werewolves (the dark side of this again being their social bottom-feeding). There is a shift in Dewey's agency from representative of the NYPD – he was already an outsider from the beginning – to siding with the Native Americans and the wolfen. Jason Read perspicuously argues that:

> In the final scene, when Wilson is cornered and surrounded by the wolf pack, he destroys the model of the new real estate development. This is an interesting reversal of the clichéd scene from horror and fantasy movies in which the protagonist has to destroy the magic amulet or other device in order to destroy the monster: in this case the monster is us, and what has to be destroyed is not some primitive magic, but a symbol of urban gentrification. In the end what makes the movie interesting is how it solves the problem of the werewolf as symbol and subtext. The wolves are not symbols of some repressed animal nature, but are the return of the repressed, the vengeance of a population subject to genocidal slaughter.[256]

In this sense, the film's true villain is killed in the opening scene, though the deed is only completed once his legacy is also demolished in the film's finale.

What makes *Wolfen* unique and its fantasy anomalous is that the wolves do not just live in a symbiotic, fantastic relationship with dispossessed Native Americans and besieged nature. They also depend on capitalist urban planning, in the sense that they thrive in the new wilderness created by planned shrinkage and 'benign neglect' (they exist not just in NY, the coroner in the film discovers, but Newark, Philadelphia, New Orleans). Scavenging on the last vestiges of the detritus the property developers are desperate to remove from the territory – those who did not escape in the opening salvos of 'urban renewal' – the wolfen literally feed on the urban crisis, while their existence is threatened by the emergence of the neoliberal city, which that cycle of urban devaluation has made possible.[257] This is a process that's even bigger and more powerful than any single individual capitalist – here Van der Veer – whose assassination is merely a sort of gentrification blowback. Rather than a street gang then, the wolfen are somewhat like the artists who move into run down neighbourhoods for studio space and cheap housing. Like them, they are the unwitting collaborators with capital, readying the neighbourhood for a new cycle of investment and development, useful in the opening stages of the process but soon to be displaced themselves. The wolfen here act unwittingly not as the stormtroopers of gentrification, but its janitors, which makes the director's claim that the film is about 'American Indians killing rich people' all the more perplexing. Simultaneously, they set the conditions for their own demise. The wolfen can only devour the most vulnerable, otherwise they would have been detected and culled a long time ago. Or rather, they are forced to go overground and kill the powerful in order to be able to continue to devour the most vulnerable. In the film's conclusion, as the wolves are running off into the sunset, they are essentially sprinting back to the South Bronx to prey on more of the poor.

Neoliberalism and/or Bust

Everything about history that, from the very beginning, has been untimely, sorrowful, unsuccessful, is expressed in a face – or rather in a death's head.
Walter Benjamin

In his excellent study of the New York fiscal crisis from 1982, William Tabb makes a prescient claim: 'I do not believe New York is "dead", as some assert, but is in the middle of a transformation in which an attempt is being made to push large numbers of poor and working people out, and to reduce the cost of local government. Should this effort succeed, the city's future as a corporate capital will indeed be bright'.[258] The murder rate would peak in 1990, but decline for the next fifteen years, and by 2005 it was back down to its 1963 level. New York is widely hailed as the safest big city in America and rents are at an all time high. At the same time, it is the most unequal large city in the most unequal state in the most unequal developed country in the world.[259] One in five New York City residents live in poverty and the Bronx today is still the poorest urban county in America.[260] The corporate business elite and the corporate headquarters complex are doing just fine but the social democratic institutions, like CUNY with its free tuition and open admissions, which were envisioned as means of providing better futures for low-income New Yorkers, have largely fallen by the wayside. The city continues to import its highly-skilled labour force while those born poor are more likely than ever to stay poor, on welfare or in low-wage jobs, and be forced out of the city by rising rents and living costs. The historical amnesia forgets the neoliberal turn, and how prior to this New York City was a place that entertained the liberal (not even necessarily socialist) dream of providing its entire population with education, housing, healthcare, cheap transit, employment, and general welfare. As David Harvey puts it, in a bitter rejoinder to Rem Koolhaas's landmark text, '"Delirious New York" erased the collective memory of democratic New York'.[261]

Not only, as argued above, was New York an iconic and highly influential example in the transformation to neoliberalism whose lessons would be learned and solutions applied throughout the nation and the world, but the policies put in place in the seventies have a direct relationship to the financial crisis of the last several years. In this respect, the conjuncture of the 1970s in New York City – as manifest in policy, political economy, social struggles, everyday life and cultural fantasies – still has many lessons for our own moment. David Harvey makes the links plain:

> [I]t was the New York City fiscal crisis of 1975 that centred the storm. With one of the largest public budgets at that time in the capitalist world, New York City, surrounded by sprawling affluent suburbs, went broke. The local solution, orchestrated by an uneasy alliance between state powers and financial institutions, pioneered the neoliberal ideological and practical political turn that was to be deployed worldwide in the struggle to perpetuate and consolidate capitalist class power. The recipe devised was simple enough: crush the power of labour, initiate wage repression, let the market do its work, all the while putting the power of the state at the service of capital in general and of investment finance in particular. This was the solution of the 1970s that lies at the root of the crisis of 2008-9.[262]

Wolfen is a film of exhaustion: it is a film about an exhausted protagonist (at one point he's told he has 'the eyes of the dead'), set in the dead zones of an exhausted city with an exhausted working-class and an exhausted left. It is also a film that registers some momentous manoeuvres in a different 'civil war', one in which the business elite trounced the working class. The film's attempt to posit a radical agency capable of intervening in the (re)development of the city comes across as absurd, deranged wish-fulfilment, eroding any sort of logical or even narrative consistency. (That said, one may wonder who can convincingly posit a revolutionary subject capable of triumphing over the forces of Finance, Insurance and Real Estate in the contemporary neoliberal metropolis any more plausible that a super breed of intelligent wolves.) Simultaneously, however, the film is successful in generating a weird and absorbing allegory, which evokes an answer to the question posed at the beginning of this discussion. What connects the South Bronx and Wall Street? The 'werewolf hunger' of capital, finance and real estate. What lies in tatters beneath the rubble is the precarious social-democratic compact of postwar New York City. What rises in its wake is a city where the memories have largely been wiped and the ruins elided, the unrestrained voraciousness of capital now but an everyday appetite.

Chapter 4

Baltimore as World and Representation
(*The Wire*, 2002-2008)

Academics? What, they gonna study your study?
Howard 'Bunny' Colvin to Dr. David Parenti, U. of Maryland
sociologist studying young violent offenders in Baltimore

Baltimore all I know. Man gotta live what he know.
Omar Little

The capitalist city is the arena of the most intense social and
political confusions at the same time as it is a monumental
testimony to and a moving force within the dialectics of
capitalism's uneven development. How to penetrate the
mystery, unravel the confusions, and grasp the contradictions?
David Harvey, *The Urban Experience*

Novel TV

Are there cultural forms adequate to evoking, analysing or
mapping the dynamics of capitalism, in its uneven and combined
geographical development? Is 'representation' a suitable concept
to grasp the critical and clinical perspicacity of such forms? As
one of the most challenging, popular and multi-faceted attempts
to give aesthetic and narrative shape to the comprehension of
contemporary society, *The Wire* provides a unique opportunity to
tackle these questions. Via the frame of the police procedural or
crime drama, the show's five seasons depict the city of Baltimore
– that 'dark corner of the American experiment', as its creator
calls it – in remarkable breadth and depth, addressing the drug
trade, de-industrialisation, city hall, the school system, and the

media. Each of these 'worlds' is mapped both vertically (making internal hierarchies explicit) and horizontally (tracking their entanglements and conflicts with the other 'worlds' spread throughout the city).[263] For example, within the world of the drug dealers the show leads us from the lookout kids all the way up to the heads of each drug gang and then even to the suppliers. Within the police force we go from the snitch, the patrolman on the beat, all the way up to the chief of police. This is repeated within each world, as bureaucratic chains of command, pecking orders and dependencies are laid bare. But we are also able to see how each world affects the ones around it, though rarely in pellucid ways. How the evaporation of working class jobs leads young men into the drug trade; how the kids of addicts and dealers cope at school; how city hall leans on the police force to employ meaningless policies (in terms of actual crime reduction) in order to 'cook the books', etc. The show descends into the hidden (if open air) abode of street-level drug distribution, not merely to sensitise the viewer to the violence and hopelessness that wracks the inner city, but to expose the complex organisations and forms of agency at stake in the drug economy[264] and their contradictory interactions – both hostile and symbiotic – with the political and economic institutions of neoliberalism.

While for a show like *CSI* technology is the real protagonist, in *The Wire* it is the urban fabric itself: the city is the critical prism through which to explore the vicissitudes of what *The Wire*'s creator, David Simon, has called 'raw, unencumbered capitalism.' As he writes:

The Wire depicts a world in which capital has triumphed completely, labor has been marginalized and monied interests have purchased enough political infrastructure to prevent reform. It is a world in which the rules and values of the free market and maximized profit have been mistaken for a social framework, a world where institutions themselves are paramount and every day human beings matter less.[265]

The themes of relentless devaluation, dispossession and decline are writ large. Simon himself, wryly tipping his hat to Chomsky and Toynbee, has portrayed the show as a study of 'the decline of the American empire'. In his words, *The Wire* 'is perhaps the only storytelling on television that overtly suggests that our political and economic and social constructs are no longer viable, that our leadership has failed us relentlessly, and that no, we are not going to be all right'.[266]

Critics have compared the series to the great Victorian novel in its painstaking attention to detail, disenchanted realism, sophisticated character development, and focus on urban depravation ('Dickensian' is a common adjective and one which the show appears to mock in season 5). Dickens and the works like Balzac's *La Comédie Humaine* or Zola's *Les Rougon-Macquart* can certainly be seen as influences on a show for which the term 'novel television' is appropriate.[267] Formally, *The Wire* has obvious affinities with Italian neo-realism, from its so-called 'style-less' style (lack of non-diegetic sound, unobtrusive camera, etc.) to its use of non-professionals actors and overall avoidance of stars.[268] But we can also consider its use of conventional speech, the loose, episodic structure rather than a tight, neatly plotted narrative, and use of actual locations. For American television, and detective series in particular, *The Wire* has an extraordinarily open narrative structure. Not only are many scenes superfluous to the main narrative, it is often difficult to ascertain what the main narrative actually is or to identify some kind of central conflict.[269] The various plot lines have at best incomplete resolution and the fate of many characters is unascertainable. While traditional narrative locates causal agency at the level of individual characters, in *The Wire* the socio-economic system – which we can provisionally identify as neoliberal US capitalism and its urban institutions – is the opaque subject, in the sense both of subject-matter and agent. The show's characters experience structural pressures in myriad ways, and they cannot but constantly try to manipulate it or temporarily circumvent it. Whether in the inevitable frustration that comes from attempting to 'buck the system' or in the fatalism of playing 'the game', the theme of systemic constraint is pervasive. When individual characters do show blatant disregard for the system – for instance McNulty in season five – the immensity of their task and the weight on their shoulders is palpable; indeed, the reason why McNulty is the closest thing the show has to a protagonist is arguably because of this aspect of his personality: we are constantly reminded how his persistent attempt to wrench agency from the system makes it impossible for him to maintain a family, drives him to alcoholism, etc.[270] It is in this light that we should consider Simon's observation that the show is not 'about' any specific character, 'It was about The City'.[271]

In what sense then is the passionate praise and slow-burning popularity garnered by *The Wire* a testament to its capacity to map capitalist reality with potency and precision? And what role does the show's condemnatory portrayal of devaluation, decline and the failure of reform – *The Wire*'s 'politics' – play in its representation of US capitalism's impact on the city? The difficulty in approaching the show with these questions in mind is that it demands a certain degree of disaggregation, allowing us to consider at one and the same time the ideological parameters of a show which is openly didactic (in the most noble sense of the term), but whose formal contribution might not be entirely flush with its aims. In other words, we want to hold together, and if need be in tension, the 'picture' of the urbanisation of capital wilfully projected by *The Wire*, with a broader reflection on the aesthetic and epistemic challenges of 'mapping' or 'representing' the contemporary capitalist world.

In the hyperghetto

Unlike in many of the works of cognitive mapping surveyed in these pages, *The Wire*'s action, *prima facie*, does not range across planetary commodity chains or international networks of intrigue and affect: the drama takes place almost completely in greater Baltimore (and primarily West Baltimore). As Wallace remarks in season one, 'If it ain't West Baltimore, I don't know it.' Even if Simon makes clear that Baltimore acts as a stand-in for any number of second-tier American cities (and has suggested a similar program could explore the mutation of 'post-industrial' ports like Liverpool or Rotterdam), a tremendous amount of attention is paid to the regional dialects, slang, and music subcultures like Baltimore Club and local hip hop.[272] There are very few scenes that take place outside of 'Bodymore, Murdaland' (as a graffito has it in the show's credits), and almost all of these depict the Baltimoreans out of their element. The scene where the drug dealer Bodie is traveling to pick up a 'package' in Philadelphia and doesn't get why the Baltimore hip hop station he's listening to fades out, as he has never been out of its range, is one of many that demonstrate for most of the characters involved the city-limits of Baltimore represent the boundaries of their world (he ends up listening to Garrison Keillor's *A Prairie Home Companion*). This also extends to the elites, as we witness the inability of Baltimore's mayor to secure a meeting with Maryland's governor in Annapolis. In its method, *The Wire* is perhaps most comparable to Hubert Sauper's harrowing documentary *Darwin's Nightmare* (2004), which takes the Nile perch industry on the coast of Lake Victoria in Tanzania as its starting point in order to depict a broad cross-section of the coastal region's inhabitants: from fishermen to street kids who smoke the fish's packaging, from a woman who picks through the rotting fish carcasses at the dump, trying to find some suitable for frying and sale at the local market, to the Ukrainian pilots who fly the fish to the EU in their beat-up cargo plains, all the way to the EU bureaucrats who give the fish processing plant a stamp of approval. Similarly, *The Wire* starts with a murder case, which morphs into a ramified narcotics investigation, and eventually expands to include different concentric and overlapping circles of Baltimore and its institutions. Geographically, however, it remains stubbornly rooted, foregoing the more regional range of other contemporary variations on the police procedural (Malmö-Copenhagen in *The Bridge*, Louisiana in *True Detective*, and so on).

The Wire, 2002-2008

Simon himself has referred to the series as a single sixty-six hour movie.[273] Contrary to the standard procedural format, single episodes have little autonomy and the show is much better suited to being watched intensely over several days rather than an hour a week for several months – feeding off but also displacing television's love-affair with repetition.[274] The sheer length of the show affords a depth that other 'cognitive mapping' films cannot possibly approach, allowing *The Wire* to move away from an individualistic narrative centred upon the trials and tribulations of one or more protagonists. Instead of plot gimmicks that allow the show to investigate certain relationships (the drug Czar's daughter becomes a crack whore in *Traffic*; an economic pundit is able to gain access to oil elites only after his son is electrocuted in a Saudi Prince's swimming pool in *Syriana*...), the serial format allows *The Wire* to map the city space to an extent unimaginable in other tele-visual formats (despite being 'always already incomplete', as John Kraniauskas has noted[275]).

Before delving into the show's treatment of the contemporary capitalist city, and the problems it raises for a consideration of the aesthetic challenges posed by the accumulation and repro-duction of capital, it is worth considering the kind of city that *The Wire* is preoccupied with. Loïc Wacquant's recent *Urban Outcasts* provides a useful starting point. Wacquant, taking Chicago as his object, tries to look behind the 'lunar landscape' of deindustri-alised and deproletarianised US black and Hispanic inner cities, those 'districts of dereliction' that have borne the brunt of drug addiction, gang and police violence, real estate speculation, withdrawal of public services and punishing poverty ever since the riots of the 1960s. He writes of the shift in the 1970s from the colour line of the 'communal ghetto' to the class-race line of the 'hyperghetto', 'a novel, decentred, territorial and organisational configuration characterized by conjugated segregation on the basis of race *and* class in the context of the double retrenchment of the labour market *and* the welfare state from the urban core, necessitating and eliciting the corresponding deployment of an intrusive and omnipresent police and penal apparatus'.[276] This is the landscape of 'advanced marginality', which Simon and his writing partner Ed Burns had already dramatized, from the standpoint of drug use and the 'petty entrepreneurialism' which orbits around it, in the book and TV mini-series *The Corner* (2000). Wacquant's thesis about the sources of advanced margin-ality is interesting, and worth considering in light of the question of *The Wire*'s figuration and critique of contemporary US capitalism, and its attention to the specifically political dimension of the city in Series 3: 'The implosion of America's dark ghetto and its flooding by extreme marginality turn out to be economically underdetermined and politically overdetermined: properly diagnosed, *hyperghettoization is primarily a chapter in political sociology,* not postindustrial economics, racial demography or urban geography'.[277]

The pivotal role is played by the 'triage' and 'planned shrinkage' undergone by US cities at the hands of political operators, which is the mere expression of a systemic process (and certainly not the psychological propensities of a putative 'underclass'). The post-1960 'brutal implosion' of the Black American ghetto is propelled from outside 'by the confluence of the decentring of the national political system, the crumbling of the caste regime, the restructuring of urban capitalism, and the policy of social regression of the federal government set against the backdrop of the continued ostracization of African Americans'.[278] Where Wacquant's take dovetails with Simon is in viewing a racialised deproletarianisation as a critical dimension of the 'structural adjustment' of the inner city. In one of the episodes in Season 1 some of the young dealers discuss the possibilities of entrepreneurship and betterment in the 'normal' economy in a comical conversation about the brilliance of the McNugget, and the huge profits it must have generated. One of them retorts that the guy who invented the McNugget is still working in the basement of McDonald's: 'nigga still working a minimum wage.'

The ideological positioning of the show is not hard to glean, and could be encapsulated as a kind of labourist social critique, infused by a dose of nostalgia for the Fordist settlement between big capital, big labour and big government. From this vantage point, it is not so difficult to read *The Wire*, in Simon's words, as 'a political tract masquerading as a cop show'.[279] As he remarks about the second season, a multi-dimensional study of the grinding downsizing of the Baltimore docks and their articulation with global flows of criminal capital, the show is concerned with 'what happened in this country when we stopped making shit and building shit, what happened to all the people who were doing that'.[280] As David Harvey, one-time resident of Baltimore, indicates, the city lost two-thirds of its manufacturing employment after 1960 – among the reasons for his judgment on the city's predicament in *Spaces of Hope*: 'Baltimore is, for the most part, a mess. Not the kind of enchanting mess that makes cities such interesting places to explore, but an awful mess'.[281] This is a development wistfully noted in the show when McNulty, the maverick detective who is the closest the show comes to a protagonist, having been demoted to work on the harbour police, reminisces with his partner as they cross the bay about how both their fathers were laid off from their factory jobs in the mid-seventies. *The Wire* in this sense has a lot in common with a nostalgic valorisation of the moral economy of work and craft (present, for instance, in the influential studies of Richard Sennett), and bears a kinship – albeit in the mode of bitter mourning – with the 'labouring of American culture' studied by Michael Denning with regards to Popular Front art in the US of the 1930s and 1940s. This theme of the end of 'real' labour, and its substitution by the vicious entrepreneurialism of neoliberal work (the drug trade) and informal economies of survival and expediency is intimately linked to that of 'unencumbered' capitalism': with the 'proletarian grotesque' being replaced by a 'neoliberal grotesque'.[282]

Despite the suggestion that Simon might be, in the words of *Entertainment Weekly*'s TV critic 'the most brilliant Marxist to run a TV show',[283] the show's worldview far more closely approximates Karl Polanyi's seminal critique of the devastating effects of 'disembedding' at the hands of so-called self-regulated markets. In *The Great Transformation*, Polanyi argues that 'the control of the economic system by the market is of overwhelming consequence to the whole organization of society: it means no less than the running of society as an adjunct to the market. Instead of economy being embedded in social relations, social relations are embedded in the economic system'.[284] Accordingly, in Fred Block's gloss, 'a fully self-regulating market economy requires that human beings and the natural environment be turned into pure commodities, which assures the destruction of both society and the natural environment'.[285] The echoes with Simon's declaration that 'pure capitalism is not a social policy' are strong. Note also the symptomatic definition of capitalism as oligarchic, as when Simon speaks of 'This money-obsessed oligarchy that we call the United States of America.' At the same time there is a 'workerist' sense in which the class struggle remains, even in its putative absence, an epistemic lens that allows one to understand the transformations of the American city. As he remarked in a talk at USC: 'When capitalism triumphs labor is inherently worth less. … It would seem that the battle has been finally won by capital.'[286] The lack of any subject of transformative class struggle, together with the depiction of a working class that continues to exist after its supposed disappearance, is the frame through which the series, particularly in Season 2, hints at the dynamics of the world-system. In this sense it is a distant echo of one of Jameson's propositions about cognitive mapping: 'successful spatial representation today need not be some uplifting socialist-realist drama of revolutionary triumph but may be equally inscribed in a narrative of defeat, which sometimes, even more effectively, causes the whole architectonic of postmodern global space to rise up in ghostly profile behind itself, as some ultimate dialectical barrier or invisible limit'.[287]

While the logic of capital is constantly pullulating under the surface of the show's narrative, *The Wire* also adroitly portrays the really-existing neoliberal city in a manner that shows how often capitalist efficiency is encumbered by everything from election cycles and black ministers' associations, to nepotism, palace politics, and the conservatism of the silent majority. The show dramatises at the city-level the dialectical relation between the territorial and capitalist logics of power.[288] Given the meticulous manner in which *The Wire* uses the dramatic and technical conceit of 'the wire' to detect and track the functioning of what Simon calls 'postmodern institutions' (the Barksdale operation, the dying unions, the police department, City Hall, the school system), it is perhaps not surprising that some have regarded the show as a critique of bureaucracies, rather than of capitalism as such, and indeed even as providing an unintentional neoliberal object-lesson on the superiority of 'pure' markets over institutions in terms of distribution and fairness. As one commentator notes: 'it seems irrefutable that Mr. Simon never uses *The Wire* to argue that capitalism is in fact the problem, whether or not that's his presupposition ... Milton Friedman could hardly object to *The Wire*'s searing portrayals of drug policy, government bureaucracies, political corruption, unions, black markets and failing schools'.[289] From the other side of the political spectrum, the show's obsession with bureaucratic and institutional vivisection has been faulted for remaining internal to a left-liberal kind of totalisation, its naturalist take on the procedural revealing a 'discord between the mode of representation and its object indicates the difficulties the show has in cognitively mapping the forms and effects of neoliberal urbanism'.[290] One could of course retort, to both these assessments, that neoliberalism (or late capitalism or capitalism *tout court*) is bureaucratic through and through.[291] But claims that *The Wire* fails truly to address or critique capitalism are worth considering with more patience.

The route of all evil

What does it mean, after all, to represent capitalism in such a way that it could be available for critique? As already indicated, several recent films have tried to rend the veil of contemporary capitalism. What is symptomatic is that in so many of them the passage from the social relations between things to the relations between people takes the guise of fantasies of conspiracy. In films like *Michael Clayton* (2007), which is emblematic of this trend, it's as though the incapacity to tackle the role of abstract domination and systemic violence in capitalism (its structural 'evil') leads to projecting real scenes of violence and sinister plots (a kind of *diabolical* evil) at its core. Fetishism is countered by fantasy, as though the absence of malicious agency in a machine that wreaks such violence (in *Michael Clayton* in the guise of environmental crime) were itself too disturbing to contemplate. It could be argued that capital is so signally absent from the American political imaginary *because* it is so often represented, in the guise of the *corporation* (invariably shadowed by the legal *firm*). The inexorable logic of capital is thus overshadowed by the personal failings of a few greedy, criminal bad apples. This individuali-sation of malign bearers (Marx's *Träger*) always retains the possi-bility that the whole might be immune to reproach or open to reform. Despite several similarities with films like *Michael Clayton*, in a *The International*, we have seen, the opposite is the case. There, it is essentially capitalism that is the problem and the evil banker is but a cog in the machine, admitting as much when he pleads for his life in the film's finale. For the most part, however, capital's criminal causalities, end up, in Jameson's characterisation of the poor man's cognitive mapping slipping 'into sheer theme and content'.[292] In a sense *The Wire*, with its refrain that 'it's just business,' reverses depictions of American capital that find some kind of diabolical, criminal evil at the core of their intrigue. Instead, we get the harsh complexities and unavoidable compulsions of the cash nexus and its associated organizational infrastructures: the universal 'institutional and systemic corruptions' of national life in America.[293] The economy of crime is never hygienically sundered from the crimes of the economy. Or, to borrow Vincenzo Ruggiero's lapidary formulation: 'the economic order contains, *ab initio*, the criminal order'.[294] This connection is made explicit by Simon when in an interview he claims that 'the Greek', probably the show's highest-ranking criminal, 'represented capitalism in its purest form'[295] – a curious claim this, as the Greek's impassive Old World malignity, leavened by an 'ethnic' attachment to family and custom, presents a very unlikely stand-in for 'pure', which is to say *abstract* capitalism.

The Wire responds to this critical and aesthetic conundrum of how to depict capital in a number of ways. By mediating the impact of urbanised neoliberal or post-Fordist capitalism through its domains of dispossession and the institutions that convey or vainly try to resist it – in other words, by tracking the mutations of American capitalism through its *effects* on organisations in a locale, Baltimore, distant from the centres of power and accumulation – it provides a 'truer' composite identification of contemporary capitalism than the vast majority of its contemporary counterparts. Moreover, by revoking moral judgment on individuals for the sake of systemic dissection and denunciation, it largely circumvents the ultimately comforting tactic of finding 'the' culprit.[296] The epistemic choice not to engage in a strategy of 'unveiling' is echoed in a statement by co-producer Ed Burns: 'we only allude to the real, the real is too powerful'.[297] It has also been perspicuously explored in a recent piece by John Kraniauskas who, in a close analysis of the first scene of the first series (McNulty's tragicomic conversation on the steps of a row house with a local youth regarding the shooting of a small-time thief by the name of 'Snot Boogie'), notes how it registers

an important, although banal, truth that is significant for the relation the series establishes between narrative form and its own historical material: the excess of history over form. *The Wire* thus signals, on the one hand, its own partiality and, on the other, its consequent status as a work of narrative totalisation that is always already incomplete. In this sense, the programme emerges not only from a realist desire to accumulate social content ... but also from a modernist acknowledgment of its own narrative limits (imposed by narrative form) and thus not so much as a representation as an invention.[298]

These limits are, as already noted, not just generic but also, and inextricably, spatial. Though the series rises from the 'sensory appearance' of the drug economy, to the 'intermediate reality' of institutions, strategies and personnel, that economy's 'ultimate structure' remains 'too abstract for any single observer to experience, although it may be known and studied—and also occasionally sensed in a representational way, as later on in *The Wire* in various forms and probes'.[299] The financial realities suffuse the opaque logistics of the drug trade are in turn farther removed, infinitely transcending if enduringly affecting life 'on the corner'.

There are a number of formal and technical aspects that may allow us to detach the 'truth' of the show, its capacity to anatomise 'a metropolitan world of chronically uneven geographical development',[300] from the ideological choice to reveal what lies 'behind the scenes'. By contrast with the absolute forensic epistemology of the 'genetic' policing of shows like *CSI* (a particular nemesis for Simon, as one can glean from various allusions), *The Wire* explores the constraints and potentialities of a lo-fi form of detection, carried out for the most part with visibly outdated technology: the wire-tap (the influence of Coppola's 1974 *The Conversation* is evident). Partiality and segmentality, rather than omniscience, determine both the specificities of the wiretap and the manner in which it can be regarded as an internal model of the show's own epistemology. The activity of surveillance does not provide some kind of untrammelled vision, requiring instead a painstaking and inevitably partial search – in some respects because, as Simon himself has suggested, one of the effects of the 'surveillance society' is a surfeit of information which, in the absence of principles of selection, generates indifference. Aside from the technicalities and tedium that dominate the wiretap, the show does dramatise the ways in which tracking the vicissitudes of criminal activity can morph – with often painful consequences – into tracking the circulation of capital. As Lieutenant Daniels remarks in the first season: 'This is the thing that everyone knows and no one says. You follow the drugs you get a drug case. You follow the money, you don't know where you're going.' 'Following the money,' which takes the wire detail from the project towers and low-rises to the proverbial corridors of power, brings the show closer to a confrontation with the challenge of registering the effects of capital accumulation. It is this aesthetics of circulation, and of the latter's opacity, which gives the lie to the simple (and, from a neoliberal vantage point, comforting) assertion that the show is not 'about' capitalism. On the contrary, what the fate of detectives doggedly 'following the money' tells us is that the opacity of accumulation and circulation is constantly enforced. It is possible to capture *that* we are tragically enmeshed in the urbanised accumulation and reproduction of capitalism through its territorially specific institutions but it is exceedingly difficult to define *how* this takes place. This problem is acutely underscored by David Harvey with reference to Marx: 'Marx's method of descent from the surface appearance of particular events to the ruling abstractions underneath ... entails viewing any particular event set as an internalization of fundamental guiding forces'.[301] The counter-intuitive vision of ruling abstractions *underneath* is crucial, suggesting as it does, for an inquiry into the aesthetic correlates of such a method, what something like a 'realism of abstraction' might be. *The Wire* is not an answer to this conundrum, but it does provide an occasion to explore it.

The Wire, 2002-2008

Attention to visual and material mediations also shows *The Wire* to be a peculiarly reflexive study on what modalities of mapping and representation are bearers of effective knowledge. Hence the key role of the case board as an epistemic tool – one with interesting resonances to the artworks of the likes of Lombardi or Bureau d'études. The case board of course cannot escape working through segments, fragments, compartments; it is never a truly 'totalising' tool, nor can it simply 'reveal' the routes of money.[302] First of all, it must be closely articulated not just with the wiretap (most of which is focused, because of the dealers' security precautions, on who talks to whom when, and not on what they say) but with seemingly ubiquitous *paperwork*: the forms that must constantly be filled in with the city courts (affidavits, etc.), but also the business and real-estate documentation that harbours the traces of those monetary 'routes'. One of the most 'political' moments in the show comes when Freamon persuades his fellow Detective Sydnor, as they sit in the 'offsite' (in itself an interesting locus of knowledge processing and production, a kind of hidden abode of information), that following bank accounts can be a much more powerful tactic than street work. The case board and its attendant paperwork are also instructively and negatively contrasted with debased modes of presenting information: the power-point, which, linked to the idea of mindless targets divorced from realities on the ground, features in a memorable montage between a spurious presentation of teaching practices in a beleaguered Baltimore school and the COMSTAT meeting of the Baltimore police department; or the homicide whiteboard, a source of constant anxiety for the detectives who must fill and clear targets. Indeed, throughout the show the statistical imperative (meeting targets, or doctoring the stats) combines with the concerted attempt to keep politicians and their networks of corruption and patronage devoid of any form of politically effective knowledge. The impossibility of 'reform', the theme of Season 3 but arguably of the whole show, as it laments the expiry of Fordist and Keynesian compromises, is thus also dramatised as a matter of knowledge and representation.

In Season 5, Detective Freamon speaks of: 'A case like this, where you show who gets paid, behind all the tragedy and the fraud, where you show how the money routes itself, how we're all, all of us vested, all of us complicit.' It is interesting to think here of the interesting tension in spatial metaphors – arguably dramatised by the show as a whole – between the idea of what lies '*behind* all the tragedy and the fraud' and the idea of money's *routes*, which may be obscured by institutional structures but do not necessarily promise knowledge as a revelation or representation or truth. In other words, what do we come to *know* when we follow the routes? The show's epistemic reflexivity also translates into a kind of formal austerity – for instance the prohibition on flashbacks (only broken once, in Season 1, at HBO's request), and the relegation of montage scenes (themselves fragmentary and evocative, rather than complacently synoptic) to the last sequence of each episode. The show's credits can themselves also be considered in this light, as a sequence of partial objects of detection that the 'wire' – and the narrative – might or might not connect (there is a distant echo here of Bresson's 'fragmentations which link up or relink fragments of space each of which is closed on its own account'[303]).

This particular strategy of mapping is not without its limitations. Kraniauskas argues that the 'paradox of *The Wire*'s accumulative compositional strategy – and the aesthetic problem it poses – is that the more of the social it reconstructs, shows and incorporates into its narrative so as to explain the present, the less socially explanatory its vision becomes'.[304] But couldn't this verdict be reversed? One could imagine the show going on endlessly, each season focusing on a different facet of the contemporary American city (the growing Hispanic population and informal workforce, the sex trade, sanitation, the emergency services, cleaners, pizza delivery guys, etc.) without it offering an 'explanation' that is any more satisfactory than the one(s) provided by the five seasons. Take the scene, nicely dissected by Kraniauskas, in which two homicide detectives search the home of Stringer Bell – the pragmatic deputy of the Barksdale operation, whom we'd earlier seen studying economics at a local college. As *The Wealth of Nations* is pulled off of his bookshelf, McNulty exclaims: 'Who the fuck was I chasing?'

The inability of the officers to wrap their head around this relation between the street gang and the (real) abstractions of political economy is an epistemological limit shared by the show itself. This is perhaps more of a hindrance in understanding what is happening in Baltimore than in other US cities because. As Harvey has noted, the banking industry has long exercised an inordinate impact on the city's development.[305] While this inability could obviously be regarded as a failure of *The Wire*'s aesthetic of cognitive mapping, it can also be seen as a materially efficacious and in a sense inescapable aesthetic and epistemological barrier operative both in David Simon's world and in that of his characters. It is this double sense of blockage that we would like to emphasise: not only does *The Wire* dramatise and use as a backdrop the failure of radicals and reformers to dull the blade of neoliberalism, as it hacks up American cities, it also stages the failure of individuals caught within this situation – police, drug dealers, mayors... – to adequately understand and master the forces at play. In other words, rather than thinking it as a successful mapping of the uneven urban development of capitalist accumulation and its social effects, *The Wire* could be seen as dramatising the struggles of any critical or political 'will to know' in the current ideological and institutional dispensation.

The opacity of domination and exploitation also transpires from the sympathetic concern of the show with 'the hell of middle management', to use Simon's caustic expression. 'Middle management' – mid-level dealers, police lieutenants, the head of a stevedore local, school superintendents, sub-editors – can be viewed, in terms of the power/knowledge couple, as that domain which is powerful enough to be actively complicit with the corrupting reproduction of an iniquitous system but not powerful enough to effect any meaningful transformations. Middle management is only allowed as much knowledge as will permit it to function without calling higher echelons into question. Hence *The Wire*'s compelling portrayal of institutional life in urbanised capitalism as a form of tragedy. As Simon notes: 'What we were trying to do was take the notion of Greek tragedy, of fated and doomed people, and instead of these Olympian gods, indifferent, venal, selfish, hurling lightning bolts and hitting people in the ass for no reason—instead of those guys whipping it on Oedipus or Achilles, it's the postmodern institutions ... those are the indifferent gods'.[306] This tragic impotence before the 'Gods' of late capitalism is reflected in the frustrations, betrayals, neuroses and humour of almost all the characters.

It receives no better summary than in the line voiced by the young 'middle manager' of the corner, Bodie who, having in an earlier episode been taught chess by a slightly senior D'Angelo Barksdale, helped by an analogy with the organisational structure of their drug operation, says to McNulty, during a melancholic and contemplative meeting at a Baltimore garden: 'This game is rigged, we're like the little bitches on the chess-board.'[307] This sentiment – the frustration of being a mere pawn, unable to understand the strategies and intricacies of not only 'the game', but the role of the game within a wider political and economic context – is yet another aspect of the show's epistemic reflexivity, and what we could call its second-order realism: not only a 'realistic' portrayal of the ramified, multi-level and contra-dictory structure of an urban political economy bearing the impact of neoliberal adjustments and austerities, but a realism about the very institutional and cognitive limits faced by anyone seeking to orient oneself in the realities of contemporary capitalism.

Not conspiracy but tragedy, not contingency but compulsion, dominate *The Wire*. In such a panorama of corruption and constraint, 'maybe the only hope is anger'.[308]

Chapter 5

Filming the Crisis
(2008-)

It's hard to build a melodrama and explain how the banks and
the economy work.
Jane Fonda

Representing crisis

At one point in Alexander Kluge's *News from Ideological Antiquity:
Marx – Eisenstein – Das Kapital* (2008) the director quizzes the
German essayist Hans-Magnus Enzensberger, born in 1929, on
the images produced in the fateful year of the stock-market
crash. Enzensberger, who bemoans his own difficulties in
writing lyric poetry on the economy, recalls newsreels showing
the destruction of mountains of foodstuffs and commodities that
could no longer find a market. This emblem of capital's
irrationality was indeed used to great effect at the beginning of
Joris Ivens's remarkable fresco of Stalinist industrialisation,
Komsomol (1933). Just a year before, it was precisely around the
destruction of tons of coffee in Brazil that Brecht and Slatan
Dudow dramatised the contrasting class perspectives on the
crisis in the final scene of *Kuhle Wampe* (1932), as a sample of
Berlin social types, crammed in a crowded train carriage, made
their political positions evident in their relation to the vicissitudes of one commodity. In his conversation with Enzensberger,
Kluge suggests that, were we to seek some emblems of the crisis
that began in 2008, we could do worse than starting with the
image of those defaulting subprime mortgage holders in the
United States, who simply left their keys behind and walked
away from their foreclosed properties. The disjunction between
Brecht and Dudow's staging of social conflict and the vision of

thousands of lone foreclosed home-owners, embarking on a kind of reverse Gold rush in the suburban sprawls of California and Florida, is indicative of the times.

Kluge's insistence on a deficit of images and narratives of the crisis is worth reflecting on. In a period when images of social and environmental collapse are ubiquitous in all spheres of culture, and television crime dramas like *Law and Order* and *CSI* have been quick to incorporate the foreclosure crisis and economic stagnation into their narratives, cinematic depictions of the ongoing economic crisis have been comparatively sparse, and rarely compelling.[309] Notwithstanding the lumbering logistics of production, which hinders most cinema from reacting to current events with celerity, depicting the drama of the economic crisis has proven arduous. Filmmakers have struggled to incorporate economic turmoil into their works without reverting to some long-standing and ultimately comforting tropes: families reuniting to overcome economic hardship, the machismo and malevolence of stockbrokers, the corrosive power of greed. Whether in fiction or documentary, the temptation has been not so much to dramatise as to *personify* systemic and impersonal phenomena, resolving widespread anxiety and hardship either into the simplistic identification of culprits or into the backdrop for the trials and tribulations of the nuclear family and the aspirational individual (a tendency that crisis films share with recent apocalypse and catastrophe cinema).[310]

Of course, this problem is hardly new: as Samuel Goldwyn once put it, 'If you want to send a message, use Western Union'. As indicated by our epigram, a remark made by Fonda in reference to Allan Pakula's *Rollover* (1981) – whose moment of ventriloquism we've already touched on – the question of how to diagram or dramatise the economy has haunted filmmakers trying to deal with previous crises too. *Rollover*, starring Fonda and Kris Kristofferson, was an explicit response to the crises of the seventies and the political panic instilled in the US by the increasing power of petrodollars. Widely panned upon its release, it might be argued that with *Rollover* Pakula – who had crystallised the paranoid style of seventies politics to such effect in *The Parallax View* (1974) and *All the President's Men* (1976) – was unable to construct a convincing melodrama *or* explain how the banks and the economy work. But have other contemporary filmmakers been more successful? While capturing the economy cinematically – both in fiction and documentary – is doubtless challenging, and doing so directly courts cries of boredom and accusations of didacticism, the aesthetic and narrative problems are not insurmountable. The examples of past filmmakers and theorists struggling with the experience of economic collapse remain alive with lessons for the present, and the ongoing financial crisis has been the object of noteworthy attempts to give narrative and visual shape to its underlying causes and effects. Representations of crisis need not be crises of representation.

Ghosts of crises past

Invisibility and connectivity, the immaterial and the systemic, are among the dimensions of modern economic life that make it so that capitalism 'itself' poses obdurate problems for plot and image. Arguably this is particularly true during periods of depression. As a 1936 *Life* article on photojournalism after the crash lamented, 'depressions are hard to see because they consist of things not happening, of business not being done'.[311] Yet at the same time, it is precisely in crises that the interruption of normal service, and its impact on everyday life and on the symbols of wealth and power, make the abstract concrete, the invisible visible. That is what the wastage of goods meant for Ivens and Brecht, or what the shiftless container ships idling in the Pacific, or the vast tracts of empty foreclosed homes, could signify for us today. These effects – on commodities, on circulation – can easily be filmed, if not necessarily emplotted, however, and it is the centrality of finance to the current crisis that poses representational problems of its own, namely the forbidding mathematical and legal complexity of the financial instruments (derivatives, CDOs, CDSs, etc.) at the heart of the crisis. Yet, though far more refractory to representation than class or even greed, finance has not been entirely absent from the silver screen.

Marcel L'Herbier, *L'Argent*, 1928

A year before the Great Crash, the French director Marcel L'Herbier, sparing no expenses, adapted Émile Zola's naturalist novel on the Paris Bourse, *L'Argent* (Money). The plot weaves together romantic intrigue, the struggle between a financial aristocrat and a crass upstart, and a transatlantic flight by a renowned aviator to find oil in Guyana. L'Herbier built up a grandiose dramatisation of the emotional frenzy and communicational complexity that make a stock exchange floor almost *too* dramatic for an audience of laypeople, which can only gawp at the numbers, the movement and the shouting as if witness to some exotic ritual. In a bravura sequence that ties together the announcement of the voyage's outcome to the breathless rhythm of stock speculation, L'Herbier's montage follows not the money, but the path of financial information in the great hall of the stock exchange (which he had remarkably gained access to for the production). Telephone exchanges and banks of typewriters (all operated by women), pulleys expediting crucial numbers to the arenas of decision, boards with the status of stocks – all are linked together in a frenetic movement in which the speed of the montage mimics the haste of profit-making.

Invisible threads connecting disparate characters and locations, sudden changes, individual fates buffeted by inscrutable structures – for all of the representational problems that they present, one can't say that finance and capital are devoid of drama. Blinded by amphetamines after the gruelling montage of *October* (as we learn from Eisenstein scholar Oksana Bulgakowa in Kluge's *News*), and inspired by Joyce's *Ulysses* (which he also wished to film), the Soviet director Sergei Eisenstein took up this very challenge in 1929, seeking to imagine, in some influential if unrealised notes, how one could film Marx's *Das Kapital*. For Eisenstein the problem was not that of matching images to Marx's text, but that of replicating his dialectical method in film. To this end, and echoing some of the didactic motifs in Brecht's work,[312] he tried to think how the vast, invisible circuits of accumulation – binding production, circulation and distribution – could be rendered by starting with the most banal moments in everyday life, like a housewife handling products in her kitchen, and moving, via the kind of montage already experimented with in *October* and other films, to the unseen economic and geopolitical forces that set the very constraints of that everyday life. For Jameson, Eisenstein was envisioning 'something like a Marxian version of free association – the chain of hidden links that leads us from the surface of everyday life and experience to the very sources of production itself'.[313]

Though production and class relations retained prominence in both militant and mainstream filmmaking after the 1930s, finance, or even the business firm itself, resisted dramatisation. When Hollywood did tackle this unglamorous theme, it did so by pitting the virtues of the firm based on real skills and assets against the depredations of profit and finance. In both *Executive Suite* (dir. Robert Wise, 1954) and *Patterns* (dir. Fielder Cook, 1956), the protagonist (a product developer and designer in the former, an industrial engineer in the latter) struggles against the perversion of 'proper' capitalism by the financial bottom line, only to end, once he's affirmed the American ethical values of work and inventiveness, by taking on leadership of the firm, with the pious promise that the making of real things will tame the rule of finance. This version of Fordist or organised capitalism was defunct by the time finance and crisis reared their head in the great conspiracy films of the 1970s and early 1980s.[314] As we've already touched on, in *Network* and *Rollover*, capitalism 'itself' speaks through the voices of a raging anchorman and an earnest financier, in monologues at once delirious and realist; it tells us that our notions of agency, nationality, and responsibility are entirely obsolescent, and that in the end the world is controlled by an impersonal force of which we can become conduits, but which it is deluded to think we can arrest. In this world, there is no kind of collective agency, of the kind affirmed in Dudow and Brecht's communist drama, which can put a spanner in the works. The system can, however, grind to a halt: a dramatic possibility envisioned in *Rollover* whose final scenes (resurrected on YouTube as presaging the current crisis) repurpose real footage of rioting across the globe to imagine the effects of economic cataclysm, closing on a striking rotating shot around the operations room of an investment firm, with the frenzy of communications brought to a halt, the lights dimmed and the computer terminals covered to look like so many sarcophagi, among which the strangely sexless couple of Kristofferson and

Fonda share their final whispers. The film poster, depicting his head buried in her cleavage on a background of stock figures reads: 'The most erotic thing in their world was money' – given their 'chemistry', this is perhaps not saying so much.

Character flaws and family value

There is considerable star power on display among recent films that have been received, or more or less advertised, as post-crisis films. Among the first was *Up in the Air* (dir. Jason Reitman, 2009), in which George Clooney plays a corporate downsizer who makes his living flying around America laying people off. The film was inadvertently timely, conceived as it was prior to the financial crisis. However, it was filmed in the crisis's aftermath and includes footage from real interviews conducted with people in St. Louis and Detroit who had recently lost their jobs. The way in which the film thematises the social and spatial disjunction between finance and management, on the one hand, and 'real' jobs and families, on the other, also resonates with a certain critical common sense about the crisis. Ryan Bingham (Clooney's character) initially gives the impression of someone fully adapted to the world of non-places (airports, corporate hotels), frequent flyer miles (his own object of desire being attaining ten million of them via American Airlines), motivational newspeak ('What's in Your Backpack?'), and tangential flings. He is forced to take stock of his life-philosophy and profession as his dalliance with a fellow corporate nomad begins to get more serious, just as his downsizing firm is itself menaced with downsizing by the rolling-out of the technique of 'remote-layoffs' via videoconferencing – an allegory of a system prone to eating itself. Detachment and family are the characterological poles in this drama, as in so much of the mass culture response to the crisis, which so often boils down to morality tales on the perils of disembedding from kith and kin. In the interviews that start and close the film, the predominant theme is the refuge the recently laid-off found in their families. But with the sentiments being expressed in lines like, 'Money can keep you warm, pay your heating bills, buy your blanket, but it doesn't keep me as warm as when my husband holds me', it's difficult not actually to side with flexibility and precarity.

The experience of what is euphemistically referred to as job insecurity is dramatised in John Wells's *The Company Men* (2010), the story of three corporate executives at a shipping and manufacturing firm outside of Boston. At three different levels of their career, and at three different percentiles in the upper-tier of American earners, each man is laid off by a firm cutting costs to keep their stock price afloat. The film hits the mark in its treatment of the stresses caused by abrupt redundancy, detailing the Sisyphean task of posting résumé after résumé in a period of high joblessness and providing an insight into how devastating unemployment can be to the (masculine) psyche (it is only the complete dearth of jobs that suggests the film has been conceived subsequent to the 2008 crisis). That said, there is cloying quaintness about the continual pleas of Tommy Lee Jones – playing ageing senior manager Gene McClary and channelling the same wrinkly, hangdog earnestness on display in *No Country for Old Men* – to the CEO, asking him to hold onto the workers because they are good men with families. Even worse is the film's naïve happy ending, which suggests that the decline of manufacturing in the United States has been a simple matter of malign individual choices by executives. Its nostalgia for the Fordist compact is one that imagines, like many reviewers of the film,[315] that the concessions offered to workers during this period were driven by managerial altruism rather than the struggles of organised labour. What is completely, almost ostentatiously, lacking in *Company Men* (as in all of the contemporary Hollywood films under consideration) is any consideration of politics; there is only family and the self-help tinged, camaraderie-in-despair of the job centre.

The family, as the arena of crisis and a possible horizon of redemption, is also at the heart of *Wall Street: Money Never Sleeps* (dir. Oliver Stone, 2010). The subtitle, which references one of the beliefs about currency that led to its theological condemnation in the Middle Ages (as narrated in Le Goff's splendid essay on the mediaeval European economy[316]), may be the most winning feature of this film. The first *Wall Street* had attained paradigmatic status as the lurid morality tale of yuppiedom qua active nihilism, the diabolical Gordon Gekko giving slick voice and body to a capital both parasitical and simulacrum-like. As testified by a scene in the compelling *Boiler Room* (dir. Ben Younger, 2000), a prescient drama on the fraudulent suburban brokerage 'chop-shops' that people the dark side of financialisation, where aspiring brokers watch *Wall Street* much like Sil in *The Sopranos* watches *The Godfather*, *Wall Street* became a kind of iconic reference *within* a financial industry enduringly enamoured with its own amorality. The class narrative of the first *Wall Street*, of the speculative destruction of the airplane company run by Bud's (Charlie Sheen's) unionised father (Martin Sheen), redolent of the Reagan's onslaught on the PATCO union, reinforces the polarity at the heart of the Hollywood Left's take on finance versus labour, and like *The Company Men* made over 20 years later, betrays a sterile if sincere longing for the world of stable jobs and stable families.

The shift to the 2008 crisis is in this regard more revealing of the waning fascination with the agents of finance and the concomitant difficulty in dramatising the social transformations wreaked by capital – of which the comical metonym is the enormous cellular phone returned to Gekko upon leaving prison. The seemingly disappeared, but more appropriately disavowed, world of the factory is replaced by the mirage of a financially-driven Green New Deal (Jake, played by Shia La Boeuf, taking Charlie Sheen's place, in this case as the investment banker boyfriend of Gekko's estranged daughter, for whom

Gekko is a kind of diabolical and beguiling role-model). Whereas the first *Wall Street* channelled the thrall of capitalism as a kind of diabolical drive, with the erotic dimensions of creative destruction, *Money Never Sleeps* struggles to generate the same dynamic. Stone has remarked, echoing Fonda, that: 'It's very hard to do a financial movie, to make stocks and bonds sexy and interesting'.[317] This may in part be because among the targets of the crisis's devaluation has been the sex appeal of financial capitalism itself. It is symptomatic that the attempt to revive the memorable if somewhat hackneyed monologues by Gekko/Douglas in the first film are so unsuccessful, parroting unpersuasive moralisms ('The mother of all evil is speculation') or nonsensical affirmations ('Someone reminded me I once said greed is good. Now it seems it's legal'). And where the décor and architecture of 1980s finance were in themselves iconic enough, they are here replaced by a somewhat unpersuasive attempt to make finance *visible*, as in a montage scene where buildings made of television screens set to finance channels alternate with traffic flows replaced by stock tickers, and the peaks and troughs of the Dow Jones are projected onto the downtown New York skyline.[318] Like *Company Men*, *Money Never Sleeps* ends with an unconvincing happy ending, not just for the Gekko clan but society as a whole. It's actually difficult to say which is more likely: whether the northeastern United States will reinvigorate its manufacturing base at the behest of a couple of well-intentioned multimillionaire CEOs or whether a California start-up will realise the dream of cold fusion. Regardless, if these are the best popular offerings of the contemporary cultural and political imagination we're in dire straits indeed.

One of the telling developments registered in *Wall Street 2* is the passage from New York to London – where Gekko holes up in a relatively non-glamorous operation after having made a killing anticipating the crisis. The City is one of the settings – the other being the dispiriting landscape of dilapidated dwellings and 'luxury apartments' of modern Britain – for the TV class and crisis melodrama *Freefall* (dir. Dominic Savage, 2009), which follows the parallel downward slopes of a banker (Gus, played by Aidan Gillen) and a security guard (Jim, played by Joseph Mawle) and his family, victims of a predatory mortgage concocted by his cocky old schoolmate (Dave, played by Dominic Cooper). From the tawdriness of built space and the commodities whose supposed attractiveness seems to drive a charmless world of work, consumption and speculation, to the vapid pep-talks and smarmy selling patter that link boardroom and mortgage call-centre in a long chain of degraded language, *Freefall* is rich in observations of a world both extremely unequal and homogeneously undesirable – where value is brutally set by forms of exchange and types of possessions that have none of the supposed glamour of twenties or eighties decadence. It also replicates some of the ventriloquisms already noted (Gus expatiates unconvincingly about 'liberating the markets'), and appropriately demotes the diabolical agents of capitalism from the boardroom to the mortgage and telephony, stripping capitalist immorality of any veneer of excitement. Most importantly, it anchors the crisis and its lived experience in the dictatorship of the home, a machine for accumulation and financialisation: a machine for not being able to live. Unfortunately, once again it seems that the crisis is employed for a kind of fruitless dialectic between the greed of individuals (and in particular of men whose self-esteem and libido are anchored to the commodity) and the families, which are both the victims of the crisis and its sole antidote (with women characterised both at the top and bottom of the class spectrum as the vectors of embedding and founts of reasonableness). The three subjective options (suicide, return to a 'sustainable' nuclear family, continued predation and bottom-feeding – interestingly by selling ecological products), all speak of a world whose imagination is stripped of collectivity and riven to a narrow horizon of finitude, in which the best one can imagine is more family and less greed, fewer commodities and more stability.

Crisis, comedy and eros

While it could be argued that in *Up in the Air*, *The Company Men*, and *Money Never Sleeps* the crisis, however dramatically central, is a mere mediator for family, it plays a key – if background – role in Steven Soderbergh's *The Girlfriend Experience* (2009). Filmed on a comparatively tiny budget in New York during the autumn of 2008, the film uses the crisis, and to a lesser extent the presidential election, as the general backdrop for its consideration of the contours of particular kinds of affective labour. The film's star, Sasha Grey, best known for another sort of affective labour (hardcore pornography), plays a young high-class escort, while her boyfriend is a personal trainer. As Grey listens semi-attentively to men fret about their lives in various boutique hotels and stylish bars – and as her boyfriend, in a lesser role, entertains his master of the universe clients – the conversations more often than not turn to the financial crisis. These worlds of generic luxury, worlds that in New York City are intimately dependent on the revenues brought in by the city's financial services, appear both totally isolated from the crisis and entirely suffused with it. Despite obliquely appearing in snippets of conversation and on television sets droning on in the background (as it does, to subtly impressive effect, in the 2012 crime film *Killing Them Softly*), when considered next to the blankness of the main characters and the milieus they inhabit, 'immanent economic catastrophe, rifted with hysteria and panic, is the most charismatic figure in the film'.[319] In treating the crisis as the impersonal backdrop of the impersonal and fragmentary yet intimate encounters between a call girl and her clients in the financial world, the film is affectively truer to the effect of economy on daily life than the melodramatic strategy of naturalist efforts like *Freefall*.

Also striking about *The Girlfriend Experience*, especially in comparison to *Company Men*, is the film's use of non-actors for all the roles (Sasha Grey made her non-pornographic debut here), the resulting stiltedness closer to the affective register of this world of communicative work. There is a kind of affinity hinted at here, in a way which chimes with the aesthetic and spatial coordinates of *Up in the Air* as well, between the non-spaces of a communicative capitalism, the non-affect of certain kinds of labour, and the oppressive, inertial invisibility of a crisis that is registered in a peripheral way. But we could also note the ways in which family, mortgage, work, and the inanity of built space (alternating between the triumphant banality of the glass skyscraper and the tawdry iteration of 'luxury apartments' and sundry cubbyholes) are 'realistically' depicted in these films. In this landscape, claustrophobic even when it is empty, an imaginary of interruption, collapse, and catastrophe becomes strangely alluring – especially as the only other possibilities appear to be loneliness, death or a return to the bosom of the family. Again, the absence of any agency which is not individual or familial is striking, and is cinematically translated into the prominence of spaces of filtering, seclusion or interdiction (the existential collapses of Gus and Jim in *Freefall* are arguably triggered by being banned from the office in which he ruled supreme in the first case, and being evicted from the 'dream home' in the second).

Perhaps surprisingly, one of the more intriguing films to deal not only with the crisis but with the aesthetic and narrative conundrums filmmakers face in tackling it is the Will Farrell and Mark Wahlberg buddy-cop comedy *The Other Guys* (dir. Adam McKay, 2010). The fourth collaboration between Farrell and McKay (following *Anchorman*, *Taladega Nights*, and *Step Brothers*), the film is not obviously framed as a post-crash comedy and much of the content actually dealing with the crisis seems to be consigned to the film's closing credits. Produced by Picture Mill Studios, also responsible for the credits to films like *The Hangover* and *Mission Impossible III*, these feature graphic representations of how Ponzi schemes work, statistics about the 2008 bailout, astronomical Wall Street bonuses and executive salaries, and income disparity in the United States. While the plot of the film centres on a white collar crime, particularly the theft of funds from the police pension by a hedge fund manager played by Steve Coogan, with the exception of a relatively obscure joke at the expense of the Security and Exchange Commission's (SEC) inability to regulate the firms involved in the 2008 crash, there is no real mention of the financial crisis (though the fact that the police captain, played by Michael Keaton, moonlights as a manager at Bed, Bath & Beyond is a corrosive allegory of the fate of work in the US today). According to Picture Mill, McKay envisioned the credits precisely as something tacked on to the end, a way of working his anger about the financial crisis and America's income disparities into the theatre without letting it 'get in the way of the movie.'[320] McKay's admission mirrors that of Stone ('I don't know how you show a credit default swap on screen'[321]) and chimes with the larger issues of financial representation facing all of the contemporary films discussed thus far.

In *The Other Guys* Will Farrell plays a 'fake cop', 'desk jockey', 'paper bitch' transferred from forensic accounting, partnered with Mark Wahlberg, who wants to be out chasing bad guys, guns blazing. When the police captain takes away Farrell's gun after some blooper, someone in the station quips, 'If you really want to disarm this guy take out the batteries in his calculator'. The film's villain gives a Gekko-esque speech at the Center for American Capitalism praising American excess. While the crime at the heart of the film is essentially financial, Mark Wahlberg can't get it out of his head that 'This guy could be connected to drug cartels, black market organ sales, human trafficking...' On their way to visit an accounting firm in New Jersey, Walhberg asks, 'So he's dealing drugs?' Ferrell responds, 'No, it's not drugs, this is not *Miami Vice*'. Still, Walhberg insists they're after

Columbian drug lords and two-thirds of the way through the film still doesn't understand the concept of the Federal Reserve. At one point in the film they visit the offices of the SEC and a guy working in the office has to didactically explain to both Wahlberg and the audience what it is the SEC is and what they do. At the end, TARP (Troubled Asset Relief Program) funds bail out the bad guys because they were 'too big to fail.'

All of this can obviously be related in various superficial ways to the crisis but what is most intriguing about *The Other Guys* is how the film conspicuously relates the epistemological issues involved with 'following the money' and the white collar crimes that contributed to the crisis to concerns with narrative and cinematic form. The difficulties of making a Hollywood film, particularly a Hollywood comedy or action film, dealing with the financial crisis are inscribed into the film itself. It is everything that makes Will Farrell's character unsuitable for a film like that – his passion for paperwork and protocol – which allows him to crack the case. Walhberg's incomprehension mirrors the inability of the director to create a comedic action narrative that doesn't resort to the tired tropes of the genre, the car chases and shootouts. The film seems reluctantly (or perhaps cynically) to function as though the crime was in fact drug dealing or weapons smuggling or whatever. Only the closing credits suggest that the film was 'about' the financial crisis, and the systemic inequalities and shady dealings that helped bring it about. This disjunction, between the deconstruction of the buddy-cop genre and the didactic diagram of economic malfeasance, makes *The Other Guys* a strangely reflexive take on filming the crisis.

The limits of denunciation

There is a scene in Michael Moore's documentary *Capitalism: A Love Story* (2009) where Moore attempts to figure out what a derivative is. He goes to Wall Street and starts asking random suits filing out of a building to inform him and is roundly ignored. He then sits on a bench with an Ivy League educated, ex-vice president of Lehman Brothers who created complex financial instruments on Wall Street. After the executive stumbles over his words, Moore acts increasingly perplexed and then asks a Harvard academic to enlighten him: his explanation is even worse. Moore then claims, backed up by the suddenly loquacious ex-Lehman vice president, that derivatives are made intentionally complex so that they'll be more difficult to regulate. The point is well taken: modern financial instruments are enormously intricate, based on advanced mathematics, and this complexity has been used to shroud dodgy dealings.[321] Still, it wouldn't be difficult to argue that this unwillingness actually to understand and present derivatives and their role in the crisis, or this feigned ignorance, severely limits one's ability to thoughtfully respond to the crisis both politically and theoretically. A sprawling dossier for the prosecution against American financial capitalism, illustrated by characteristic interventions by Moore and tear-jerking interviews with the working class victims of the crisis (invariably described as middle class in keeping with American ideology), as well as a rich archive of clips and cartoons, *Capitalism: A Love Story* portrays the crisis's brutal impact in the context of a long wave of deindustrialisation and the dispossession of an indebted majority. Unlike most other films or documentaries on the crisis, it does insistently point towards the collective dimensions of a response to the crisis – the possible awakening of the 'friggin' people'. Yet it does so without truly digging into what might be done to surmount a Fordist pact that is a nostalgic figure rather than an option (poignant strolls through the devastated industrial landscape of Flint, Michigan with his father notwithstanding). Though Moore is sensitive to the limits of American Fordism (in racism and imperialism), his observations on 'democratic socialism' are frustratingly vague, so that the agency of the fat cats who have stripped American democracy does not find a counterpart, except in forms of ethical production that hardly seem to be the foundation for resistance.[323]

In a less overtly polemical, but more penetrating mode, Charles Ferguson's *Inside Job* (2010), as the title designates, is another documentary exploring finance's depredations of American capitalism (the fact that Moore's film ends on the flag and Ferguson's on the Statue of Liberty is no mere detail). For Ferguson, however, denunciation and explanation are more closely woven together, in a documentary that seeks to structure itself as a kind of interview-driven citizen's inquiry rather than populist agit-prop. In laying out its argument about the collusion of government, academia and finance (above all Goldman Sachs) in preparing the way for the crisis through a fierce campaign of deregulation, *Inside Job* resorts to a familiarly eclectic palette of techniques familiar from many other recent documentaries. Though interviews predominate, they are supplemented by graphics (efficiently pedagogical charts, economic diagrams and textual excerpts), TV clips, music-video montages and long outdoor takes to accompany and illustrate the narration provided by Matt Damon. From the swooping National Geographic-like landscapes of its Icelandic prologue to its vertical overviews of Manhattan skyscrapers (shared with just about *every* one of the works in this survey), *Inside Job* partakes in a contemporary trend to represent global capitalism and its effects through a kind of slick naturalist sublime. Always prone, and often legitimately, to instrumentalism, the documentary form is treated here primarily as a vehicle – ideally an enter-taining one – for delivering knowledge to an otherwise disori-ented public. In view of the aversion that audiences allegedly feel toward the dry and didactic, it may be argued that it is only sensible to ornament a complex narrative with familiar and slickly attractive visual forms.

Yet there is a kind of aesthetic dishonesty in illustrating the ecological effects of speculation with luscious and filtered God's-eye-views of 'Nature', in the clichéd fascination with the geometry of skyscrapers, in the all-too-brief and unpersuasive shots of an empty Chinese factory to indicate the downturn in manufacturing, or indeed in the shady footage of financial johns (the ones too broke for the likes of Sasha Gray, one surmises) hanging around night-clubs. These somewhat hackneyed illustrative moments in *Inside Job* can be contrasted with a far more effective delineation of the relations between capitalist crisis, real estate, nature and social decomposition in the final and very striking section of Andrew and Leslie Cockburn's politically superior, if more lo-fi, *American Casino* (2009). There, guided by an eloquent young employee of Riverside, California's 'Northwest Mosquito Vector Control District', we learn of the potentially lethal effects of the crisis on the mosquito populations breeding in the putrescent pools of abandoned foreclosed homes in California and becoming viral vectors (snakes, vermin, and meth labs are among the other effects of the credit crash in real estate). Combined with the Cockburns' patient interviews with those bearing the brunt of practices of racist predatory lending in Baltimore, this is the kind of materialist epiphany sorely absent from most documentary narratives of the Great Recession.

In *Inside Job*, social relations are not so much represented as gestured at, with predictable and unenlightening means. Conversely, it is at its most abstract – in the minimalist graphic explanations of the crisis, detailing, among others, the exposure of insurance giant

Leslie Cockburn, *American Casino*, 2009

AIG in the tangled geometry of trades in collateralised debt obligations and credit default swaps – that *Inside Job* is at its most realist, providing a sense of the systemic patterns in which individual greed and collective suffering find their place. This is not to say that one should turn documentaries into PowerPoints – though the closing credits of *The Other Guys* are pretty effective in this genre – but the capacity to connect individual fates and systemic developments, which is both a thematic and a formal question for these contemporary documentaries, is ill-served by the ubiquity of visual clichés, which in *illustrating* the social fail to represent or comprehend it.

Didactic graphs are also a mainstay in *The Flaw* (2010), in a sense a more modest endeavour than either Moore or Ferguson's films. It uses many of the same tropes (aerial and street shots of NYC, news clips, expert interviews, and, as in Moore, the use of film and television excerpts for ironic effect), but builds up a story and an explanation which are considerably more nuanced than the pitting of the real economy against the depredations of finance. The whole movement of the film is dramatised by the footage of a laid-off stockbroker who takes tourists on a crisis-themed tour of Wall Street, laying out the workings of the financial system. Unlike the academics who are in many ways the target of Ferguson's inquiry, *The Flaw* relies very heavily on critical and neo-Keynesian economists (Robert Shiller, Robert Wade, Louis Hyman, etc.). They put the emphasis on the long-term tendency of stagnation in real incomes, the tenuous compensatory effects produced by the real estate market, the increasing scissor of income distribution, the pernicious perfor-mative effects of 'efficient market hypothesis', and the deregu-lation agenda of Greenspan and his ilk. In doing this, it moves beyond the vision of greed and malfeasance as the key driving forces of the process, to a much more systemic perspective on the shifting shape of American capitalism (and it is worth noting that, despite the minor second pole in London, and the peripheral presence of China and India as rising rivals, all of these films are fiercely American-centric[324]).

Mapping the crisis

We possess incisive Marxist accounts of the economic causalities behind the crisis,[325] and detailed ethnographic investigations into the exotic world of hedge funds and collateralised debt obligations.[326] Yet we are still, arguably, far short of a way of thinking through 'the problems of history, the problems of biography and the problems of social structure in which biography and history intersect', to quote C. Wright Mills, in any way that would allow us to locate the strategic levers of which he spoke. Finance still remains both insidiously pervasive and refractory to totalisation. Symptoms of this can be seen in recent works seeking to map it. In films like *Freefall* and *The Company Men* we have potent representations of the biographical impact of the credit crisis, which links personal troubles to public issues. However, we could say that the glimpses of a more sociological map are lost in the urge to personify greed or suffering, and that any sense either of the broader dynamics or of the possible levers of change vanishes into the background.

In December 2010, during a meeting of a bipartisan commission created by the US government to investigate the causes of the financial crisis of 2008, the four Republican members of the ten member panel formally proposed that the words 'Wall Street', 'shadow banking', 'deregulation', and 'interconnected' be banned from the commission's final report. The five Democrats and one independent voted against the proposal and a week later the Republicans left the panel, and later released their own account, blaming the government for the crisis.[327] In the face of such anti-cognitive mapping, which wards off any conception of the economic whole, or of the names with which to indicate and represent it, it is all the more important to have cogent narratives of the crisis that acknowledge and explore the very interconnectedness the contemporary world and the systemic nature of the crisis. Documentaries like *Capitalism: A Love Story, Inside Job, American Casino,* and *The Flaw* have begun to do this, though when they are not conduits for the explanations (or refutations) of economists, they can struggle to find forms that can effectively span the complexity of economic phenomena and their individual and collective repercussions.

In fiction films, where the cognitive payoff is less at stake, the risks of framing the crisis in familiar narratives and clichéd images have been even greater. For films like *The Company Men*, and to a lesser extent *Freefall* and *Up in the Air*, the crisis offers us the opportunity to take stock of our lives, to realise – after years of speculative madness and predatory and consumerist greed – what is really important, and to carve out a more sensible future for both ourselves, our family and our country. In each case however, this is either framed as a personal, family, or entrepreneurial project and politics is absent without leave. In *The Girlfriend Experience* the crisis is omnipresent, an abstract atmosphere of sorts, while in *The Other Guys*, the crisis is there in its very absence. As two films that circumvent the dramatic themes of individual hopes and family fates, casting doubt on the linear satisfactions of generic constraints, the latter are much more faithful to the affectively disorienting and intellectually enigmatic character of the crisis, not to mention to the challenges it poses for representation. In their oblique views on the worlds of labour, these films also take a step away from the tiresome tendency to view the turbulence in our social and economic life as an occasion to take refuge in the interiority of the psyche or the home.

Cherchez la femme (de chambre)
Whereas, six years after the Lehman Brother bankruptcy, mass culture continues to register capitalist crisis either clumsily or obliquely, things seem different in the world of art.[328] Even an infrequent acquaintance with biennales and white cubes, not to mention the art press, offers a welter of anecdotal evidence that the desire called cognitive mapping has not in the least been

quenched, a quarter of a century from Jameson's original proposition. Capital may be the invisible logic structuring our daily miseries, but it is also everywhere on display, especially in the shape of works that thematise its representability (and the limits thereto) in a context of crisis. In Isaac Julien's *Playtime* (2013), art's moment of capital can be judged to have reached a kind of crystallisation, which doubles as a record of exhaustion and redundancy, a reflection of times in which a pall of uncertainty shadows the imperative of accumulation.

Doubles are ubiquitous in the seven-screen feature-length installation, shown at the Victoria Miro gallery from 24 January to 1 March. Not only are images relayed and displaced across the projection screens, but faces and gazes are often cross-cut by reflecting surfaces, while the entire piece is suffused by an effulgent glossiness, a grit-less visual field familiar from advertising, nature documentaries and the aesthetics of finance itself. Yet these are not the materialist mirrors that Louis Althusser found in the work of Leonardo Cremonini, surfaces of mis-recognition, delay and over-identification, which allowed the Italian artist to 'paint the real abstract', thereby thwarting any identification of materialism with the theory of reflection.[329]

Neither are these spaces – like the preternaturally speckless counter-tops we see a Filipina domestic stoically polishing in *Playtime*'s Dubai episode – the uncanny habitats of an alien modernity, similar to those Jacques Tati traversed in the 1967 film from which Julien borrows his title. Notwithstanding the inspiration supposedly drawn from Eisenstein's cinematographic 'libretto' for *Das Kapital*,[330] Julien does not film the real abstract; instead of representing capital, *Playtime* merely re-presents it. This failing is rendered all the more acute by the fact that at Victoria Miro we enter the fictional superstructure of *Playtime* via the discursive base of *Kapital*, a filmed conversation with David Harvey on the topic of capital's visibility, which is interspersed with footage of a traders' riot in the city (reminiscent of Kanye

West and Jay-Z's *No Church in the Wild*, if considerably less compelling) and the now ineluctable shots of LED ticker tape and server banks.

Kapital is presented on two screens, in a manner more distracting than dialectical, and there is a further doubling in that the audience at Victoria Miro watch another audience watch Harvey and Julien's talk. This select public is composed among others of Paul Gilroy, Colin MacCabe, and the late Stuart Hall, all of whom pose somewhat foreseeable if partly warranted challenges to Harvey's unalloyed faith in classical Marxism, giving the proceedings a rather early nineties vibe, despite the topicality of crisis (MacCabe's question, as to why the renascence of Marxian analysis has been unaccompanied by a reprise of socialist politics goes unanswered). It is difficult, especially when the conversation turns to the composition of the contemporary working classes, not to feel that the loop between the art world and academia, however radical, is uncomfortably narrow.

A phrase by Harvey serves as the leitmotiv for both works (and is voiced by one of the characters in the film-installation): capital is like gravity, invisible, only discernible through theoretical abstraction, and yet tangibly present in its effects. Yet as you ascend from the brightly lit ground floor into the cavernous carpeted twilight of *Playtime*, the potential promise of this axiom comes unravelled. What we encounter instead is a kind of inventory of the impasses which increasingly confront the theory and practice of representing capital.

Harvey's analogy of gravity is curiously disregarded in Julien's own installation. Where Eisenstein's gambit was to transpose Marx's *method* into film, by articulating, through montage, the affective dimension of capital's effects with its invisible, abstract processes, Julien resorts, in what does not appear an ironic or dialectical gesture, to *repeating* the representational clichés through which we typify capitalism. The conjuncture of financialised capital and crisis does not call forth any true *formal* innovations, any ruptures in our perceptual habits and visual forms.

The abundance of mirrors and doublings seems merely to connote, statically, capitalism's spectrality. Landscape, as in popular documentaries on the financial crisis such as *Inside Job* (which like *Playtime* travels to post-crisis Iceland), becomes a site of sublime contemplation, a static Other to capital, not the uneven battlefield of a production of nature and society – Caspar David Friedrich in the age of Goldman Sachs.

Playtime is organised around highly stylised 'portraits' of a set of archetypical figures – the Art Dealer, the Bankrupt Artist, the Domestic Worker, the Auctioneer, the Hedge Fund Manager. The personifications of capital are more dramatic cyphers of occupations than figures who may render a specifically filmic insight into how capital turns its subjects into bearers of anonymous processes, ventriloquised by abstraction (with the exception of the real auctioneer, whose manic panegyric to his craft carries a weird allure). They do not, as a Lukácsian realism might propose, generate cognitively and politically revealing types; nor, as in effective satire or caricature, do they effectively deploy a method of exaggeration. Indeed, when the characters, mostly alone or in pairs, pacing the voided spaces of finance, foreclosure or art, turn and speak to the camera, their social ventriloquism is more reminiscent of the wooden asides peppering recent crisis films like *The Bank, Margin Call, Le Capital, Krach,* or *Arbitrage,* than of the magnificently psychotic monologues in *Network* or *Rollover.*

Most symptomatically, and in keeping with contemporary melodramas of global finitude and economic anxiety like *Babel* (dir. Alejandro Gonzalés Iñarritu, 2006) and *Mammoth* (dir. Lukas Moodysson, 2009), class and exploitation are metonymically embodied in the maid, a woman of colour, in this case a Filipina trapped in the postmodern wastes of Dubai – here represented, as has already been noted,[331] through the most resilient visual clichés of Orientalism, from the immaculate undulating desert through which she contemplatively strides to the apparently vacant skyscrapers, with the accompaniment of vaguely Arabic music.

That Julien notes his desire to base his characters on people he has met, and their experiences of the crisis, is revealing – as in those Hollywood films, it's as if domestic workers have become the only conduit for a transnational elite to access the lived reality of exploitation. None of the workers who build Dubai are visible in Julien's tableaus, just as any proletarian labour other than domestic is effectively absent from Iñarritu's California or Moodysson's New York City. There would be nothing to object to sustained reflection on the closure of the 'art world', on its disjunction from the predicaments of everyday life and labour (we could think here of Godard's gesture, refusing to 'go to Vietnam' in the 1970s, filming himself in *Loin du Vietnam* on a Parisian roof with an enormous camera ruminating the aporias of solidarity), but there is more indulgence than reflexivity in this *mise-en-scène* of the crisis. Following the maid *in this way* – as a lone individual adrift in the Gulf dystopia – means not following the money, nor indeed articulating how crisis is a *collective* experience. Nor does the drama of the Icelandic photographer, haunting his own unfinished modernist home – his life fractured and suspended by the crash, architectural hubris giving way to geometric ruin – really serve as more than a dispatch of *déclassement* from strata whose experience it is hard to treat as emblematic.

Julien's film ultimately reiterates a widespread cognitive and aesthetic impasse in what concerns giving form to capital, crisis and contradiction. It does so with glossy elegance – itself a connotation, as he recognises, of the kind of art that requires much... capital, as the presence of Hollywood starts James Franco and Maggie Cheung further underscores. What is writ large, in this depopulated world which resembles nothing so much as those neutron-bomb car advert fantasies of digitised nature, is the seemingly panoramic but in fact extremely parochial 'view' of capital afforded by the habitus of the metropolitan 'artworld' (one that shares so much with the visual culture of contemporary commerce and entertainment).

In *Playtime*, all three elements of one possible definition of capital – as a *social relation* of *production* – are screened out. The de-socialisation of the economy is relayed by the fact that the seven-screen installation is more or less devoid of true montage, relying on juxtaposition, rhythmic alternation of shots, and the continuity of ambient soundtracks. It triggers no flashes of insight, no clashes of form and content, no unexpected connections, no break with the smooth empty time of financialised capital, here 'represented' by data banks, flashing stock displays, and empty trading floors. Tellingly, at Victoria Miro the sizeable audience all sat dutifully on the perimeter of the carpeted floor, craning heads and scanning eyes quietly labouring to compose a familiar cinematic experience, no one really compelled to move around – fearing to interrupt the others' enjoyment, perhaps, but also, one imagines, because *Playtime* doesn't call for that kind of work, of montage and perambulation, from the viewer.

What Julien's *Playtime* finally demonstrates is that the representation of capital can also turn into one of the 'mythologies' of our time. The more we are bewitched by 'the' crisis and financialisation, the more we risk treating a capitalist aesthetic as an aesthetic of capital, mistaking the redundancy of re-presentation for the complex seeing that our times demand. To echo Brecht, as our reality continues to 'slip into the domain of the functional', a tracking shot past a stack of servers running algorithms, or the mere ventriloquising of capital's ceaseless chatter, is unlikely to reveal any more about the institutions of contemporary finance than a photograph of the Krupp works or the AEG could tell the spectator of the 1930s about those pillars of German militarism. 'The reification of human relations … no longer discloses these relations. So there is indeed "something to construct", something "artificial", "invented".'[332] To make such constructions possible, it will be necessary to take a far greater distance from capital's ubiquitous *clichés* than works 'about' the crisis and finance have done hitherto, to leave the echo chambers in which the language of commodities natters incessantly. The 'art world' is possibly not the best place to start.

Part III

Monsieur le Capital and Madame la Terre

The world only appears before my eyes as a solid 'landscape',
lustrous like plastic.
Takuma Nakahira, 'Rebellion Against the Landscape'

Prologue

Cargo Cult

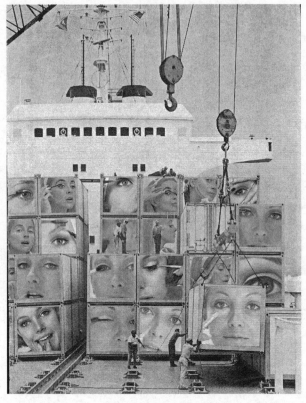

Martha Rosler, *Untitled (Cargo Cult)*, from the series, *Body Beautiful,
or Beauty Knows No Pain*, 1965-1974

Cargo Cult is a photomontage from Martha Rosler's series *Body
Beautiful, or Beauty Knows No Pain*, produced between 1966 and
1972. The series, starkly inter-cutting the devices of female
domestic labour (fridges, washing machines) and commodified
nudity, was produced – initially for political circulation and intervention rather than gallery display – concurrently with *Bringing
the War Home: House Beautiful* (1967-72), which projects the

imperialist carnage of the Vietnam War into the feminised décor of American domesticity. Though its theme – the profitable 'industrialisation' of women's beauty – is blunt enough, the possible connotations of the image are not exhausted by its apparently direct feminist-materialist intent.

The term 'cargo cults' is commonly used to refer to the collective ritualistic practices of certain groups, principally in Melanesia and Micronesia in the Pacific, who reacted to the traumatic encounter with colonial power and capitalist technology by mimicking the appearances of the devices of alien domination (say, by building a wooden airport and airplane) in the messianic belief that this would bring the 'cargo', the unexplained plethora of goods which the white man – who could never be seen *producing* these goods – seemed to dispose of in unlimited amounts. In the 1950s and 1960s radical anthropologists – most memorably Peter Worsley, in his 1957 *The Trumpet Shall Sound* – demonstrated, against a condescending gaze on this 'primitive' reaction, that many facets of the cargo cults expressed a rational response to both the trauma and the fluctuations of colonising capital (viewed from these islands, capitalism seemed to involve no production and a thoroughly irrational and unpredictable fluctuation in values).

Affixed to an image of shipping containers which might contain the components of the export of the Western beauty myth (be these cosmetics, domestic appliances, or indeed the military ordnance needed to 'open doors' to US capital), the term cargo cult echoes the anthropological inversion already at work in the history of the idea of commodity fetishism – beauty under capital is a monetised social relation between things, just as the beauty industry is in turn an irrational, ritualised invocation of future 'cargo'.

Against the tendency to take the preponderance of logistics as warrant for the disappearance of labour, Rosler juxtaposes the standardised singularity of female beauty with the black, male labour on the ship (the foreman appears to be white). Alongside the articulation of the opacity of trade and the surface spectacle of glamour, and of these in turn with the disavowed physicality of work, *Cargo Cult* also opens up to another dimension of an aesthetics of logistics, if we link it to *Bringing the War Home* (2004) – the reprised version of the Vietnam series, now with reference to the Iraq invasion.

Though open to a variety of organisational understandings, and critical to the spatial and temporal logics of contemporary capitalism, logistics is first of all a military preoccupation. As Sergio Bologna writes, the original function of logistics was:

> to organise the supplying of troops in movement through a hostile territory. Logistics is not sedentary, since it is the art of optimizing flows. ... So logistics must not only be able to know how to make food, medicines, weapons, materials, fuel and correspondence reach an army in movement, but it must also know where to stock them, in what quantities, where to distribute the storage sites, how to evacuate them when needed; it must know how to transport all of this stuff and in what quantity so that it is sufficient to satisfy the requirements but not so much as to weigh down the movement of troops, and it must know how to do this for land, sea and air forces.[333]

While developments in logistics have been pivotal to the ongoing transformations of contemporary capitalism, from the just-in-time organisation of production of 'Toyotism', to the world-transforming effects of containerisation (itself accelerated by its military-logistical use in the Vietnam War[334]), they have long influenced the strategies and tactics of war.

The history of the container itself, that exquisitely banal keystone of the subsumption of the planet by trade, is in this regard an almost perfect synthesis of the military and the economic. Having launched the world's first container ship (actually a converted oil tanker), in 1956, the trucking impresario and 'father of containerization' Malcolm McLean made massive strides in his hegemony over and revolutionising of the transport industry when in 1967 his company Sea-Land garnered the contract to ship war material in containers from the port of Oakland (to which we'll return) to Da Nang in Vietnam.[335] In a war in which, as Paul Virilio delineates in *War and Cinema*, the 'logistics of perception' played as much of a role as material logistics, containerisation was a response to the military risks incurred by the laborious process of unloading ships (whereas in 'peaceful' scenarios, it was mainly the economic struggle to lower labour costs and undermine dockworkers unions that was critical). In this light, we can read *Cargo Cult* as a multi-layered dialectical image that presages, but also preemptively criticises, much of the concern of contemporary art with the question of logistics.

Chapter 6

The Art of Logistics

Chains of dissociation

Though it's thousands of miles away
Sierra Leone connects to what we go through today
Over here it's a drug trade, we die from drugs
Over there they die from what we buy from drugs
The diamonds, the chains, the bracelets, the charmses
I thought my Jesus piece was so harmless
'Til I seen a picture of a shorty armless
Kanye West, 'Diamonds are Forever'

The opening credit sequence of Andrew Niccol's *Lord of War* (2005) – scored to Vietnam film soundtrack staple 'For What It's Worth' by Buffalo Springfield ('Stop children, what's that sound?') – is shot from the point of view of a bullet as it makes its way from a munitions factory somewhere in Eastern Europe into the head of a child soldier in an anonymous African warzone, via ports in Eastern Europe and Africa. Officially endorsed by Amnesty International, the film tells the story of a Brooklyn arms dealer of Ukrainian descent whose career implicates him in the Lebanese civil war, Colombian drug cartels, arms-for-hostage scandals, and the depredations of Liberian warlords. This three-minute long sequence – the most engaging part of the film, a feature it shares with some of its contemporaries (like the 2007 *The Kingdom*) – neatly encapsulates a trend that has emerged throughout the visual arts over the past decade, in which the narrative structure of the work is parasitic on the global movements of a particular commodity.

Twenty years ago Terence Hopkins and Immanuel Wallerstein

190

coined the term 'commodity chains' – later commonly referred to as 'global commodity chains' – to describe the network of labour and production processes that lead to a finished commodity.[336] Since then a body of academic literature has developed that examines specific commodity chains in minute detail, not only reconstructing the journey from production to consumption, but examining each link, and conceptualising what such chains tell us about the structure and dynamics of contemporary global capitalism. Recent years have seen the emergence of a wide array of works in the visual arts and popular culture, which in various forms and genres track the production and distribution of particular commodities and the societies they transverse. These works are too many to exhaustively catalogue, but a quick list would include feature films like *Blood Diamond* (dir. Edward Zwick, 2006), *Traffic* (dir. Steven Soderbergh, 2000), *Syriana* (dir. Stephen Gaghan, 2005)[337]; as well as works in the fine arts like Steve McQueen's *Gravesend* (2007) and Lucy Raven's *China Town* (2009). Variants of this theme can be seen in film-essays like Ania Soliman's *Natural Object Rant: The Pineapple* (2007-9), which

Steve McQueen, *Gravesend*, 2007

poetically investigates the fruit's history and its tie to the politics of colonialism, and Herbert Sauper's documentary *Darwin's Nightmare* (2004), which traces the perturbing effects of Nile perch on the communities off the coast of Lake Victoria in

Tanzania.

This contemporary variant of 'it-narratives' – a genre of fiction popular in the eighteenth and early nineteenth centuries written from the point of view of objects in circulation[338] – often fit under the rubric of what's been called 'hyperlink cinema'. Hyperlink films feature multilinear plots, and part of the film's suspense is generated by the viewer wondering how the narratives of the characters are interwoven or will intersect.[339] In these commodity chain films, the narrative link is the characters' relation to the film's product of choice, whether it be guns, cocaine, oil, or Nile perch.[340] Fears of didacticism from this subgenre might be overstated, but at times, especially within the Hollywood variants, the films are forced to resort to plot gimmicks that allow the work to investigate particular relationships: in *Syriana*, for instance, an economic pundit is able to gain access to oil elites only after his son is electrocuted in a Saudi Prince's swimming pool. In the fine arts, unsurprisingly, a subtler, if more contemplative approach, has prevailed. Raven's *China Town* traces the production of the copper wire used in light bulbs from an open pit mine in Nevada to a smelter in China, at which point the ore is smelted and refined. The work is a 52-minute photographic animation featuring sound recordings from various sites along the way. In many film-works about globalisation, there is a focus on speed: in *Lord of War*, the bullet's journey from the assembly line to the child-soldier's forehead takes three action-drenched minutes. In *China Town*, by contrast, the viewer experiences the full weight of grinding temporality in this slow, labour- and travel-intensive process. This is also the case in Steve McQueen's *Gravesend*, which takes its title from the port town just east of London on the southern bank of the Thames from where Charles Marlow sets off for his journey in Conrad's *Heart of Darkness*. It features scenes of miners prospecting for coltan in caves and a river bed in the Congo, images from a high-tech refinery in England, as well as stills capturing a bright orange-red sunset over the Thames, intercut with a black-and-white animation that tracks the Congo river from its origin in the highlands of Zambia to its mouth in the Atlantic.

Coltan, the industrial name for columbite-tantalite, is a metallic ore whose element tantalum is used in electronic equipment: mobile phones, DVD players, video games, and computers. Two-thirds to fourth-fifths of the world's coltan reserves are thought to be located in the Democratic Republic of Congo and export of the ore is widely cited as one of the main sources for funding the country's murderous civil war. McQueen's elegant work not only references Conrad but contains a clear allusion to Gustave Courbet's *The Stone-Breakers* (1849), perhaps indicating an effort to articulate a realism shorn of didacticism. As T.J. Demos has noted, this 'moving image of globalisation' reveals the latter's dark underside, yet does so obliquely, only alluding to the horrors involved in coltan extraction.[341] There are no subtitles, narration, or text explaining the nature of the images or how they are linked, but the global chain around coltan can distinctly be inferred – we could say it is presupposed, as a kind of virtual caption or subtext.[342]

Works such as McQueen's can be seen to dislocate the fetish of the commodity by bringing to the fore, however tentatively, the social relations largely shrouded by the final products, to disclose the violence behind the anodyne surface of exchange. It was in this spirit that the Colombian poet and lawyer José Eustasio Rivera wrote a letter to Henry Ford in 1928, where he exclaimed that, were rubber to speak, 'it would exhale the most accusing wail, formed by the cries of flesh torn away by the whip, the moans of bodies devastated by hunger and swollen by *beriberi*, and the screams of the exploited and persecuted tribes'.[343] Today, to quote the extraordinarily underwhelming website WikiChains, they could be seen 'to encourage ethical consumption and transparency in commodity chains.' Case in point is Mike Daisey's one-man performance *The Agony and*

Ecstasy of Steve Jobs (2011), largely a self-aggrandising narrative of the performer congratulating himself for informing the audience they should not get completely swept up by their gleaming gadgets and think a moment about where their iPads came from. At their worst, as China Miéville notes, many of these discussions digress into a crass commodity-fetishism themselves: properties that are the result of the social relations between human beings are yet again confused for innate properties of objects themselves. As in neoliberal warnings of 'resource curses', commodities themselves are given the power to ruin economies, corrupt statesmen and launch wars: 'the social dynamics causing the very decried crises are obscured, and the mindless nuggets with which capital accumulation is effected instead sternly blamed.'[344] The focus on infamous commodities frames them as an exception in a world where 'normal' trade is thought to unfold with complete transparency and free of gross exploitation, often occluding a more systemic conception which may conclude with Miéville that 'Every Pritt stick bought on a London high street is Hot Glue. Every toilet-roll procured legitimately in a Toronto suburb is Conflict Tissue. Every branny breakfast item in a New York Starbucks is a fucking Blood Muffin.'

The best examples of this narrative and visual trend avoid conjuring up tidy chain in which each link can be clearly differentiated, and responsibilities duly apportioned, in a horizon which is ultimately that of ethical consumption. Rather than focusing on, for example, the rather simple linear connection between a Foxconn factory in Zhengzhou and the Soho Apple store, these works would put the iPhone in a larger geopolitical context that includes coltan extraction in eastern Congo, trade pacts and shipping lanes, the 55 kilograms of carbon emissions it produces over its lifetimes, as well as the Foxconn factory and high street shop. Commodity-chain works have perhaps been tainted by their association with more anodyne fair trade politics, though it's worth noting that even linear mapping can pose a threat, witness Apple's rejection of *Phone Story* – 'an educational game about the dark side of your favourite smart phone' where you 'follow your phone's journey around the world and fight the market forces in a spiral of planned obsolescence' – from their app store.[345]

Ideal X, or, the poetics of containerisation

By and large, the commodities that transfix today's artists spend most of their journey in uniform containers that have themselves generated a diverse array of works. In thinking through the aesthetics and poetics of containerisation, and through the ways in which it has been thematised in recent narratives and artefacts, it is perhaps worth noting how McLean's innovation – he did not *invent* the container – can itself be chalked up to an 'aesthetic' shift. The management guru Peter Drucker takes the logistics of the 'box' as a crucial example of the distinction between invention and innovation. As he observes:

> whatever changes the wealth-producing potential of already existing resources constitutes innovation. There was not much new technology involved in the idea of moving a truck body off its wheels and onto a cargo vessel. This 'innovation', the container, did not grow out of technology at all but out of a new perception of a 'cargo vessel' as a material handling device rather than a 'ship' which meant that what really mattered was to make the time in port as short as possible. But this humdrum innovation roughly quadrupled the productivity of the ocean going freighter and probably saved shipping. Without it, the tremendous expansion of world trade in the last sixty years – the fastest growth in any major economic activity ever recorded – could not possibly have taken place.[346]

For all the disavowal of the dynamics of capital and war in such a managerial conception of logistics, its notion of a new perception does point us to the fact that containerisation is shorthand for a complex assemblage of labour (living and dead), capital (fixed and variable), law, politics, energy and geography. The container is widely taken to be a crucial factor in the emergence of capitalist globalisation, as it accelerates the volume, speed, and scope of trade and production through a number of politically and aesthetically significant features: standardisation, homogeneity, modularity, fungibility and efficiency. But viewed in terms of social relations of production and their geographical determinants, it also signals the devastation of port and ship-labour, the dislocation of transport and production centres in new spatio-temporal fixes, the separation of the harbour from the social life of the city, dematerialisation, as well as a kind of radical opacity or invisibility that comes to affect commerce and industry alike. The container is thus both a crucial operator *and* a symbol of an all-encompassing regime of materialised abstraction. Like the ex-tanker that carried 48 containers from Newark to Houston in 1956, 'the box' is not just a terribly banal entity, but an *Ideal X*.

The increasing presence of the container as a synecdoche for logistics, circulation and capital in the arts – unlike the best work on commodity chains – is often too prone to obscure its 'relational' properties (arguably the only ones that truly count) and remain mesmerised by its modularity, homogeneity, and opacity.[347] If it can be said that a cartographic desire continues to animate much contemporary artistic practice, it's also notable how the container has come to serve for some as the 'cell-form' or 'box-form' of this aesthetic: a dumb, indifferent, interchangeable materialisation of capital's abstract circulation; a concrete identical *noumenon* for the proliferating differences of phenomenal consumption. Allan Sekula articulated the most perceptive criticism of the fetish of the container in his *Fish Story*, starting from the sensory experience of the port:

If the stock market is the site in which the abstract character of money rules, the harbour is the site in which material goods appear in bulk, in the very flux of exchange. Use values slide by in the channel: the Ark is no longer a bestiary but an encyclopaedia of trade and industry. This is the reason for the antique mercantilist charm of harbours. But the more regularized, literally containerized, the movement of goods in harbours, that is, the more rationalized and automated, the more the harbour comes to resemble the stock market. A crucial phenomenological point here is the suppression of smell. Goods that once reeked – guano, gypsum, steamed tuna, hemp, molasses – now flow or are boxed. The boxes, viewed in vertical elevation, have the proportions of slightly elongated banknotes. The contents anonymous: electronic components, the worldly belongings of military dependents, cocaine, scrap paper (who could know?) hidden behind the corrugated sheet steel walls emblazoned with the logos of global shipping corporations: Evergreen, Matson, American President, Mitsui, Hanjin, Hyundai.[348]

Container lit

Some of the more sustained efforts at narratively thematising the constraints on individual and collective action posed by global capital have treated the container as narrative emblem and device, as well as an allegory of sorts for the condition of disorientation and lacking knowledge. Consider three of the most feted and accomplished efforts at mapping the impasses of contemporary agency and knowledge in terms of the structures of power that subtend the circulation of commodities (including, and at times principally, that critical commodity which is labour-power and the human bodies that bear it). *Gomorrah* (the 2006 book by Roberto Saviano and the 2008 film by Matteo Garrone), the TV series *The Wire* (Season 2 in particular) and William Gibson's 'speculative fiction of last Tuesday' *Spook Country*

(2007), all give dramatic prominence to that singularly undramatic technology. In *Gomorrah* and *The Wire* the port, as it sheds labour and is prised away from the urban texture of Naples or Baltimore, is a privileged observatory for grasping the mutations of power, profit and production. At first, though, there appears to be nothing to see, save for the seamless standardised movement of a space that resembles nothing so much as an extruded factory, or even better an outdoor distribution centre, having more in common with one of the gigantic boxes employed by Amazon or Sainsbury's than with the chaotic, conflictual, odorous, romantic and dangerous space of the historic commercial habour.

Saviano's rather overwrought prose captures some of the contradictions of this space – this hidden abode of circulation that logistical innovations (with their legal and political preconditions) have rendered possible.[349] The containerised port defeats our scalar sense: 'It is necessary to refound your imagination to try to understand how the immensity of Chinese production can rest' on the port of Naples; 'Entire cities of commodities are built up in the harbour only to be taken away'; the port is an 'immense structure, but which seems to have no space, instead it seems to invent it'. Just as the choreography of invisibility that governs the movement of commodities through this space defeats our spatial conceptions of quantity, so is the lived density of time evacuated: 'Here every minute seems murdered. A massacre of minutes'. This massacre is *silent*, stripping the port of its traditional association with the labour of loading and unloading ship, the spectacle of shipping, the culture of dockers and sailors: 'One imagines the port as a place of noise, the coming and going of men, the rush of people. Instead there rules within it the silence of a mechanised factory'.

Saviano tries to force a contrast with this factory harbour, in which commodities 'don't leave the slime of their trajectory', by stacking up digestive metaphors. The port is not just a black hole on the map, it is a wound, or rather an anus. But it is also segregated: 'The harbour is split from the city. An infected appendix that never degenerates into peritonitis, always preserved in the abdomen of the coast'. Not one to keep his metaphors in much order, the port is also a place of parturition, not just excretion, at least when Saviano imagines – as so many do – the possibility of following the commodities, of unweaving the warps of capital:

> It's like staring at the origin of the world. In a few hours there pass through the port the clothes that Parisian kids will wear for a month, the fish sticks that will be eaten in Brescia for a year, the watches that will cover the wrists of Catalans, the silk for all the English dresses for a season. It would be interesting if one could read somewhere not only where a commodity are produced, but even the kind of path it's taken to arrive in the hands of its buyer. Products have multiple, hybrid and bastard citizenship.

But the starkest contrast between seamless opacity of containerisation and the dramas of the kind of social life it makes possible (and which makes it possible in turn), is to be found in the book's opening scene, as dozens of dead Chinese migrants are disbursed by a broken container – supposedly being shipped back to China for burial while their passports are acquired by a new levy of living labour. It is worth noting that this tableau is among the many produced by Saviano whose veracity has been queried, in this case by Chinese migrant associations who have condemned him for recirculating an urban legend with an evident racist undercurrent.[350]

The investigation that spans Season 2 of *The Wire* is also set off by a container, revealed to hold a number of dead Eastern European women, trafficked for prostitution. The criminal occasion provided by the 'dead girls in a can' leads the police detail and the show far afield, into the industrial decadence of the Eastern seaboard, the contradictions of security in the age of the Patriot Act, the racial rifts within city and union, and the fateful advance of gentrification. Though the means and results differ widely, the pattern is similar: as though answering to some primordial anxiety about logistics, the banality of the box is broken to reveal its pound of flesh, the bodies in pain that its abstraction erases. The networks and violence of crime become a pretext, but also a model, for investigating the more impersonal and mediated dynamic of capital (as we segue from finding bodies to following the money). The containerised port stands revealed as a latter-day Golgotha for a labouring body whose collective, political power is an object of nostalgic contemplation.

Cleaving much more closely to the abstractive powers of the container, Gibson's *Spook Country* employs it, fittingly, as a kind of Hitchcockian McGuffin, a 'nothing that makes something', a narrative magnet around which to arrange emergent features of a hyper-mediated experience. This is perhaps most evident in the book's preoccupation with 'locative art' and the aesthetic potentials of GPS – the virtual container that 'occupies' an artist's studio being perhaps the emblem of a late, and libidinally rather etiolated, postmodernity. We should perhaps add to this list *I Am the Market*, a remarkable ghosted interview book with a logistics expert for drug cartels, patiently laying out the momentous but unsung character of the innovations that allowed him to design some of the logistical 'solutions' that make possible the gigantic volume of global drug trade, and whose 'hiddenness' is intimately interwoven with the 'legitimate' economy.[351]

If we could speak of something like a *poetics of containerisation* with reference to these works – as perhaps a more pure variant on the poetics of circulation of commodity-chain narratives – it would be marked by a certain fixation on the 'box' as refractory to feeling and cognition, but also as the possible source, when cracked open, of an insight into the freight of bodily suffering that the seamlessness of circulation renders invisible. But there is also a sense that the tale of secrecy, mystery, and revelation pales in front of the narratively refractory function of the box (whatever its contents, mainly unexceptional) as the atomic support of a globe-spanning system, one whose consequences are much more momentous than any single intrigue, and for which the bodes in a can are but a strained allegory.

The pattern is one of impasse (the container as stand-in for the opacity of circulation, compounding the opacity of production), followed by a trope of revelation (bodily suffering, 'true stories'), relayed in turn by a new kind of opacity. As the narrative imagination comes up against the formidable questions of scale, agency, and space-time thrown up by the world market, we can perhaps identify a different, if perhaps complementary, pattern in the visual arts, which, more than interpellated by the opacity of the box, are lured by its seriality, repetition and modularity.

The perception of logistics

The landscape transformed by logistics, which is to say the social factory as a physical, visible form, is a landscape that appears to signal the becoming concrete of the abstract; not just the moulding of everyday life by the homogenising power of abstract social forms (value, money, exchange) but their physical embodiment in 'really abstract' spaces. Scanning the spaces created by what we could call the *flexible homogenisation* that logistics renders possible, Keller Easterling observes how '[o]bdurate physical material ideally behaves more like information, sorting itself and thus further enticing the distribution addict to his obsession. In this landscape of machines and vehicles, materials are not belts or cogs in the machinery, but chips or bits in an information *Landschaft*'.[352] In a kind of social psychosis that realises the dream of cybernetic domination, information is no longer a *post facto* formalisation of material exchanges, or a programme for manipulating action, but a feature of the world. Even floors in warehouses are turned into informational maps or infrastructures. The mapping function is a technical problem: 'FROG, a company that develops vehicles for industry, transport, and entertainment, has developed an AGV with internal mapping able to navigate areas of 100,000 square feet. Automatic warehouses also literally perform like the motherboard of a computer, combining and redistributing goods as bytes and containers like software containers'.[353]

McLean's intermodal innovation – a box smoothly moving from train to truck to ship, indifferent to contents, to language, to labour – becomes a kind of paradigm for a vision of the world in which information, forms of transport and materials are fully 'compatible, combinable and divisible'. As is often the case in descriptions of such socio-technical phase-shifts, Easterling is overly quick to identify, albeit critically, with its metaphysics – writing, in quasi-Deleuzian language – that though the system is hierarchical it does not generate 'arborescence'. Less speculatively, we can note that the spatial and temporal imperatives behind the proliferation and intensification of this logistical, informational landscape are those which, at a certain level of abstraction, have long governed the capitalist use of machinery: minimising the cost and ratio of living labour, breaking union combinations, resolving the problem of idle stocks, increasing the turnover of capital, expanding the scale of accumulation, and so on. In that general sense, a container port is just the gigantic externalisation of the Fordist factory (and weirdly resembles utopias of full automation which accompanied the interwar infatuation with 'Americanism').

But refocusing on logistics can allows us to think through some of the material and economic characteristics of the ongoing urbanisation of capital. The fantasy of frictionless integration that possesses the 'logistics orgmen' does leave its stamp on reality. Drawing on the power of the 'grid' – already remarked upon by authors as diverse as Lewis Mumford, Michel Foucault and Rem Koolhaas – the logistical transformation of the urban combines 'the repertoires of cars, elevators, robots, and rapid transit'; in this scenario, 'conveyance devices are germs or technological imperatives that shape larger urban fields', geared to posing and resolving 'repetitive, modular problems'.[354] This logistical space can be regarded as both generalising in tendency – pushing its horizon of integration ever further – and as wielding its logic over circumscribed 'laboratory' spaces, compartmentalised enclaves of which the distribution warehouse and the containerised port are paradigmatic cases. As Easterling notes: 'The quarantined territories of ports and parks are ... another iteration of the dream of optimized frictionless passage'.[355]

This fantasy, of minimising or abolishing all obstacles to the turnover of money and goods, all costs of stockage and circulation, is a specifically capitalist fantasy, anchored in the real and inexorable imperatives of capital's spatio-temporal logic. Jameson has rightly underscored how this centrality of logistics to late capitalism is the locus of an exquisitely dialectical problem for political imagination and practice. The streamlined distribution systems of Wal-Mart enact, in a horizon of ruthless deregulation and precarity, aspects of the utopias of consumption that have enduringly characterised certain strains of socialism. Jameson indicates two technological innovations that powerfully embody the ubiquity of capitalist logistics, as well as its utopian potentials: the bar code and the container.

Both resolve, under novel conditions, the immemorial capitalist problem of stocks, of overproduction and stagnation; they also point towards forms of integration between previously segmented or compartmentalised firms along the commodity chain, now forced beyond a purely competitive stance by interdependency. Jameson cites Hosoya and Schaeffer's conceptualisation of the bar code as one among a series of 'bit structures': 'a new infrastructure in the city, providing unprecedented synchronization and organization in seeming formlessness. Bit structures reorganise the pattern of the city and allow its destabilization'. It is worth pausing on Jameson's suggestion that we treat the bar code and containerisation, both of which partake in the logistical revolution's shift of power onto the side of retail, in terms of the 'utopian' dimensions of their shift from production to distribution. As he declares: 'both these ends of the so-called supply chain demand philosophical conceptualization and stand as the mediation between production and distribution and the virtual abolition of an opposition between distribution and consumption'.[356]

In this respect, the logistical revolution would express a collapse of the dialectic between production, distribution and consumption, a dialectic which, in Marx's famous formulation from the 1857 Introduction to the *Grundrisse*, was always one where production doubled as a moment and as the totality of the process or cycle. Arguably, whereas the bit structures of contemporary capital have been taken up by narrative as allegories of secrecy or McGuffins occasioning the desire for cognitive mapping, there has been a tendency in the visual arts, and photography in particular, for a fixation with the symmetrical and homeomorphic properties of the logistical landscape, whose paradoxically photogenic character stems in many ways from its inadvertent mimesis of a modernist, minimalist geometry whose rules of representation are already deeply incorporated into the grammar of artistic form.

These landscapes, not made to be seen (by contrast with the classic architecture of industry and transport, or indeed the modern designer airport), generate a kind of collateral aesthetic effect which has a magnetic draw for the kind of photography that wishes to fuse together or sublate the distinction between the documentary and the artistic. We'll return below to Allan Sekula's powerful analysis of the problematic transcoding of instrumental images into artistic (and sentimental) ones, but his comments on the aestheticisation of war-landscape photography remain very relevant to the abiding fascination of photography with the man-altered landscapes of logistics, and of containeri-sation in particular: 'A landscape possessed of humanly made features can be translated into the realm of a nonreferential abstract geometry. The deployment of roads, trenches, city grids and cultivated fields over the rectangular space of the image is lifted into a universe of spiritualized affect or simple enjoyment'.[357]

Logistical landscape easily affords such spiritualisation. Consider the feted work of Edward Burtynsky, who has devoted himself for two decades or so to depicting the planetary effects and appearance of forms of life and material organisation entirely reliant on non-renewable fossil fuels – following a curiously 'totalising' epiphany, in which he realised that he'd driven to shoot fossil fuels in a car driven by them using a camera all of whose components relied on non-renewable energy. Inevitably, the logistical revolution is an abiding presence in his work, but its form of appearance shows the limitation of his particular mix of eco-liberalism and an aesthetic concern with monumental scale.

Scale and symmetry – along with focused detail, a divine panoramic view, and the absence or insignificance of human presence – dominate this work. The container port presents a kind of pre-established logistical harmony between the manifes-tations of global capitalism and a type of photographic gaze – the apex of the tendency, already crucial to the 'new topographics' moment, to turn one's eye and camera towards the abstracted landscapes of capital. The spiritualisation of this abstraction can be criticised for its fetishisation of scale and symmetry (this is most evident, in Jennifer Baichwal's documentary *Manufactured Landscapes* (2006), in Burtynsky's elaborate staging of his photographs in Chinese factories; stressing, much as techno-fantasies might, depersonalising symmetry and scale over exploitation, friction, or indeed the waste and consumption of energy, human and machinic). This landscape, somewhat like the

Philip Glass-scored film *Koyanisqaatsi: Life Out of Balance* (dir. Godfrey Reggio, 1982), and other liberal totalisations of ecological systems and the crises of Gaia, elides both the inapparent logics at work in these processes and the enduring role of collective labour and agency. It presents us with beautiful monuments to alienation without any inquiry into the processes of their production. In the depiction of cycles of energy extraction, circulation and waste, cause and effect implode into a kind of entropic destiny, which we can nonetheless artistically enjoy (while we simultaneously arrive at some kind of mindfulness of our total and terminal dependency).

The photographed container may also serve to pose the problem of the invisibility of social relations, the problem of defetishisation in the midst of the logistical revolution. This is what Jacques Rancière has suggested about the port photographs of Frank Breuer:

From afar the spectator perceived them as abstract scenes or reproductions of minimalist sculptures. Upon approaching, however, one discovered that the coloured rectangles on a white background were containers stacked in a large deserted space. The impact of the series was down to the tension between this minimalism and the signification that it concealed. These containers were to be, or were to have been, filled with merchandise unloaded at Antwerp or Rotterdam, and probably were produced in a distant country, perhaps by faceless workers in Southeast Asia. They were, in short, filled with their own absence, which was also that of every worker engaged to unload them, and, even more remotely, that of the European workers replaced by these distant labourers. The 'objectivity' of the medium thus masks a determined aesthetic relation between opacity and transparency, between the containers as brute presence and the containers as representatives of the 'mystery' of the merchandise – that is to say, of the

206

manner in which it absorbs human work and hides its mutations.[358]

However, though the short-circuit between the geometry of built and logistical forms and photographic abstraction is strongly grounded in the history of the genre, one wonders whether Rancière's 'reading' is not simply a meditation on the container that could have been applied to the photographs of Burtynsky with similar aptness. If the narrativisation of the container risks defetishing too fast – what appears to be a seamless technical apparatus for distribution hides, beneath its blank metal surface, bodies in pain – its photographic depiction can slide mechanically into an implicit celebration of the fetish, relishing the revelation that the physical and social world has been transformed into an orthogonal space, the social factory approximating an infinite assemblage of depersonalised minimalist or suprematist views. Neither perspective truly confronts the deeper challenge that logistics poses to the image. This is to be found not so much in the representation of logistics – which is inevitably covered by the much-quoted Brechtian warning about the impotence of industrial photography in a moment when 'reality has slipped into the functional', as good a definition as any of the logistical revolution – but of the logistics of representation, of information and images.

The traffic in instrumental images

Histories of cartography often remark upon the critical role that military requirements imposed on how geography was represented. Similarly, European visual culture is pervaded with the demands of a military gaze, superiority in sighting capacities translating into a control over space (by means of anticipating in time the movements of one's adversary), and a mastery of humans and materials. Jacques Lacan once quipped that every action represented on a canvas appears to us, be it implicitly, as a battle scene.[359] It is possible to trace numerous parallels, entanglements and intersections between military and artistic representation – in different registers this is what we encounter in Sekula's reflections in *Fish Story* on the shift from the panorama to the detail, or in Paul Virilio's inquiries into the logistics of perception in *War and Cinema*.

Logistics, as we've already noted, is a martial term, and to approach the art image from a logistical angle is to approach it in terms of how it may be affected by the incorporation of representational considerations into the management and movement of resources (informational, material, destructive, human) in war. The study of the logistical image in the age of mechanised and later informational warfare tends to the common conclusion that this is an image which has broken with the mode of panoramic overview that we readily associate with the traditional 'theatre of war'.

To think the image in the field of logistics is thus to think of an image shorn of the subjective, reflective, contemplative features generally ascribed to an artistic representation, as a representation produced *for* a viewing, judging subject (individual or collective). The logistical image – whether the particular domain of logistics is military or commercial is of minor importance here – is to be considered primarily in its informational functionality, as an element in a concatenation of actions, or in a *flow*. In the final analysis, such an image does not differ in kind from other logistical components. As logistics becomes more significant in the preparation and operation of totalising, if not total wars, the representation of war (in emblems, uniforms, historical paintings, and so on) is replaced by representations in war, or wars of representation.[360]

Though there is a marked contemporary resurgence in the kind of aftermath photography of war landscapes that finds its origin in Fenton's photographs of the Crimean war (consider for instance the works of Simon Norfolk or Sophie Ristelheuber),[361] military topographic images – outside of their important propagandistic uses – might be said to be largely shorn of aura. But to see the logistical image, that is, to see that it is an image not made for contemplation, and to draw the consequences from this, remains a feat of de-fetishisation.

That was precisely the task that Allan Sekula set himself in responding, in 1975, to the curatorial identification of Edward Steichen's role as overseer of aerial reconnaissance photography in World War I as an origin-story for modernist photography. Aerial photographs taken under Steichen's military directorship (and ascribed his authorship with no clear factual basis), had been extracted from their context of use. Originally, they were tasked with providing information for immediate use in the tracking and targeting of the enemy. Curatorship had also abstracted them from their mode of production – a veritable assembly line, subjected to principles of standardisation, speed and efficiency. It was this decontextualisation and desocialisation that allowed them to be anointed as 'works of art': individual photographs whose precise referents are long lost, now free to serve as occasions for disinterested visual pleasure.

Bucking this trend to spiritualise images that operated as functional moments in the strategic deployment of destructive force, Sekula wants to return us to an understanding of their reality as 'instrumental images', all the better to understand the ideological coordinates of their transubstantiation into inadvertent precursors of a dispassionate modernist gaze (a curatorial move which in turn appears as symptomatic of a certain affinity between 'cold' modernism and military anti-humanism). Airplane photography appears here as a point of crystallisation in the logistics of representation: 'With airplane photography ... two globalizing mediums, one of transportation and the other of communication, were united in the increasingly rationalized practice of warfare'.[362] The instrumentality of these images involved representation as a mode of anticipation – foreseeing the manoeuvres and siting of the enemy, in time to 'move' one's arsenal of destruction to the correct place, at the correct time. Sekula stresses the 'fundamental *tactical* concerns which governed the reading of aerial reconnaissance photographs':

> The meaning of a photograph consisted of whatever it yielded to the rationalised act of 'interpretation'. As sources of military intelligence, these pictures carried an almost wholly denotative significance. Few photographs, except perhaps medical ones, were as apparently free from 'higher' meaning in their common usage. They seem to have been devoid of any rhetorical structure. But this poverty of meaning was conditional rather than immanent. Within the context of intelligence operations, the only 'rational' questions were those that addressed the photograph at an indexical level, such as 'Is that a machine gun or a stump?' In other words, interpreting the photograph demanded that it be treated as an ensemble of 'univalent', or indexical, signs – signs that could only carry one meaning, that could point to only one object. Efficiency demanded this illusory certainty.[363]

Now, the spiritualising *détournement* of these images extracts them from the uni-valence of their instrumentality, and from the factory logic that made their 'applied realism' possible, by way of the author-function (the imprimatur of Steichen's creative mind), anointing them with a strangely poly- or non-valent reference: their denotation shifts from the moment of targeting to the generality of war, and they enter into a peculiar mimesis, already referred to, with a kind of modernist artistic abstraction that was miles away from their inaugural intent.

They become 'found' modern art, but only because of their supposed 'signature' by Steichen – though his relationship to the photographs was mainly that of a 'high-level military bureaucrat', who as it happens was 'especially good at solving procurement problems'. Sekula's analysis of the spiritualisation and commodification of these photographs, of their entrance into 'a new order of instrumentality', is exemplary and subtly devastating; what we wish to emphasise here is his attention to the vast domain of instrumental images and to the ideological pitfalls of their translation (or *abstraction*) from a logistical, functional domain to an artistic and representational one.

Sekula hints here at an inhuman elective affinity between aerial photography and a kind of sovereign modernist gaze, mediated by the activity of abstraction. Referring to Malevich's use of aerial photographs of cities in *The Non-Objective World* and his view of Suprematism as somehow 'aeronautical', he notes that,

> Malevich may have kept air war from his mind when he praised the new technology for its aesthetic potential. But although abstraction may try to excuse itself from any ideological stance in relation to its sources, it remains implicated by the very act of denial. One abstracts these photographs at the expense of all other meanings, including the use to which they were originally put.[364]

Most significant to developing a critical stance on contemporary images of logistics are Sekula's reflections on Steichen's move beyond instrumental image-production, and beyond what he perceived as the sterile legacy of painting, to an affirmation of photography as a humanistic art.[365]

Another avenue into this question – of the disavowals of military and capitalist instrumentality in image-making – is Sekula's identification of the liberal paradigm of photographic representation as being split and articulated between efficiency and ethics, *instrumental* realism and *sentimental* realism. The former is 'an ambitious attempt to link optical empiricism with abstract, statistical truth' (as evidenced, for instance, in the uses of photography for the scientific management of industrial labour, or the identification and policing of 'dangerous individuals'). The latter can be met with in the family photograph, the humanist portrait and such projects as Steichen's *Family of Man*, what Sekula terms a 'Cold War utopia'. From this liberal antinomy between technology and humanism we can draw various unstable third ways, among which Sekula numbers symbolism and bourgeois realism.[366] But to try and understand the logistical image and its instrumental realism without attending to capital, to the exchange abstraction and monetisation, is to deprive ourselves of the comprehension of what is at stake in these practices of abstraction, and what the ultimate determinant of instrumentality is.[367]

The factory logic that conditions the production of these instrumental images, with its separation of intellectual and manual labour, its Taylorist intensification and deskilling of work (accompanied, or rather compensated, by a romantic lionisation of the producer-designer-ideator as author), is intimately tied up with a monetary logic of commensurability and accumulation. Reference to the US Supreme Court Justice's Oliver Wendell Holmes's essay 'The Stereoscope and the Stereograph' allows Sekula to explore the way in which the universalism of the nascent art and technology of photography was explicitly likened, or even identified, to money as a universal equivalent in the exchange of commodities. The question of form was paramount. As Holmes writes, with photography 'Form is henceforth divorced from matter'. This is the very fantasy that we encounter in paeans to the seamless shaping of architecture by computer design, or in the spurious, but nonetheless influential (for a time) view of the 'new economy' as a domain of immaterial flows and immaterial work. The fantasy is one of 'dematerialised form' in the guise of 'photographic sign[s] [that] come to eclipse [their] referent'. Circulation, storage and 'traffic' are brought together in this vision of abstraction, in which photography and money come together as media of exchange, equivalence and universality. In Holmes's words:

> Matter in large masses must always be fixed and dear; form is cheap and transportable. ... The time will come when a man who wishes to see any object, natural or artificial, will go to the Imperial, National, or City Stereographic Library and call for its skin or form, as he would for a book at any common library.

What's more:

> as a means of facilitating the formation of public and private stereographic collections, there must be arranged a comprehensive system of exchanges, so that there might grow up something like a universal currency of these banknotes, on promises to pay in solid substance, which the sun has engraved for the great Bank of Nature.[368]

Holmes also wrote of *carte-de-visite* photos as 'the sentimental "greenbacks" of civilisation'. For him, Sekula concludes, 'photographs stand as the "universal equivalent", capable of denoting the quantitative exchangeability of all sights', they are imagined 'to reduce all sights to relations of formal equivalence ... Like money, the photograph is both a fetishized end in itself and a calibrated signifier of a value that resides elsewhere, both autonomous and bound to its referential function'.[369]

A consideration of the logistical image can thus open onto an aesthetic and political inquiry into the conjunctions between circulation and abstraction, the traffic in photographs and their abstraction from use, the role of images in logistical flows (military, productive, financial) and their modes of exchange and commensurability. Attention to the traffic in and of photographs, to their integration into logistical apparatuses of production and destruction, provides a critical counterpoint to the lures and impasses of images and representations of 'traffic', of the circulation of goods and people.

Complementary observations can be drawn from the work on eyeless vision by Harun Farocki. Videoworks like *As You See It* (1986), *Images of the World and the Inscription of War* (1989), *Eye/Machine I, II and III* (2001-3) and *War at a Distance* (2003) – or indeed, in the domain of retail logistics and design *The Creators of Shopping Worlds* (2001) – are so many reports on the vast realm of what Farocki, echoing Sekula, calls 'operative images'. These are images 'that do not try to represent reality but are part of a technical operation' – and thus arguably transcend any ordinary use of the term 'image'.[370] Where Sekula's emphasises how the commodity exchange-abstraction mediates between the instrumental image and its re-instrumentalisation into a sentimental realism or a spiritualised modernism, Farocki repeatedly locates the genesis of the operative image in the replacement of manual by mechanical labour, that is in the (contradictory) capitalist tendency to try to shed living labour, with all of its frictions, fallibilities and antagonisms, for the sake of machine-work. The rising organic composition of capital, of the proportion of dead to living labour, has its counterpart in the domain of representations, impelled by the very imperatives of profit and the expediencies of war which, as we've already noted, find one of their crucial points of synthesis in the domain of logistics.

As Farocki observes: 'Just as mechanical robots initially took workers in the factory as their model, shortly afterwards surpassing and displacing them, so the sensory devices are meant to replace the work of the human eye'. Inventorying Farocki's explorations into this 'anaesthetic' domain of eyeless vision – which occasionally trespasses from the operative to the representational, as in the images broadcast from the nosecones of 'smart bombs' in the first Gulf War[371] – Georges Didi-Hubermann writes of '*images that dispense with the very human beings they were intended*

to represent', of *'images for destroying human beings',* and, importantly – since this is another key instance of image-fetishism – of:

> images of technical processes, divided into squares by the
> viewfinder and saturated with explosions, ... abstract and
> perfectly 'contemporary' images [that] took the place of the
> *images of results* which a journalist could have – should have –
> brought back from the ruins caused by all these 'surgical
> strikes' (and those images would not in the least have seemed
> 'new', since nothing looks more like a burnt corpse than
> another burnt corpse).[372]

Here too, in these images of targeting and surveillance, images
primed for expedient action, a kind of abstraction is at work.
Didi-Hubermann has in this light tried to bring Farocki into
contact with the Horkheimer and Adorno of *Dialectic of
Enlightenment*:

> While surveillance certainly produces 'an abstract existence
> like the Fordist factory produced abstract work; as Farocki
> once wrote, the word *abstract* must here be considered in the
> precise understanding it was given by Adorno and
> Horkheimer in *Dialectic of Enlightenment*, when they wrote
> that 'abstraction, the instrument of enlightenment, stand [...]
> to its objects [...] as liquidation;. To convince oneself of this it
> suffices to watch again, in *Gefängnisbilder* (Prison Images,
> 2000), this chilling moment where the camera has detected a
> fight in the prison yard, and the gun that is *linked* to it – for
> such is the complete device: to monitor and to destroy – fires
> a shot at one of the two prisoners without warning.[373]

'Compressing the kill chain' – this sinister military-managerial
expression encapsulates the process that Farocki has so meticu-
lously tracked and diagnosed in the visual field. Its combination

of labour-saving devices and unlimited force, deskilling and desk killing, has reached its (no doubt temporary) apex with the ongoing drone 'wars'. The imperial drive 'to put warheads on foreheads', as one military motto goes, is in great part the product of an aesthetic and political fantasy, a fantasy about the perfect match between omnipotence and omniscience. In this new political techno-theology of total vision and unbounded jurisdiction, instrumental and operational images come together – mediated by forms of algorithmic rationality and calculated over 'big data' in ways that neither Farocki nor Sekula could have fully factored.

In an acute philosophical inquiry into 'drone theory', Grégoire Chamayou has synthesised the drone's 'revolution of the gaze' into six principles, which go some way to outlining the political and aesthetic problem of the logistics of perception today.[374] First, *the principle of the persistent gaze or permanent wakefulness* – not just through 24hr automated processing, but through the round-the-clock shifts of operators, since the organic composition of surveillance has its lower limits, and a residuum of labouring agency remains. Second, *the principle of the totalisation of perspectives or the synoptic view* – this can be seen in the technical attempt to transform the gaze of the drone into something resembling the eyes of a fly, but we could also think of how GIS systems totalise and unify a vast amount of different images into one view, as in the contemporary images of the planet we mentioned in our introduction.[375] Third, *the principle of total archiving or the film of all lives* – the dreamed capacity of stocking and reviewing at will all past actions, through cognitive systems of surveillance that combine the techniques of contemporary sports television with legal, and lethal, protocols of judgment, in which every life would be 'searchable'. Fourth, *the principle of fusion of data* – the drone as a site of synaesthesia, correlating visual, auditory and other forms of information. Fifth, *the principle of schematisation of forms of life* – the algorithmic profiling of 'dangerous individuals' and groups, producing a cartography of their 'patterns of life', a 'generic identification' allowing military power to direct deadly force without needing to actually know or recognise the target *as such* (this is the principle behind the infamous 'signature strikes'). Sixth and last, *the principle of the detection of anomalies and of preventive anticipation* – drone strikes operate on the basis that deviation from 'normal' patterns of life is an index of danger, so that a kind of automated human geography, or what Derek Gregory terms 'militarised rhythmanalysis', would allow specialists of violence to compress the operative connection between the perception of a pattern of life and the exercise of the power of death.

The imperialist utopia of a 'boundless informant', made public by the NSA scandal, is deeply entangled with a practice of uncircumscribed power, in which vision is at once centralised and ubiquitous, and lethal force can be projected anytime, anywhere, against anyone – the classical monopoly of violence seeking to translate itself also into a monopoly of sight and information. Remarkably precarious in its own control over the interlocking causalities of geopolitics and political economy, this is contemporary power's own purely military 'solution' to the problem of cognitive mapping.

Chapter 7

Landscapes of Dead Labour

Drabness and decline, or, The problem of England

In a recent catalogue essay for the exhibition of L.S. Lowry's paintings of 'the industrial scene' in the English North, which he curated along with Anne Wagner, T.J. Clark notes the aesthetic sea-change that affected European modernism's orientation as the twentieth century advanced beyond the age of empire into that of extremes. Addressing not just the figurative concerns but the spatial determinants of painting, the English art historian notes how the drive, by the likes of van Gogh, Seurat and Pissarro, to register 'a new kind of evenness and openness to sensation' across the whole of the picture frame also depended on their intense receptivity to 'emergent, unorchestrated still *unknown* forms of life', that had the city and its industrialising environs as their stage. For Clark, the dissipation of this surmise about the bond between everyday life and novelty – in both figurative and urban forms – marks a threshold in modern art. Though we wouldn't countersign them, his observations about this 'scene-change' are certainly germane to this book's concerns:

> There must have been a newly determinant character to modernity ... that came to make any kind of investigative recording of social forms, social behaviour, however studied or elliptical or deliberately limited, impossible – or if done, plodding and superficial. There must have been something in the twentieth-century that meant that looking for modernity's *location,* or its typical subjects, was in itself to misrecognise the way we live now ... modernity no longer presented itself as a distinctive territory, a recognisable new form of space ... the ordinary life of the 'modern' had become unglamorous,

unspectacular, neither familiar nor unfamiliar – *un-exotic*.[376]

One of the objectives of this chapter and the previous one is to explore how the 'logistical scene', so to speak, has been thematised as the elusive location, or better territory, of our late- or post- or indeed anti-modernity. But before returning to that preoccupation, it is worth dwelling for a moment on how Lowry's industrial landscapes – provocatively raised by Clark from minor, if immensely *popular* works, to a veritable *unicum* in modern English painting – cast a peculiarly English light on the problem of a realism of capital. Lowry's articulation of the 'world-historical mystery' of industrialisation is one which, even when its scale is at its most capacious, is resolutely anti-sublime.[377] Refusing, as Clark remarks, the 'grand view', Lowry's ambition, in the painter's own words, was 'to put the industrial scene on the map because nobody had done it, nobody had done it seriously'.[378] The map returns in Clark's own commentary. Against the grain of first (and second) impressions – which would designate Lowry's work as 'static, local and subjectively repetitious'[379] – Clark claims for it an exceptional status: to have produced an 'astonishing panorama' (in other words: a 'great view'!). This would be 'truly a map of the whole of class struggle' in England, as evidenced in the scope and number of Lowry's subjects.[380] This feat, for Clark unmatched by any English artist of his time, ends up itself being a matter of location. Not just the 'milky pool' of light and landscape of the Midlands and the North of England, which Berger highlights as a key ingredient of Lowry's aesthetic, but the *class* location of Lowry as a rent collector, a 'small cog in the machinery of exploitation' who was also, therefore, a 'crosser of boundaries'.[381] Sedentariness, immobility and repetition, at least within certain very clearly defined bounds of space and experience, would thus double as conditions, productive constraints, for this insistent, methodical mapping – which, it should not be forgotten, is actually a very 'synthetic' realism, not matched to any individual location if nevertheless 'typical' of many.

Such attentiveness to the unexotic sites of quotidian struggle – a term which here resonates more with effort or ordeal than conflict or combat – comes at a price (at least from the vantage point of our discussion): modernism's concern with the invisible if wrenching dynamics of social novelty and transition, with what some have conceived as the 'capitalist sublime', are ignored for the sake of a dogged attention to its felt and visible effects. The everyday life of class, as is so often the case in the political aesthetics of England and the United Kingdom, blots the more abstract machinations of capital from the frame. Up to a point. For, as Berger perspicuously notes the 'atmosphere of dramatic obsolescence' that characterises Lowry's industrial scene – what Clark more modestly dubs its 'drabness' – is the index of a more comprehensive theme, the registering and foretelling of *British decline* from the 'privileged' vantage of parts of England, where this decline was tangible long before the 1960s (the time of Berger's writing).[382]

But in what sense is drabness an index of decline? What are the latter's 'forms of appearance'? And is it an even process – or rather one that asymmetrically affects different types and factors of capital? Patrick Keiller's work – both his films *London* (1994), *Robinson in Space* (1997), *The Dilapidated Dwelling* (2000),[383] *Robinson in Ruins* (2010), and his essays – is a matchless exploration of these questions, precisely because of its capacity to address the aesthetics of English political economy through a unique assemblage of theoretical reflection, historical attentiveness and visual invention. Needless to say, the pleasures and demands of Keiller's work transcend the dialectic of drabness and decline, yet it stands out as an exemplary case of how a question whose proper ambit seems to be historiographic or theoretical ('Is the British economy in decline?') can be newly illuminated by an aesthetic investigation into the *appearance(s) of capitalism.*

Both *London* and *Robinson in Space* can be seen to take their cues from, among other catalysts (the Situationist International, Lefebvre, the lived experience of defeat under Thatcherism, the unfulfilled aspirations of British revolutionary history), from the debate over the 'Nairn-Anderson theses' that occupied many of the theoretical attentions of the British Marxist left in the 1960s.[384] Very synthetically, Tom Nairn and Perry Anderson, then young editors of the *New Left Review*, perceived the protracted post-imperial crisis of British polity, economy and, crucially, culture, as a distant, compound effect of its 'peculiar capitalism', in pioneering the advance of other capitalist states yet, because of its originating role, still encrusted with the pathological features of a recombinant aristocracy and the related debilities of a non-revolutionary working class. What had for Marx been the exemplary heartland of capital appeared in retrospect as a landscape marred by prematurity and retardation, having never truly experienced the events and traumas of *political* (and not just industrial) modernity, namely bourgeois revolution and the emergence of an autonomous, forward-tending bourgeois culture. This last dimension of the theses was a more than plausible prism through which Keiller's avatar, Robinson, could make sense of the galling discrepancy between his desire for urban modernity and the dispiriting realities of John Major's (and the City's) London ('The failure of the English revolution is all around us', Robinson observes).[385] The drabness and disappointment of a denizen's existence in the capital seemed to gain a certain clarity from placing the contemporary predicament in the *longue durée* of capital accumulation in England, with its deep-rooted prejudices against modernity and in favour of the conservation of privilege. The following jeremiad by Nairn, which Perry Anderson saw fit recently to revive in a brief comparative estimation of urban life in Britain and France,[386] speak acerbically to the experiences driving *London*:

The very urban world, the bricks and mortar in which most of the population lives, is the image of this archaic, bastard conservatism—an urban world which has nothing to do with urban *civilization*, as this is conceived in other countries with an old and unified bourgeois culture. ... [The] aberrant obsession with the countryside is still a powerful feature of our culture—the country house, as the image of true civilization and social cultivation, has sunk so deeply into the national soul. The modern British town is merely the obverse of this, in its meaninglessness. Culturally, as an artefact of real civilization, it has never existed, because civilization went on elsewhere, in the residences of the territorial aristocracy and gentry (or, just possibly, in the West End of the metropolis, where they customarily spent part of the year, and in the institutional embodiments of gentlemanly culture at Oxford and Cambridge). The squalid, crassly utilitarian town with neither shape nor centre; the suburb, which grotesquely mimics the rural ideal; the dignified country home in its landscaped park, an inevitable focus of taste, ideal social relations, and natural authority, all that the merely bourgeois town is not and has renounced: in this contrast of environments (as in a thousand other contrasts and contradictions) the heterogeneous, paradoxical character of English society and culture is revealed—the true meaning of the 'slow evolution', the conservative empiricism of which (until yesterday) apologists were so proud.[387]

The great, and intended, irony of Keiller's treatment of this problem – as Robinson and his narrating companion take their queerly methodical investigations from London into (English) 'space' – is that it is by gently corroding the bucolic veneer of 'the' countryside that Keiller comes to question the visual and cultural evidence of decline.[388] Accompanying the growth and speculation in finance, real estate and services that would be given a kind of ideological cohesion by New Labour (and whose travails its 2010 crisis sequel investigates), *Robinson in Space*'s Defoesque trajectories[389] take in – with the unsettling attentiveness of Keiller's fixed framings of the 'unexotic' landscapes of late twentieth-century England – the vast distribution centres, suburban complexes, transport systems, and energy networks that comprise the territory of a new regime of accumulation, as well as the outposts of the repressive apparatus (US army bases, privatised prisons for asylum seekers) that makes possible the reproduction of this logistical state. We can even hear resonances of the conservationist lament against the militarisation of the landscape in Hoskins's *The Making of the English Landscape*:

> And those long lines of the dip-slope of the Cotswolds ... how they have lent themselves to the villainous requirements of the age! Over them drones, day after day, the obscene shape of the atom-bomber, laying a trail like a filthy slug upon Constable and Gainsborough's sky.[390]

Robinson in Space corroborates, in a specifically visual register, Ellen Meiksins Wood's rejoinder to the urban dimension of the Nairn-Anderson theses. Her contention that England's was not a 'peculiar capitalism', but that it was 'peculiarly capitalist', was supplemented, in *The Pristine Culture of Capitalism*, by the related argument according to which the 'urban culture' whose absence Nairn and Anderson rue is actually an index of the 'purer' character of capitalism in the British isles, not intermixed with a pre-capitalist burgher culture.[391] Keiller's film updates this counter-thesis, describing the reasons for Robinson's 'erratic' behaviour in terms of the arduous unworking of the lived, visual 'evidence' of decline, and the discovery of a transition within British capitalism that cannot be so easily read off the landscape, or registered at the level of the misery of everyday life: 'the appearance of poverty that characterizes so much of modern

Britain is not the result of the failure of the UK's capitalism, but of its success'.[392] Or, as the narrator of Robinson has it: 'Those of us aesthetes who view the passing of the *visible* industrial economy with regret, and who long for an authenticity of *appearance* based on manufacturing and innovative, modern design, are inclined to view this English culture as a bizarre and damaging anachronism, but if so, it is not an unsuccessful one'.[393] It is only attention to the new spaces thrown up by capital, the new, and often unexceptional or hidden footprint of different

Patrick Keiller, *Robinson in Space*, 1999

patterns of accumulation, which can extricate us from the political-aesthetic fallacy of decline, the wrong inference from the drabness of our lives to the poor health of capital.

These exterior spaces seemed to be developing something of the feel of other kinds of space that, while not inaccessible, are largely hidden from view – the space behind a television, perhaps, or on top of a wardrobe. In the rural landscape, too, there was a similar quality. With but of effort, one could imagine that parts of it were as unexperienced as if they were merely access space for the maintenance engineers of mobile phone networks.[394]

At its extreme, the 'dilapidated *appearance* of the visible landscape, especially the urban landscape, masks its prosperity'.[395] The *détournement* of Defoe's journeys through the British Isles – along with the recent evocative physical montage of the Robinson Institute at the Tate Britain, with its own attention to the logistical – is an aesthetic, narrative and experiential method, which counters the linear thesis of decline in a manner that theoretical argument alone could not.[396]

As we move from the industrial scene to what we could call the logistical scene reality does indeed 'slip into the functional', and the conditions of legibility, the capacity to read symptoms off the landscape, are further strained. And yet it is precisely by attending to these inaesthetic, anaesthetic, unexceptional spaces of production and distribution, that Robinson and his companion can resist the fallacy that consists in inferring from their undesirable, silently hostility, that English capitalism is affected by a terminal malady.[397] Critical to this effort is a nuanced understanding of the (in)visibility and (un)representability of capital. Labouring through 'port statistics'[398] to match abstract process with physical flows and infrastructures, or stalking commodities as they wend their way through distribution centres – impassive, featureless boxes – also invites quiet if momentous realisations, such as the recognition that it is not a passage from the visible to the invisible, the material to the immaterial which is at stake here, but the preponderance of '*less visible* manufactured items, in particular intermediate products (for example, chemicals) and capital goods (power stations, airports, weapons)'.[399]

New spaces also demand an attention to new symptoms. The

keen sensitivity to new sensations and new experiences, as well as to epiphanies of non-contemporaneity and of futures lost, which never leaves Keiller, is tempered in Robinson by a sober consideration: the vitality of capital bears no linear relationship to our livelihoods or the liveliness of our perceptions.[400]

The equator of alienation

What modern capitalism – concentrated and fully established capitalism – inscribes within life's setting, is the fusion of what had been opposed as the positive and negative poles of alienation into a sort of *equator of alienation*. "Urbanism as Will and Representation" in *Internationale Situationniste*, 1964[401]

That landscapes are manufactured or man-altered is no late-capitalist discovery. Though the landscape as genre, or even ideology, may have allowed an emergent modern subject to frame his propertied metaphysic and mastery of nature (crucially by clearing the land of indigenous, insurgent and independent inhabitants), it has also traded in the depiction of human artefacts, imprints of social intercourse – though tending towards singularity, be it salient or submerged. Thus we read in the first systematic European account of landscape painting:

Those who have shown excellence and grace in this branch of painting, both in private and public places, have discovered various ways of setting about it – such as fetid, dark underground places, religious and macabre, where they represent graveyards, tombs, deserted houses, sinister and lonesome sites, caves, dens, ponds and pools; [secondly] privileged places where they show temples, consistories, tribunals, gymnasiums and schools, [or else] places of fire and blood with furnaces, mills, slaughterhouses, gallows and stocks; others bright with serene air, where they represent palaces, princely dwellings, pulpits, theatres, thrones and all the magnificent and regal things; others again places of delight with fountains, fields, gardens, seas, rivers, bathing places and places for dancing. There is yet another kind of landscape where they represent workshops, schools, inns, market places, terrible deserts, forests, rocks, stones, mountains, woods, ditches, water, rivers, ships, popular meeting places, public baths or rather *terme*.[402]

This indeterminacy of the landscape as subject matter, and of its markers, continues into the present, but in a very different guise. When it is not scoured for traces – aftermaths of trauma, indices of futures past – the indeterminacy of landscape is most often coded as indifference: the indifference of modularity and iteration across social spaces, the indifference of concrete abstraction. It is an indifference remarkable for its ubiquity and magnitude, as well as for the sheer scale of its continued reproduction – tract homes all the way into a vanished horizon, container terminals that never sleep, banks of screens in a stock exchange.

That landscape – that prime terrain for the assertion of the view from power – should have been thematised with such insistence in the 1970s as the emblem of a kind of inhuman subsumption (though one not devoid of its own grim splendour, to which we'll return) should not surprise. With the urbanisation of capital going well beyond the expansion of cities into a transmutation of the lived and visible landscape into that of a social factory – especially evident in once-rural suburban and functional spaces – built space attained an experiential, as well as an allegorical function it didn't previously have. This was especially so in those places where postwar 'planner-states' enabled an accelerated industrialisation, quickly saturating landscapes with the infrastructures of accumulation. Think, for instances, of the massive industrial establishments in Antonioni's seemingly depopulated Po Valley. Or, to turn to two cases worth dwelling on in a more comparative vein, to the 'new topographics' moment in US photography,[403] with its attention to the suburbanisation of habitation and business in the American West, and the 'landscape theory' (*fûkeiron*) proposed by militant artists in the late sixties and early seventies in Japan.

Aside from their foregrounding of 'landscape' as medium, object, and in a sense subject of their work, these unconnected proposals share some telling formal traits. Vistas are vanquished (and if they open up, it is only into a kind of orthogonal feature-lessness), the built world is encountered frontally, deadpan. Captions are minimal, doing little of the critical work famously invoked by Brecht and Benjamin. Spaces are depopulated or humans appear in the kind of routine everyday that has them circulate obediently in deserts of architecture (ironically, given that demographic density is often a dimension of the phenomena at stake). These are not landscapes virtually possessed by a subject, but ones that either refuse to afford any grip for an imagined presence or simply crowd agency out.

Jean-Luc Godard, *Weekend*, 1969

One of the proponents of *fûkeiron*, the photograper Takuma Nakahira, noted this tendency in Godard's *Weekend*, where 'the central "characters" are a series of traffic accidents and a sea of draining blood, while the human couple running away plays only a small role'. But this inversion is for Nakahira the bearer of an aesthetic and political truth: 'it seems very vivid and pertinent for us, because we are actually living in such a time, more than ever before'; this in turn calls for the artist to make 'our age's syndrome more explicit, to expose it for what it is'.[404] Where an urban landscape 'covered over with expressionless smoothness',[405] is still looked at by practitioners of *fûkeiron* in the context of rebellion (be it the impasses of the student struggles or the shootings by Nagayama Norio, the absent subject of the key *fûkeiron* film *A.K.A. Serial Killer*),[406] in the new topographics the inhuman homogeneity of built space is presented without comment, in a studied aesthetic of anonymity, of style-less style.

Abstracting the land

It was precisely this aesthetic of the new spaces of suburbanising US capital that beckoned the critical rebuke of Allan Sekula against the 'new topographics' photographer Lewis Baltz. In a postscript to his own photo-essay on the kind of schooling, exploitation and discipline at work in the same 'new industrial parks near Irvine' that were the object of a 1974 book by Baltz, Sekula queried the manner in which this photographic trend, lured by the pictorial examples of modernist minimalism, approached these new spatial phenomena – inextricable from a certain spatial logic of capital – by evacuating their social and labouring referent. This is a bad abstraction, one that 'finds an exemplary aesthetic freedom in the disengaged play of signifiers'.[407] Baltz's images, like those of what Sekula sarcastically dubbed 'the neutron bomb school of photography', would thus be led by their own economic unconscious – chiefly, modernism's reassertion of the separation between intellectual and manual labour – to a complicity with the 'mystifying translation of a site of production into a site of imaginary leisure' synthesised in the oxymoronic blandness of the term 'industrial park'.

Though this is a suggestive line of criticism, which Sekula has developed at length elsewhere, there is a parenthetic qualification in his postscript on Baltz that bears reflecting on. He writes: 'To his credit, Baltz's ambiguity [between documentary photography and abstraction] echoes an ambiguity and loss of referentiality already present in the built environment'.[408] In other words, there would be an element of realism, though perhaps not of a critical kind, in depicting landscapes that capital has rendered fungible, homogeneous, faceless. What we would have is a kind of short-circuit between abstraction as an artistic theme and abstraction as a real, concrete product of the spatialisation of capital. Though Baltz's *The New Industrial Parks near Irvine* appears unprefaced, its captions simply vouching for the precise locations they record, his occasional comments and writings suggest that the abstract reality of these spaces, and the social mutations they reveal, were very much at the heart of the project.

It's interesting to contrast the seemingly anti-political character of the seventies turn to landscape – a reductive reserving of judgment for the sake 'describing the surfaces of the phenomenal world in a manner unique to [photography]'[409] – with what, at least for Baltz, were its motivations. As he stated in an interview: 'Coming from Orange County, I watched the ghastly transformation of this place – the first wave of bulimic capitalism sweeping across the land, next door to me, I sensed that there was something horribly amiss and awry about my own personal environment'.[410] But, in what we could call a mimesis, or indeed an ascesis, of abstraction, the aim was, on the basis of the 'vernacular model'[411] of real-estate photography to deny the singularity of image or subject-matter (even if this didn't stop certain interpretations from reintroducing a rather ideological sense of 'American beauty').

In this respect, non-judgment was a prelude to a kind of typology. In his 1974 'Notes on Recent Industrial Developments in Southern California', Baltz shows some of the research involved in the visual inventorying of these new spaces:

> *Typical functions:* Such developments typically house industries that have become significant in the years since the Korean War. These include: aerospace, data processing and information storage; leisure time industries, such as the fabrication of recreation vehicles and equipment. Often these developments house storage and distribution centres for firms whose manufacturing occurs in other parts of the country or abroad.[412]

The typological abstraction of these denatured landscapes is also the product of a process of real abstraction, which allows us to see the mimesis of modernism and minimalism that so fascinates our pictorial sensibility as the product of a dynamic of profit and planning that is in many ways incommensurable with its artistic capture:

> One of the most common views capitalist society takes of nature is among the most rigorous and most appalling. 'Landscape as Real Estate'. This was the view of nature presented to me in Park City and the viewpoint I showed in my photographs. To know that an apparently unbroken expanse of land is overlaid with invisible lines demarcating the pattern of future development is to perceive it in a very different way than one would otherwise. That these divisions only coincidentally pertain to topography and are the arbitrary result of financial speculation, illustrates the casually rapacious disdain that out culture has of the natural world as such. This attitude holds all non-productive land as

marginal; 'nature' is what's left over after every other demand has been satisfied.[413]

It is worthy of note then, that in the Irvine photographs criticised by Sekula, the spatial logics of capital that Baltz gestures towards are not just elided but there is an explicit aesthetic decision to depict homogeneity, modularity and opacity as just that, and without further elucidation.[414] How to approach this anti-cognitive aesthetic is one of the conundrums thrown up by the work of Baltz and those associated with the *New Topographics* exhibition, as well as by some of the work inspired by *fûkeiron*. As Baltz has famously noted, looking at these new industrial landscapes, at these seemingly limitless tracts of boxes, 'You don't know whether they're manufacturing pantyhose or megadeath'. Sekula's response, that what we need is not a topography of abstraction but a 'political geography, a way of talking with words and images about both the system and our lives within the system' remains valid.

Rebellion against dead labour

Yet work like *The New Industrial Parks near Irvine* (and its many, sometimes desultory epigones) also suggests that we take serious stock of the peculiarity and political intractability of such spaces of abstraction. Though the trajectories leading them could perhaps not be more different, the thematisations of landscape in *fûkeiron* and 'new topographics' both emerge from the felt saturation of a certain mode of artistic militancy. Their evacuation of the subject can of course signal many things. In the American photographers one could detect, depending on the angle, cynicism, aestheticism, restraint or even a kind of ecological consciousness. Japanese landscape theory is instead marked by a maximum of antagonism. 'Landscape' is the closure of the space of politics and experience by capital, nation and state. Hence the relentless face-off between its imperviousness and the violence or sexuality of individuals who, in the end, leave no trace. The allegory that is Oshima's *The Man Who Left His Will on Film*, where a vanished activist filmmaker leaves a handful of actuality shots as his legacy, and characters seek to revitalise these bland spaces with violent action, in a 'war of landscapes', speaks to this aesthetic and political impasse. So does Nakahira's apocalyptic humanism:

> A day will come when a single crack will nick this 'landscape' which is uniformly covered over with expressionless smoothness, and a fissure will gradually deepen until this 'landscape' is completely turned inside out like a glove being taken off. There will undoubtedly be a revolt. When that time comes, the 'landscape' will already not be a 'landscape', but will instead become a crucible of confusion, trampled over by the bare feet of vivid human kind. The fire will engulf the entire surface of the city. There, people will run amok. Fire and darkness. Barefoot people running around recklessly. In ancient times, people must have scrambled about in the midst of fire and darkness barefoot. It's an old fashioned image but when I envision urban rebellion, this is the scene I always imagine.[415]

What remains unimaginable, in this seventies moment of landscape, be it in militant anxiety or disenchanted coolness, is instead what could *become* of this landscape whose unassailability – to use Nakahira's term – seems to belie its character as 'manufactured' or 'man-altered'. From De Chirico's arcades for human marionettes to the crushing volumes of *Metropolis*, from Antonioni and Welles to Gursky and Burtynsky, the dwarfing (or expunging) of the human by the built has been frequently seen as an index of alienation. A reflection on the contemporary depiction of landscape should allow us, however, to repel the temptation to treat such alienation by way of some cod-existentialist reflex.

The aesthetic, cognitive and political problems thrown up by *fûkeiron* and 'new topographics' are related to the difficulty we have in confronting the logistical spaces of the social factory, precisely those spaces which most evidence Brecht's demand that we re-invent realism in light of reality slipping into the functional. Though industrial parks are certainly not devoid of their own pseudo-bucolic managerial aesthetic,[416] one of the most significant aesthetic, disciplinary and political-economic aspects of such spaces is that – unlike the monumental spaces of metropolitan capitalism – they're not there to be seen. Their opacity is no accident. Nor is the relative fungibility between underwear and overkill. What's more, the short-circuit between artistic and social abstraction, rife as it may be with its own mystifications, among them the fetishisation of landscape, also points us towards the concrete processes that do shed labour (or shunt it into windowless sheds); that witness the abiding mutation, in certain regions, of the organic composition of capital, of the proportions between living labour and accumulated dead labour. In a nutshell, the problem of landscape theory, of new topographics, is the problem of dead labour, a problem that Marx encountered in the factory, but which we strangely strain to recognise as it is written, visibly and invisibly, into space:

Here too past labour — in the automaton and the machinery moved by it — steps forth as acting apparently in independence of [living] labour, it subordinates labour instead of being subordinate to it, it is the iron man confronting the man of flesh and blood. The subsumption of his labour under capital — the absorption of his labour by capital — which lies in the nature of capitalist production, appears here as a technological fact. The *keystone of the arch* is complete. Dead labour has been endowed with movement, and living labour only continues to be present as one of dead labour's conscious organs. The *living connection* of the whole workshop no longer lies here in cooperation; instead, the system of machinery forms a unity, set in motion by the *prime motor* and comprising the whole workshop, to which the living workshop is subordinated, in so far as it consists of workers. Their *unity* has thus taken on a form which is tangibly autonomous and independent of them.[417]

In a logistical, exurban landscape, this dead labour appears in all its banal 'bad infinity'. One opaque box after another. Yet the gnawing anxiety that meets this affect-less space, which in *fûkeiron* is claustrophobia, suffocation, is also the index of a problem of scale and magnitude (and we can note here the recent drift of 'topographic' photography to the vast results of man and capital's geological agency). The unsettling desublimation of shed architecture is also part of a kind of capitalist sublimity, though a sublimity with no foothold for an introspective, centred subject (it is not a shipwreck with a spectator, to quote Hans Blumenberg, but the shipwreck *of* the spectator). With the intensification of exploitation under the impetus of extracting relative surplus value, we witness 'a dialectic of scale embodied in the machinery itself':

It is not past labor and its structural relationship to the present which 'extinguishes' it that is different, but rather the immense quantity of that past labor now deployed. ... At the same time the dead labor embodied in machinery suddenly swells to inhuman proportions (and is properly compared to a monster or a Cyclopean machine). It is as though the reservoir, or as Heidegger would call it, the 'standing reserve' (*Gestell*) of past or dead labor was immensely increased and offered ever huger storage facilities for these quantities of dead hours, which the merely life-sized human machine-minder is nonetheless to bring back to life, on the pattern of the older production. The quantities of the past have been rendered invisible by the production process ... and yet they now surround the worker in a proportion hitherto unthinkable.[418]

Ever huger storage facilities, indeed.

The seventies aesthetic of landscape can be provisionally and partially interpreted then as the thematization of the spatial, material and experiential impact of capital's rising organic composition. The crucial paradox here is that this quantitative raising of the dead over the living is properly invisible. In an insight into the 'postmodern condition' arguably deeper than that which calls on its disorienting complexity, or its multinational spread, Jameson is pointing towards the logic whereby the domination of past, dead labour (and of the relations it is instantiated in) can appear as the disappearance of the past (of the past as experience, as visibility). It is an antiseptic, air-conditioned nightmare that weighs on the brains of living. Similarly, a landscape periodically destroyed by speculation, riven by unevenness and generative of inequality, may appear suffocatingly smooth. The theories and practices of landscape we've discussed testify to the petrifying effects that such a domination by dead labour can have over landscape-altered women and men. In so doing, to paraphrase Nakahira, they make the syndrome more explicit but, at the same time, risk mutating it into a fetish, a petrifying Medusa of real abstraction.

Conclusion

The landscapes on which we closed the last chapter suggest that the visual and narrative cartography of contemporary capitalism may serve to delineate a limit – to both our actions and our imaginations – rather than to identify the levers of social transformation. That impression would not be incorrect, and there may indeed be something salutary in the harsh realisation, after trying to establish one's place in a far-flung and mystifying totality, that one, that 'we', may constitute the limit itself. If capital is indeed a relation, then it is not a relation that we can angelically call ourselves out of, and its contradictions run right through us. To some degree, we *are* those contradictions. In the lapidary words of the Italian communist poet Franco Fortini: 'In the list of your enemies, write your own name first'.

Efforts to forge figures and images that register or mediate the new spaces and times of capital are also caught in this predicament. As Keiller has wryly observed, an oppositional survey of the topography of exploitation is always also, to an extent, an observation of defeats both collective and personal, and sometimes even a kind of enjoyment extracted from them. Reminiscing about the experience of seeing the landscape of England's postwar compact overtaken by that of a bullish neoliberalism, he writes: 'As we felt ourselves losing ground, both politically and economically, our sense of loss was partly mollified by observing these visible changes in the detail of the landscape, as spectators at some sporting event might watch the opposition winning'.[419] Being a spectator at one's own shipwreck, with all the dissonance that entails, is a common experience among those privileged enough to maintain some foothold amid the waves of dispossession that have made this particular contest an increasingly unedifying one.

It's perhaps no surprise in this respect that the everyday

barbarism that characterises our recessionary times has found a home in works that dwell pitilessly on the corruption of bodies and wills at the mercy of capital's indifference and instrumentalism. A bleak naturalism of crisis transpires from a novel like Rafael Chirbes's 2013 *En la orilla* (On the Shore), which plunges into the wreck of devalued life in a Spain casually devastated by real estate speculation, and quietly corroded by the afterlives of civil war and dictatorship. The protagonist engages in passing attempts to put his failed life in communication with the social forces beyond – no more so than in a bravura section where he avows his curiosity at the infinite chains of labour that spur him to imagine, beyond the abstract surface of cellophane, where these goods originate from, what kinds of desires their producers entertain, as though these could be registered in the commodities themselves. These forensic fantasies devolve either into ephemeral nostalgias for craft (he is the son of a broken and senescent Republican carpenter, and carries on the trade with no conviction), or into a livid pessimism, the recurrent recognition that man is but a finite sack of refuse. Yet though death and putrefaction frame the narrative, the panorama of the crisis in the Spanish provinces (on the outskirts of Valencia) makes for a compelling if dismaying journey through the wastage and human obstinacy that persists after the pipe-dreams of the boom have been terminated, as well as a potent record of the half-finished spaces left behind. One wonders whether the decomposing dead bodies with which Chirbes entices us into a neo-noir atmosphere – only to unfold a national allegory of epochal dejection – are a necessary goad, making possible those lateral illuminations of the landscape of crisis which turn out to be the book's most compelling aspects.

We've already touched on this dialectic of death and realism in recent container narratives, and could push it further to encompass the sheer violence that characterises some of the more illuminating representations of the social terrain of contemporary capitalism. In Jia Zhangke's *A Touch of Sin* (2013), in the galling absence of any civic redress against the crass corruption of local bosses, amid the turbo-capitalist kitsch, dilapidated dwellings and dead zones of development, the *wuxia* genre of the martial art revenge films is retooled to give a kind of affective rhythm to an otherwise numbing, if revealing, survey of the new spaces of Chinese accumulation and the lives straining to adapt. *A Touch of Sin* ties together dramatisations based on those symptomatic bursts of everyday violence that punctuate the ravenous advance of money as the community that admits no other, of which Marx wrote in *Grundrisse*: a migrant worker much like *AKA Serial Killer*'s Nagayama Norio takes a cold artisanal pleasure in killing strangers; a humiliated sauna attendant retaliates against the misogyny of small-time businessmen; a young man, modelled on the Foxconn suicides, is tracked across the labour market to his eventual demise; a miner goes from petition to payback against corrupt village authorities. As in *En la Orilla*, there is nothing sublime here about the overpower of capital, just a grinding away of dignity and a saturation of everyday life, against which the sterility of individual violence against self and other seems the sole retort.

The way in which these bleak, stylistically accomplished, narratives wear away at any prospect of *collective* anger – the atmosphere of inexorability in which they're bathed – might be 'true' to our present's structure of feeling, but that precisely is one of their potential pitfalls: that we *recognise* our horizon as closed. Even, or especially, when it expresses itself as both political and aesthetic realism, the recognition-effect that accompanies some efforts at representing capital should make us vigilant, like any amplification of what, more or less consciously, we always already knew. In this respect, and remaining with narrative figurations of crisis, it is telling that one of the most incisive explorations of the centrality of real estate, of the psychic life of property, to our current economy – Pang Ho-cheung's 2010

Dream Home – succeeds in opening up the tribulations of the Hong Kong lower-middle classes by means of a brilliant disjunctive synthesis a social realist narrative and an arrestingly gory slasher film. The dialectic of structural and 'real' violence manages to upend the 'humanistic' motivations of revenge: the protagonist, Cheng Lai-sheung, slaughters the inhabitants of a condominium not out of any animus, but merely to depress the asking price for the apartment she has been working two jobs to attain, and which she can no longer afford following a combination of bureaucratic mishaps regarding her father's medical bills and insurance and the fluctuations of the housing-market, which take the property beyond her reach. Conversely, the reduction of all desire to home-ownership, already oppressive enough in its social-realist rendering, is revealed as a kind of property horror where the home is no longer the haunted container of malignant properties, which are borne instead by the social structure of ownership. The way that the film's fantastical violence is fully absorbed by the concluding return to normality (but for a television reporting about the possible effects of the US mortgage crisis on Hong Kong), is a more enlightening, if by no means more hopeful, index of the anxieties of the present than Chirbes or Zhangke's panoramas of debased everyday life.

Anxiety is perhaps the dominant mood of today's efforts at cognitive mapping. We could consider this in a psychoanalytical vein, where it signals the mortification of the symbolic order by the real,[420] the paralysing abrogation of sense, but here it is perhaps more apt to return one of its inaugural modern formulations from a great thinker of the visual and of the problems of representation, Thomas Hobbes. In *Leviathan*, Hobbes links anxiety to curiosity, in the seeking of causes and the coming up against invisible power:

Anxiety for the future time disposeth men to inquire into the causes of things: because the knowledge of them maketh men the better able to order the present to their best advantage. Curiosity, or love of the knowledge of causes, draws a man from consideration of the effect to seek the cause; and again, the cause of that cause; till of necessity he must come to this thought at last, that there is some cause whereof there is no former cause.[421]

That this quote is about religious belief, and the uncaused invisible power is God – as projected by men who, in Hobbes's wonder formulation, 'stand in awe of their own imaginations, and in time of distress invoke them' – should make us reflect on capital's theological attributes. Where can our curiosity take us, when it comes to capital? How not to transmute into paralysing awe?

In our discussion of the virtues and vices of socialist transparency we touched on some efforts to think the aesthetic and social forms through which powerlessness could be undone, the inescapable invisibilities and complexities of social life brought under some kind of collective control. Anticipatory reflection on these questions, and on how the existing apparatuses of capitalist representation could be repurposed or terminated to emancipatory ends, remains vital. But our predicament remains, for the time being, that of the view from the 'trough',[422] and not the revolutionary prospect. In that respect, it is worth revisiting the articulation of knowledge (of capital's abstractions) and (collective) action with which we began. Though the significance of orientation can't be gainsaid, and the predicament explored by Jameson and Mills remains our own, it would be mistaken to think that a politics with a totalising impetus presupposes some kind of visualisation or cartography in the strict sense. Yes, we need to name the system, but a global challenge is of necessity partisan, and with it also, at least initially partial. Overview, especially when it comes to capital, is a fantasy – if a very effective, and often destructive, one. Because we can't extricate ourselves from our positions in a totality that is such through its unevenness and antagonism, there is in the end something reactionary about the notion of a metalanguage that could capture, that could represent, capitalism as such.[423]

This is also why it is necessary to insist on the question of form. Having surveyed many of the 'maps' thrown up by anxious desire to represent our mode of production, it is difficult not to conclude that, bar some inspiring exceptions, capital has been a theme or content, not an occasion truly to rethink and refunction our available genres, styles, figures and forms, to recast our methods of inquiry in the arts as in the sciences of society. This need is not unconnected to the political search after modes of organisation, communication and solidarity, political *forms* adequate to our moment. It is in this sense that we can understand a communist poetic proposal from half a century ago, which still beckons for present response: 'Try to create in the literary or poetic work a stylistic structure whose internal tensions are a metaphor for the internal tensions and structural tendencies of a social "body" moving by a revolutionary path towards its own "form".'[424]

Eisenstein's libretto remains unfilmed.

Notes

1. See Laura Kurgan, *Close Up at a Distance: Mapping, Technology & Politics* (New York: Zone Books, 2013), pp. 19-20.

2. Stuart Ian Burns, 'Scene Unseen: All the President's Men', *Feeling Listless*, 6/25/2012. Available at: http://feeling listless.blogspot.com/2012/06/scene-unseen-all-presidents-men.html

3. Fredric Jameson, *The Geopolitical Aesthetic: Cinema and Space in the World System* (London/Bloomington: BFI/Indiana University Press, 1995), p. 79. We can note in passing how the zoom-out can have an inverse cognitive valence, as when the trading floor of the Paris Bourse appears as a teeming vortex of insect-like energy in Marcel L'Herbier's film of Zola's *L'Argent* (1928). On the theme of providence see also Jameson's 'The Experiments of Time: Providence and Realism', in *The Antinomies of Realism* (London: Verso, 2013).

4. *The Geopolitical Aesthetic*, p. 82.

5. There will come a time in the future when these great repositories of human knowledge, together with the traces of humanity's existence, will have been vanquished from the face of the earth, yet some of our satellites and other spacecraft will continue to circle the planet. Responding to this ineluctable horizon of extinction, in the Fall of 2012, a communication satellite was launched into the Earth's orbit from southern Kazakhstan, carrying a project by artist and geographer Trevor Paglen. Paglen and his collaborators micro-etched a collection of a hundred black-and-white images onto a tiny silicon wafer affixed to the side of the satellite. This portfolio of the species was poised to last until the sun turns into a red giant in approximately five billion

243

years – in the meanwhile, it will orbit in geosynchronous orbit in the Clarke belt. Drawing obvious parallels to the Pioneer Plague and the Voyager Golden Record launched into deep space in 1972 and 1977 aboard unmanned probes, Paglen's *The Last Pictures* (New York/Berkeley: Creative Time Books/University of California Press, 2012) is a cogently idiosyncratic attempt at summarizing human history, experience and knowledge, the singularity of whose aesthetic may be said to undermine the hubris of a totalising view, and the fantasy of perfect communication, while being true to the desire that drives these aspirations.

6. *The Geopolitical Aesthetic*, p. 82.

7. Hito Steyerl, 'In Free Fall: A Thought Experiment on Vertical Perspective', in *The Wretched of the Screen* (Berlin: Sternberg Press, 2012), p. 26. See also Eyal Weizman's seminal reflections on the politics of verticality, and some of the responses they elicited at *Open Democracy*. Available at: http://www.opendemocracy.net/conflict-politicsverticality/debate.jsp. For a compelling historical treatment of the role of views from above in the development of postwar (French) social science, in particular in the formation of the idea of *social space*, which also draws on the significance of colonial anthropology, see Jeanne Haffner, *The View from Above: The Science of Social Space* (Cambridge: The MIT Press, 2013).

8. Henri Lefebvre, *The Explosion: Marxism and the French Upheaval*, trans. A. Ehrenfeld (New York: The Monthly Review Press, 1969).

9. Anselm Franke, 'Earthrise and the Disappearance of the Outside', in *The Whole Earth: California and the Disappearance of the Outside*, ed. Diedrich Diedrichsen and Anselm Franke (Berlin: Sternberg Press, 2013), p. 14. This essay collection/exhibition catalogue provides fascinating documentation, analysis and critique of the *planetary paradigm*'s Californian origins, and the enduring effects of 'cybernetic neo-

animism'. As Iain Boal acerbically reminds us: 'Universalists of various stripes – neo-Kantians, humanitarian liberals, UN one-worlders – remain wedded to the imagery of the earthscape, which shows no borders, and for that matter no traces of humanity. Transnational corporations like it too. British Petroleum, for instance, recently spent millions on greenwashing and renaming itself simply "BP", initials now standing for "Beyond Petroleum", together with a floral yellow-and-green "solar earth" logo which matches their new interest in GMOs. BP's search for biomass-derived alcohol to replace fossil fuel for cars is already driving worldwide deforestation and the enclosure of millions of hectares of commonland in the global South in anticipation of biofuel monoculture'. See his 'Globe Talk: The Cartographic Logic of Late Capitalism', *History Workshop Journal*, 64 (2007), p. 345.

10. Kurgan, *Close Up at a Distance*, pp. 11, 15, 26.

11. 'The conception of cognitive mapping proposed here therefore involves an extrapolation of Lynch's spatial analysis to the realm of social structure, that is to say, in our historical moment, to the totality of class relations on a global (or should I say multinational) scale. ... The incapacity to map socially is as crippling to political experience as the analogous incapacity to map spatially is for urban experience. It follows that an aesthetic of cognitive mapping in this sense is an integral part of any socialist political project.' Fredric Jameson, 'Cognitive Mapping', in *Marxism and the Interpretation of Culture*, ed. C. Nelson and L. Grossberg (Champaign: University of Illinois Press, 1988), p. 353.

12. Jameson makes this distinction with reference to the problem of representing war: 'Abstraction versus sense-datum: these are the two poles of a dialectic of war, incomprehensible in their mutual isolation and which dictate

dilemmas of representation only navigable by formal innovation ... and not by any stable narrative convention.' 'War and Representation', in *The Antinomies of Realism*, p. 256. Representations of war and capital are intimately intertwined, so much so that the former can serve as the occasion for some of the more accomplished figurations of the latter, as in Döblin's *Wallenstein* (p. 245).

13. Fredric Jameson, *Postmodernism, or, The Cultural Logic of Late Capitalism* (Durham: Duke University Press, 1991), p. 51.

14. Ibid., p. 50.

15. Fredric Jameson, 'Modernism and Imperialism', in *The Modernist Papers* (London: Verso, 2007), p. 157.

16. Ibid., p. 152.

17. Ibid., p. 160.

18. Ibid., p. 156.

19. *Postmodernism*, p. 412.

20. Ibid., p. 51.

21. Ibid., p. 416.

22. We discuss Lukács's contribution to thinking through the representability of capital in Part I, in terms of his understanding of crisis as revealing the grounding coordinates of our social life.

23. C. Wright Mills, *The Sociological Imagination* (Oxford: Oxford University Press, 1959), p. 11.

24. Ibid., p. 116.

25. Ibid., p.176.

26. Ibid., p. 131.

27. Ibid., p. 150.

28. Quoted in Daniel Geary, *Radical Ambition: C. Wright Mills, the Left, and American Social Thought* (Berkeley: University of California Press, 2009), p. 37.

29. Fredric Jameson, 'Third-World Literature in the Era of Multinational Capitalism', *Social Text*, 15 (1986), p. 69.

30. We owe to Benjamin Noys the observation that this gloss on

Jameson's essay renders only a partial truth regarding Woolf's fiction. In an incisive unpublished note, 'Phantom India: Writing the "Other" in Virginia Woolf', Noys, takes his cue from Neville's observation, in *The Waves* – 'We are walled in here. But India lies outside' – quite a confirmation, in its own right of Jameson's suggestion about the spatial and subjective disjunction that characterises imperial modernism. Noys astutely shows how the phantom presence of Empire insists in Woolf's writing, and is refracted, in a potentially destabilising way, across the axis of gender, as 'the "Outside" – as a space of masculine achievement and success – against the "walled in" interiors of the characters in London – especially for women'.

31. For the debate around Jameson's text, see Aijaz Ahmad, *In Theory: Classes, Nations, Literatures* (London: Verso, 1992); Neil Lazarus, *The Postcolonial Unconscious* (Cambridge: Cambridge University Press, 2011); Madhava Prasad, 'On the Question of a Theory of (Third World) Literature', *Social Text*, 31-32 (1992), pp. 57-83; Neil Larsen, 'Fredric Jameson on "Third-World Literature": A Qualified Defence', in *Fredric Jameson: A Critical Reader*, ed. D. Kellner and S. Homer (London: Palgrave, 2004), pp. 42-61; more recently, Jernej Habjan, 'From Cultural Third-Worldism to the Literary World-System', *CLCWeb: Comparative Literature and Culture*, 15.5 (2013), available at: http://docs.lib.purdue.edu/clcweb/vol15/iss5/13/.

32. 'Third-World Literature in the Era of Multinational Capitalism', p. 69.

33. Ibid., p. 85.

34. Jean-Paul Sartre, 'A Plea for Intellectuals', in *Between Existentialism and Marxism* (New York: Basic Books, 1974), p. 244.

35. David R. Roediger, 'Plotting Against Eurocentrism: The 1929 Surrealist Map of the World', in *Colored White:*

Transcending the Racial Past (Berkeley: University of California, 2002), p. 175. The essay was originally published in *Race Traitor* 9 (1998). See also the critical and historical contextualisation in Denis Wood, *Rethinking the Power of Maps* (New York: The Guildford Press, 2010), pp. 198-9. Wood suggest that the 1929 map (whose authorship he assigns to Paul Éluard) may be the first *counter-map*, not just 'appropriated and recontextualised, but *made against* another map'.

36. This map is discussed, along with the surrealist map of 1929 and numerous contemporary works, in a stimulating pamphlet on anticolonial (anti-)cartography: Estrella de Diego, *Contra el mapa. Disturbios en la geografía colonial del Occidente* (Madrid: Siruela, 2008). Wolman and Debord published their 'A User's Guide to Détournement' in the same issue of *Les lèvres nues*.

37. Roberto Schwarz, 'A Brazilian Breakthrough', *New Left Review* 36 (2005), p. 92. Reprinted in Roberto Schwarz, *Two Girls and Other Essays* (London: Verso, 2013). For a richly informative illustration of how shifting the field of inquiry to the semi-periphery and its uneven development can also elicit quite different periodisations of the link between narrative and value forms, see Ericka Beckman, *Capital Fictions: The Literature of Latin America's Export Age* (Minneapolis: University of Minnesota Press, 2013), which covers the period 1870-1930, and the 'imaginative apparatuses enlisted to explain' and advertise, or project into the future, the 'mysteries of value' pivoting around the export commodity.

38. Though it has informed our approach, especially in Part III, we have not systematically explored the aesthetic dimension of Neil Smith's crucial insight into the unevenness of capital's geography: 'Uneven development is social inequality blazoned into the geographical landscape and it

is simultaneously the exploitation of that geographical unevenness for certain socially determined ends'. *Uneven Development: Nature, Capital and the Production of Space*, 3rd ed. (Athens: University of Georgia Press, 2008), p. 206.

39. *Distant Reading*, p. 58.

40. Raymond Williams, *Modern Tragedy* (London: Verso, 1979), p. 193.

4 . Colin MacCabe, 'Preface', in *The Geopolitical Aesthetic*, p. xiv.

42. Neil Smith, 'Afterword to the Second Edition', in *Uneven Development*, pp. 223-4.

43. See http://www.iniva.org/exhibitions_projects/2010/who se_map_is_it. Several journals have also dedicated issues to mapping. See, among others, *Printed Project* 12, and *Afterall* 27. Consider too Alighiero Boetti's *Mappa* series of large embroidered maps of the world (1971-1994); the indispensable political atlases produced by *Le Monde Diplomatique* geographer and journalist Philippe Rekacewicz; the vast maps of graphic designer Paula Scher; Ashley Hunt's *A World Map* – to name but a tiny sample.

44. *Postmodernism*, p. 409. See also 'Modernism and Imperialism', where Jameson remarks that 'cartography is not the solution, but rather the problem, at least in its ideal epistemological form as social cognitive mapping on a global scale' (p. 158).

45. The same could be said for the following claim by Bruno Latour, which channels what has become a theoretical common sense about the present irrelevance of the notion of totality: 'People will go on believing that the big animal [i.e. Society] doesn't need any fodder to sustain itself; that society is something that can stand without being produced, assembled, collected, or kept up; that it resides behind us, so to speak, instead of being ahead of us as a task to be fulfilled'. Bruno Latour, *Reassembling the Social: An Introduction to Actor-Network Theory* (Oxford: Oxford

University Press, 2002), p. 184.

46. Guy Debord, *Considerations on the Assassination of Gérard Lebovici*, trans. Robert Greene (Berkeley: TamTam Books, 2001) pp. 21-2.

47. Debord, *The Society of the Spectacle*, trans. D. Nicholson-Smith (New York: Zone Books, 1995), p. 15.

48. For a (disputable) account of Debord's relation to vision see Martin Jay, *Downcast Eyes: The Denigration of Vision in Twentieth-Century French Thought* (Berkeley: University of California Press, 1993). pp. 416-35.

49. *The Society of the Spectacle*, p. 17.

50. Ibid., p. 12.

51. Ibid., p. 19.

52. For an account of Debord's conception of the spectator, see Kinkle, 'The Emaciated Spectator', in *That's What A Chameleon Looks Like: Contesting Immersive Cultures*, ed. K. Menrath and A. Schwinghammer (Cologne: Harem Verlag, 2009).

53. *The Society of the Spectacle*, p. 37.

54. Ibid., pp. 12-13.

55. Guy Debord, *Comments on the Society of the Spectacle* (London: Verso, 1990), p. 2.

56. We are grateful to Jason Smith for turning our attention to these images of the planetary in the film of *The Society of the Spectacle*. A proper consideration of this *leitmotiv* would require approaching the film in terms of Debord's borrowings from and controversies with contemporary thinkers of *mondialité*, namely Henri Lefebvre and Kostas Axelos.

57. Letter to Mirabeau, originally quoted in David McNally, *Political Economy and the Rise of Capitalism: A Reinterpretation* (University of California Press, 1988), p. 110; now in Susan Buck-Morss, 'Envisioning Capital: Political Economy on Display', *Critical Inquiry*, 21.2 (1995), p. 440. See also Marx's

revision of the *tableau* in his letter to Engels of 6 July 1863. Available, with diagram, at: http://www.marxists. org/archive/marx/works/1863/letters/63_07_06.htm

58. See Michel Foucault, *Security, Territory, Population: Lectures at the Collège de France, 1977-1978*, ed. M. Senellart, trans. G. Burchell (Palgrave, 2007), pp. 17-18.

59. Timothy Mitchell, 'Fixing the Economy', *Cultural Studies*, 12.1 (1998), p. 86. A descendant of Fisher's hydraulic apparatus, Bill Phillips's MONIAC, provides the subject-matter for an ingenious artwork by Michael Stevenson, *Fountain of Prosperity* (2005), which tries to trace the fortunes of the model bought by the Bank of Guatemala shortly before the US-backed coup of 1954. See Michael Stevenson, 'The Search for the Fountain of Prosperity', *Printed Project*, 12, *Circulation*, ed. K. Sander (2009), pp. 19-26.

60. 'Envisioning Capital', p. 447.

61. Karl Marx, *Capital: A Critique of Political Economy, vol. 1*, ed. F. Engels, trans. S. Moore and E. Aveling (Mineola, NY: Dover, 2011), p. 195.

62. 'Envisioning Capital', p. 452.

63. Ibid., p. 463.

64. Ibid., p. 455.

65. Ibid., p. 456.

66. Ibid., p. 460fn66.

67. To borrow the title of Hans Blumenberg's erudite essay on the precursors of Kant's aesthetic of the sublime.

68. Marx, *Capital, Vol. 1*, trans. S. Moore and E. Aveling, p. 60.

69. See also Mark Neocleous, *Imagining the State* (Milton Keynes: Open University, 2002), on the personification of capital and legal personality, pp. 78-87, and Eyal Weizman, *The Least of All Possible Evils* (London: Verso, 2011), pp. 103-11, on the role of prosopopeia and material witnesses in humanitarianism's forensic turn.

70. Karl Marx, *Capital, Vol. 1*, trans. B. Fowkes (London:

Penguin, 1976), p. 92.

71. Slavoj Žižek, *In Defense of Lost Causes* (London: Verso, 2008), p. 454.

72. Both soliloquies can also be found on YouTube. Here are their texts, a much impoverished substitute. Ned Beatty as Arthur Jensen (script by Paddy Chayefsky): 'You have meddled with the primal forces of nature, Mr. Beale, and I won't have it! Is that clear? You think you've merely stopped a business deal. That is not the case! The Arabs have taken billions of dollars out of this country, and now they must put it back! It is ebb and flow, tidal gravity! It is ecological balance! You are an old man who thinks in terms of nations and peoples. There are no nations. There are no peoples. There are no Russians. There are no Arabs. There are no third worlds. There is no West. There is only one holistic system of systems, one vast and immane, interwoven, inter-acting, multivariate, multinational dominion of dollars. Petro-dollars, electro-dollars, multi-dollars, reichmarks, rins, roubles, pounds, and shekels. It is the international system of currency which determines the totality of life on this planet. That is the natural order of things today. That is the atomic and subatomic and galactic structure of things today! And YOU have meddled with the primal forces of nature, and YOU... WILL... ATONE! Am I getting through to you, Mr. Beale? You get up on your little twenty-one inch screen and howl about America and democracy. There is no America. There is no democracy. There is only IBM, and ITT, and AT&T, and DuPont, Dow, Union Carbide, and Exxon. Those are the nations of the world today. What do you think the Russians talk about in their councils of state, Karl Marx? They get out their linear programming charts, statistical decision theories, minimax solutions, and compute the price-cost probabilities of their transactions and invest-ments, just like we do. We no longer live in a world of

nations and ideologies, Mr. Beale. The world is a college of corporations, inexorably determined by the immutable bylaws of business. The world is a business, Mr. Beale. It has been since man crawled out of the slime. And our children will live, Mr. Beale, to see that... perfect world... in which there's no war or famine, oppression or brutality. One vast and ecumenical holding company, for whom all men will work to serve a common profit, in which all men will hold a share of stock. All necessities provided, all anxieties tranquilized, all boredom amused. And I have chosen you, Mr. Beale, to preach this evangel.' Hume Cronyn as Maxwell Emery (script by David Shaber): 'When the Arabs learn of word of what they've been doing is out they may panic... move a big chunk of funds too fast or the wrong way...really destabilize the monetary markets. Then the dollar will collapse. Whereupon there will be a lot of jaw boning by the President, and that won't work. Then they'll go to selling gold, and that won't work either. Then they'll have to go to capital controls, freeze foreign assets, stop any money from going in or out, and that will be the end of all the markets. That'll really be the finish. Then you'll see a worldwide depression that'll make the 1930's look like a kindergarten. In two months you'll have bread lines in Detroit, riots in Pittsburgh. In six months you'll see grass right over Rodeo Drive, and Michigan Avenue and 5th Avenue. And I won't have done it, Hub, you will. All because you tried to stop a movement that couldn't be stopped anyway. Listen to me, Hub. Money, capital, has a life of its own. It's a force of nature. Like gravity. Like the oceans. It flows where it wants to flow. This whole thing with the Arabs and gold is inevitable. We're just going with the tide. The only question is whether you want to let it go like an unguided missile and raise hell, or whether you want to keep it in the hands of responsible people. Keep it channelled, keep it quiet. Believe me, Hub, the dollar will hold, the system will be fine... provided nobody panics.'

73. Marx, *Capital, Vol. 1*, p. 254.

74. Slavoj Žižek, *How to Read Lacan* (London: Granta, 2006), p. 116.

75. Mladen Dolar, *A Voice and Nothing More* (Cambridge, MA: The MIT Press, 2006), pp. 73, 81, 113.

76. Karen Knorr-Cetina, 'From Pipes to Scopes: The Flow Architecture of Financial Markets', in *The Technological Economy*, ed. A. Barry and D. Slater (London: Routledge, 2005), pp. 127, 132.

77. See, for example, JK Gibson-Graham, *Postcapitalist Politics* (Minneapolis: University of Minnesota Press, 2006), pp. 23-52; also the remarkable proto-communising anti-workers' inquiry by *La parole au capital* (Paris: UGE, 1976), which collects and analyses the statements of precarious textile workers 'spoken by capital', in explicit polemic with the Maoist search for affirmative proletarian speech.

78. Film and materials available at: http://www.crisisinthecreditsystem.org.uk/.

79. *Institutes of Oratory*, Book 9, Chapter 2, trans. Rev. J.S. Watson, available at: http://rhetoric.eserver.org/quintilian/9/chapter2.html.

80. On the art and social history of the panorama, see Dolf Sternberger, *Panorama of the 19th Century* (Oxford: Basil Blackwell, 1977); Ralph Hyde, *Panoramania! The Art and Entertainment of the 'All-Embracing' View* (London: Trefoil, 1988); Angela Miller, 'The panorama, the cinema, and the emergence of the spectacular', *Wide Angle*, 18.2 (1996), pp. 34–69; Stephan Oetterman, *The Panorama: History of a Mass Medium* (Cambridge, MA: The MIT Press, 1997); Bernard Comment, *The Panorama* (London: Reaktion, 2002).

81. Jonathan Crary, 'Géricault, the Panorama, and Sites of Reality in the Early Nineteenth Century', *Grey Room*, 9

(2002), p. 19. See also Walter Benjamin, *The Arcades Project*, ed. R. Tiedemann (Cambridge, MA: The Belknap Press, 2002) and *Berlin Childhood around 1900* (Cambridge, MA: The Belknap Press, 2006).

82. 'Géricault, the Panorama, and Sites of Reality in the Early Nineteenth Century', p. 20.

83. Bruno Latour and Emilie Hermant, *Paris ville invisible* (Paris: La Découverte, 1998), pp. 7-9; *Paris: Invisible City* (2006), p. 2, available at: http://www.bruno- latour.fr/virtual/PARIS-INVISIBLE-GB.pdf.

84. Latour and Hermant, *Paris ville invisible / Paris: Invisible City*, p. 125/88.

85. *Paris ville invisible / Paris: Invisible City*, pp. 19-20/7-8.'Nature at a glance' was the name under which Robert Barker first patented in 1787 what later came to be known as the panorama. Oetterman, *The Panorama*, p. 6.

86. *Paris ville invisible / Paris: Invisible City*, p. 134/91.

87. Bruno Latour, *Reassembling the Social: An Introduction to Actor-Network Theory* (Oxford: Oxford University Press, 2002), pp. 21, 43.

88. Ibid., p. 166.

89. Ibid., p. 184. Tellingly, Latour treats the notion that there 'is a pecking order from top to bottom', as a political and epistemological 'prejudice' (p. 183).

90. *The Pasteurization of France* (Cambridge, MA: Harvard University Press, 1993), p. 173.

91. *Reassembling the Social*, p. 167.

92. The same could be said for the claim that 'People will go on believing that the big animal doesn't need any fodder to sustain itself; that society is something that can stand without being produced, assembled, collected, or kept up; that it resides behind us, so to speak, instead of being ahead of us as a task to be fulfilled' (p. 184). One supposes that Latour would argue that the myriad theories of repro-

duction put forward by Marxists, Bourdieusians, feminists, etc., are just not theories of reproduction.

93. *Reassembling the Social*, p. 179.

94. See the writings of the economic sociologist Donald Mackenzie, in particular his articles for the *London Review of Books*, available at: http://www.lrb.co.uk/contributors /donald-mackenzie.

95. *Reassembling the Social*, p. 188.

96. For a brilliant reading of Marx in this direction, see Nicole Pepperell, *Disassembling Capital*, PhD thesis, RMIT University, Melbourne, Australia. Available at: http:// www.roughtheory.org/wp-content/images/Disassembling-Capital-N-Pepperell.pdf. A version of this text will be published in the *Historical Materialism* book series with Brill.

97. *The Arcades Project*, p. 532.

98. Ibid., p. 536.

99. 'Géricault, the panorama, and sites of reality in the early nineteenth century', p. 21. Allan Sekula has made a similar observation: 'The panorama is paradoxical: topographically "complete" while still signalling an acknowledgment of and desire for a greater extension beyond the frame. The panoramic tableau, however bounded by the limits of a city profile or the enclosure of a harbor, is always potentially unstable: "If this much, why not more?" The psychology of the panorama is overtly sated and covertly greedy, and thus caught up in the fragile complacency of disavowal. The tension is especially apparent in maritime panoramas, for the sea always exceeds the limits of the frame' Allan Sekula, *Fish Story* (Rotterdam: Witte de With and Richter Verlag, 1996), p. 43.

100. 'Mapping Ghosts: Visible Collective talks to Trevor Paglen', in *An Atlas of Radical Cartography*, eds. L. and A. Bhagat (Los Angeles: Journal of Aesthetics and Protest Press, 2007), pp. 42-4. Of particular interest here is Paglen's stress on the

difference between geography and cartography, and the distancing of his work from the 'very lazy read' of it in terms of 'mapping'.

101. Cited in Robert Hobbs, *Mark Lombardi: Global Networks* (New York: Independent Curators International, 2003), p. 118.

102. Hobbs, *Mark Lombardi*, p. 32.

103. George Pendle, 'The Numbers Game', *Frieze*, 124 (June-August 2009), available at: http://www.frieze.com/issue/article/the_numbers_game. A similar remark could be made regarding Paolo Sorrentino's film *Il Divo* (2008), about the life and times of Giulio Andreotti.

104. The term 'overworld' is used here in specific reference to the work of Peter Dale Scott, who is credited with coming up with the term 'parapolitics' in 1972, in his book *The War Conspiracy* (see the endnote below). He defines the overworld as 'That realm of wealthy or privileged society that, although not formally authorized or institutionalized, is the scene of successful influence of government by private power. It includes both (1) those whose influence is through their wealth, administered personally or more typically through tax-free foundations and their sponsored projects, and (2) the first group's representatives.' Importantly, he stresses that 'The overworld is not a class but a category.' Peter Dale Scott, *The Road to 9/11: Wealth, Empire, and the Future of America* (Berkeley: University of California Press, 2007), pp. 268-9.

105. See Hobbs, *Mark Lombardi*, pp. 20-6. From its description by Hobbs, *On Higher Grounds* would appear to sit well in the burgeoning field of parapolitics. Parapolitics can be usefully defined as a field preoccupied with 'systemic clandestinity', or as 'the study of criminal sovereignty, of criminals behaving as sovereigns and sovereigns behaving as criminals in a systematic way'. See Robert Cribb,

'Introduction: Parapolitics, Shadow Governance and Criminal Sovereignty', in *Government of the Shadows: Parapolitics and Criminal Sovereignty*, ed. Eric Wilson and Tim Lindsey (London: Pluto Press, 2009), pp. 2, 8. If traditional political science looks at the 'overt politics of the public state, so parapolitics as a field studies the relationships between the public state and the political processes and arrangements outside and beyond conventional politics'. See Eric Wilson, 'Deconstructing the Shadows', in *Government of the Shadows*, p. 30. As an emergent and anomalous research field it has been tainted by its similarities to traditional conspiracy theory, but also by the widespread failure of researchers themselves to investigate the systemic coordinates of these phenomena, often resorting to presenting crisis events as the work of rogue elements or corrupted individuals.

106. *Fish Story*, p. 44. Sekula is also extremely attentive to the material and strategic conditions of possibility of this shift: 'Coal-fired boilers, torpedoes and long-range naval guns introduced a new abstractness to the maritime space of combat. Abstract measured distance – from coaling stations, from one gun to another – came to matter more than the immediate and local vagaries of the wind. ... The ultimate and likewise contradictory result of the "distancing" of determining factors [coaling stations, link to the land, targeting, etc.] was that the detail, rather than the panorama, became crucial. At the level of naval "intelligence" details became the analytic fragments that had to be entered into a vast statistico-taxonomic grid, a grid that compared and weighed the fleets of the world' (p. 107). Sekula's own totalisations are results of concrete processes of abstraction, full of actors and devices, not seamless overviews of a homogeneous Capitalism.

107. *Fish Story*, p. 106.

108. Ibid., p. 107.

109. Allan Sekula, 'Between the Net and the Deep Blue Sea (Rethinking the Traffic in Photographs)', *October* 102 (2002), p. 7.

110. 'The arrogant conceit of the cyber-economy, for that matter of the very idea of the postindustrial era, is that we disavow our dim but nagging awareness that nearly all energy – whether converted to electricity or derived from direct combustion – comes from oil or other hydrocarbons, or from fissionable uranium refined from yellow-cake ore: solids, liquids, and gases that are extracted from the earth and transported in bulk ... the contemporary persistence of slow, heavy transport flows'. 'Between the Net and the Deep Blue Sea', p. 33.

111. It is fruitful in this regard to contrast Sekula's work with that of Edward Burtynsky, which we touch on in Part III.

112. Trevor Paglen, *Blank Spots on the Map: The Dark Geography of the Pentagon's Secret World* (New York: Dutton, 2009), p. 246.

113. Gail Day and Steve Edwards, 'Global Dissensus: Art and Contemporary Capitalism', in *Art and Visual Culture, 1850-2010: Modernity to Globalisation*, ed. S. Edwards and P. Wood (London: Tate Publishing, 2012), p. 311.

114. *Blank Spots on the Map*, p. 4. The ironies of this terminology, especially in light of the critical role played by the US covert state in the repression of black politics in the US (for instance via the CONTELPRO programme), is all too obvious.

115. Peter Galison, 'Removing Knowledge', *Critical Inquiry*, 31 (Autumn 2004), pp. 229-43.

116. The visible, and partly unclassified, global footprint of the US military has recently been given a more concrete shape by Josh Begley, in a project inspired by Paglen, entitled 'Mapping United States Military Installations'. See: http://empire.is/. See also a recent piece on Begley's work in

The Daily Mail, available at: http://www.dailymail.co.uk /news/article-2524082/All-US-Armys-secret-bases-mapped-Google-maps.html.

117. See Trevor Paglen and A.C. Thompson, *Torture Taxi: On the Trail of the CIA's Rendition Flights* (Cambridge: Icon, 2007).

118. *Blank Spots on the Map,* p. 93.

119. Ibid., p. 190.

120. Hannah Arendt, 'Lying in Politics: Reflections on the Pentagon Papers', *New York Review of Books* 18, 8 (18 November 1971).

121. *Blank Spots on the Map,* p. 277.

122. Ibid., p. 280.

123. See 'Mapping Ghosts: Visible Collective talks to Trevor Paglen', in *An Atlas of Radical Cartography,* pp. 42-4.

124. 'Cognitive Mapping', p. 356.

125. Richard Hofstadter, *The Paranoid Style in American Politics and Other Essays* (New York: Knopf, 1966), p. 6.

126. *The Geopolitical Aesthetic,* pp. 2-3.

127. Michael Barkun, *A Culture of Conspiracy* (Berkeley: University of California Press, 2006), pp. 3-7.

128. Hobbs, *Mark Lombardi,* p. 95.

129. Alasdair Spark, 'Conjuring Order: The New World Order and Conspiracy Theories of Globalization', in *The Age of Anxiety: Conspiracy Theory and the Human Sciences,* ed. J. Parish and M. Parker (Oxford: Wiley-Blackwell, 2001), pp. 52, 53.

130. Skip Willman, 'Spinning Paranoia: The Ideologies of Conspiracy and Contingency in Postmodern Culture', in *Conspiracy Nation: The Politics of Paranoia in Postwar America,* ed. P. Knight (New York: NYU Press, 2002), p. 21.

131. Barkun, *A Culture of Conspiracy,* p. 3. In this sense, conspiracy theory is similar to populism as defined by Žižek (see, among others, 'Against the Populist Temptation', *Critical Inquiry,* 32 (2006), pp. 551-74). Rather than identi-

fying a central antagonism as the principal driver and stakes of politics, it projects a source of evil either invading the true community from without or growing within the community as a blight that must be eliminated.

132. Willman, 'Spinning Paranoia', p. 28.

133. Ibid., p. 33.

134. Sissela Bok, *Secrets: On the Ethics of Concealment and Revelation* (New York: Vintage, 1989), p. 199.

135. Owen isn't even allowed vengeance, as an Italian hit man beats him to it. The film's final lines imply Owen's bloodlust and sense of justice made him the pawn of another ruthless firm.

136. Jean-Patrick Manchette, 'Five Remarks on How I Earn My Living' (1976), available at: http://www.marxists.org /archive/manchette/1976/earn-living.htm.

137. 'Cognitive Mapping', pp. 352-3.

138. Georg Lukács, *History and Class Consciousness* (Cambridge, MA: The MIT Press, 1972), p. 70.

139. Marx, *Capital, Volume 1*, trans. B. Fowkes, p. 172.

140. *History and Class Consciousness*, pp. 72-3.

141. Ibid., p. 74.

142. Ibid., pp. 74-5.

143. Ernesto Laclau, 'Psychoanalysis and Marxism', trans. A.G. Reiter-Macintosh, *Critical Inquiry* 13:2 (1987), pp. 331-2.

144. Sergei Eisenstein, 'Notes for a Film of *Capital*', trans. M. Sliwowski, J. Leyda, A. Michelson, *October* 2 (1976), p. 9.

145. Ibid., p. 26.

146. Ibid., p. 12.

147. Ibid., p. 15.

148. Ibid., p. 17.

149. Ibid., p. 18.

150. Bertolt Brecht, 'On the Popularity of the Crime Novel', quoted in Ernest Mandel, *Delightful Murder: A Social History of the Crime Story* (London: Pluto Press, 1984), pp. 72-3.

151. 'The situation is complicated by the fact that less than ever does the mere reflection of reality reveal anything about reality. A photograph of the Krupp works or the AEG tells us nothing about these institutions. Actual reality has slipped into the functional. The reification of human relations – the factory, say – means that they are no longer explicit. So something must in fact be *built up*, something artificial, posed'. Bertolt Brecht, 'The Threepenny Opera Trial: A Sociological Experiment', quoted by Walter Benjamin in 'Little History of Photography', in *Selected Writings, Volume Two, Part Two, 1931-1934* (Cambridge, MA: Harvard University Press, 2005), p. 526.

152. Bertolt Brecht, 'Über Stoffe und Formen' (1929), in *Brecht on Theatre*, ed. J. Willett (London: Methuen, 1978), p. 30.

153. Elisabeth Hauptmann, quoted in Frederic Ewen's *Bertolt Brecht: His Life, His Art, His Times* (New York: Citadel, 1992), pp. 160-1.

154. See Richard Stites, *Revolutionary Dreams: Utopian Vision and Experimental Life in the Russian Revolution* (Oxford: Oxford University Press, 1988).

155. Perry Anderson, 'Sweden: Study in Social Democracy' (Part 2), *New Left Review*, 9 (1961), p. 44.

156. Robert Linhart, *Lénine, les paysans, Taylor*, new ed. (Paris: Seuil, 2010), p. 151.

157. Trotsky devoted to the seventh chapter of *The New Course* to refuting criticisms of this Order.

158. Ibid., p. 162.

159. Ibid., p. 169.

160. Dziga Vertov, *Kino-Eye: The Writings of Dziga Vertov*, ed. A. Michelson, trans. K. O'Brien (Berkeley: University of California Press, 1984), p. 52.

161. Ibid.

162. Ibid., p. 14.

163. Ibid., p. 19.

164. *Lénine, les paysans, Taylor*, p. 166.
165. Ibid., p. 174.
166. Manfredo Tafuri, 'Il socialismo realizzato e la crisi delle avanguardie', in Alberto Asor Rosa et al., *Socialismo, città, architettura URSS 1917-1937* (Rome: Officina Edizioni, 1971), p. 51.
167. Ibid., p. 58.
168. Bruno Latour and Peter Weibel (eds.), *Iconoclash: Beyond the Image Wars in Science, Religion and Art* (Cambridge, MA: The MIT Press, 2002).
169. See Alberto Toscano, *Fanaticism: On the Uses of an Idea* (London: Verso, 2010).
170. Edmund Burke, *A Letter to a Noble Lord*, ed. A.H. Smyth (Boston: The Athenaeum Press, 1903). The quote is from Dario Gamboni, *The Destruction of Art: Iconoclasm and Vandalism since the French Revolution* (London: Reaktion, 1997) p. 35.
171. Jean-Joseph Goux, *Les iconoclastes* (Paris: Seuil, 1978).
172. Consider also Jameson's provocative observation about money and utopia, according to which money is 'the source of all the bad Utopian solutions to the dilemma of capitalism. From Thomas More (abolish it altogether) to Proudhon, who envisages its control and sanitation as labor certificates, as the just price of labor-time. These illusions are as pernicious in their anti-capitalism as the accompanying propaganda of the political economists for the system itself; and both emerge from the way in which the fact of money occults and represses the law of value from which it emerges. The obsession with money as cause and disease alike condemns us to remain within the market system as such, the sphere of circulation, as the closed horizon of our knowledge and our scientific questions and explanations'. *Representing Capital* (London: Verso, 2011), pp. 45-6. For a more nuanced estimation of the abolition of money as a

moment of disruption in utopian narratives, see *Archaeologies of the Future: The Desire Called Utopia and Other Science Fictions* (London: Verso, 2005), pp. 229-31.

173. Leon de Mattis, 'What is Communisation?', *SIC: International Journal for Communisation*, 1 (2011), p. 27.

174. Alfred Sohn-Rethel, *Intellectual and Manual Labour* (London: Macmillan, 1978), p. 45.

175. Louis Althusser, 'Cremonini, Painter of the Abstract', in *Lenin and Philosophy and Other Essays*, trans. B. Brewster (New York: Monthly Review, 1971), p. 237.

176. Louis Althusser, 'From *Capital* to Marx's Philosophy', in Louis Althusser and Étienne Balibar, *Reading Capital*, trans. Ben Brewster (London: Verso, 2009), p. 20.

177. Bertolt Brecht, 'The manifesto', trans. D. Suvin, *Socialism and Democracy*, 16.1 (2002), p. 3.

178. See Alberto Toscano, 'Gaming the Plumbing: High-Frequency Trading and the Spaces of Capital', *Mute Magazine*, 16 January 2013, available at: http://www.metamute.org/editorial/articles/gaming-plumbing-high-frequency-trading-and-spaces-capital.

179. For an introduction to Bunge, his work, methods and politics, see Nik Heynen and Trevor Barnes's 'Foreword to the 2011 Edition: Fitzgerald Then and Now', in William Bunge, *Fitzgerald: Geography of a Revolution* (Athens: The University of Georgia Press, 2011 [1971]), pp. vii-xv. See also 'Wild Bill Bunge' (along with its links), available at: <http://indiemaps.com/blog/2010/03/wild-bill-bunge/>. We first came across Bunge's work in a fine text by some French geographers, Gatien Elie, Allan Popelard and Paul Vannie, 'William Bunge, le géographe révolutionnaire de Detroit', *Visions Cartographiques* blog at *Le Monde diplomatique*: <http://blog.mondediplo.net/2009-12-29-William-Bunge-le-geographerevolutionnaire-de>.

180. See the fine summary in Dennis Wood's *Rethinking the Power*

of Maps, pp. 166–71.

181. *Fitzgerald*, p. 7. In the same pages, Bunge talks about wielding the 'steel-hard hammer of humanism' against the forces of capital.

182. For a map that inherits the same intention to diagram racialised exploitation in the US house market, see Andy Vann's 'Reverse Redlining Atlanta: Predatory Mortgage Lending and Structural Racism' (2011), available at: http://urban-gsapp.tumblr.com/post/3260760966/2-feature-mapping-visualization.

183. For a further discussion of von Thünen, see David Harvey, 'The Spatial Fix: Hegel, von Thünen and Marx', *Antipode*, 13.3 (1981), pp. 1–12.

184. *Fitzgerald*, p. 132.

185. As a recent study of the history of racial urbanism notes: 'land markets are the one capitalist institution in which race-infused economic interests became consistently and increasingly important in the division of cities, even arguably becoming the single most important segregationist force in cities today'. Carl H. Nightingale, *Segregation: A Global History of Divided Cities* (Chicago: University of Chicago Press, 2012), p. 7. See also the articles by Keeanga-Yamahtta Taylor on black housing in the US, and her *Rats, Riots and Revolution* (Chicago: Haymarket, 2014).

186. *Fitzgerald*, p. 134.

187. On the 'cult film' label, see: http://www.cineaste.com/articles/cult-film-a-critical-symposium.

188. See Joshua B. Freeman, *Working Class New York* (New York: The New Press, 2000), pp. 55-71.

189. John Walters Interviews Michael Wadleigh, *Front Porch*, New Hampshire Public Radio, 6 October 2004. Available at: http://www.nhpr.org/node/7381.

190. In fact, Wadleigh didn't even finish directing the film

himself: he was removed by the studio after submitting a four hour and four minute cut and it was actually finished, uncredited, by the director John Hancock, best known for *Bang The Drum Slowly* (1973). For this, and other information on the film's production and reception, see CEJ, 'Wolfen: Leading the Pack as the First, Best, and Only True *Political Thriller*, *The Gull Cottage / Sandlot* blog, April/May/June 2012, available at http://www.gullcottageonline.com/Bur.html.

191. *Front Porch* interview with Michael Wadleigh.

192. The luxury residential neighbourhood Battery Park City was being built a few blocks from the park while the film was being shot. Also, the area where Van der Veer was intending to build is not actually on the shore. Short of some even more extreme urban engineering, the marina doesn't make much sense.

193. Jameson signals this element in 'Totality as Conspiracy', but also with reference to the rag-tag detail in *The Wire* (on which more in the next chapter). See Fredric Jameson, 'Realism and Utopia in *The Wire*', *Criticism*, 52.3-4 (2010), pp. 363-4.

194. In an arresting political and aesthetic short-circuit, Wadleigh has Ferguson show the same footage of helicopter wolf-hunts with which Chris Marker closes his great film about the 'red decade' straddling the sixties and seventies, *Grin Without a Cat (Le Fond de l'air est rouge)* (1977). That Wadleigh would have re-refunctioned this footage, which Marker had turned into an allegory courage defeated, further complicates our sense of the film's political response to its moment.

195. The NAM is an obvious nod to the AIM (American Indian Movement), arguably the most militant political group struggling for indigenous sovereignty in the US. The AIM, along with the Panthers, the Young Lords and numerous other seventies anti-systemic groups was devastated by the

COINTELPRO programme.

196. This is built on the site of Federal Hall, which was erected as New York's City Hall in 1700 and briefly served as the US's first capitol building. It is also the site of the first 'car bomb', where Italian anarchist Mario Buda exploded a horse-drawn wagon in 1920. See Mike Davis, *Buda's Wagon: A Brief History of the Car Bomb* (Verso, 2007).

197. The South Bronx is not an exact location and its boundaries are not universally agreed upon. In the 1960s it was designated as the area south of Robert Moses's Cross Bronx Expressway, finished in 1963, but later the border moved further north to Fordham Road. Robert Jensen claimed it is 'a condition of poverty and social collapse, more than a geographical place'. Jensen quoted in Jeff Chang, *Can't Stop Won't Stop: A History of the Hip-Hop Generation* (New York: Picador, 2006), p. 17.See also Katherine Simpson, 'Media Images of the Urban Landscape: the South Bronx in Film', *Centro Journal*, XIV.2 (2002), p. 101; Marshall Berman, 'Among the Ruins', *The New International*, Issue 178, December 1987, available online at: http://www.newint .org/features/1987/12/05/among/.

198. Marshall Berman, *All That's Solid Melts Into Air* (New York: Verso, 1983),p.290.

199. Mike Davis, *Dead Cities* (New York: The New Press, 2002), p. 386.

200. Manny Fernandez, 'In the Bronx, Blight Gave Way to Renewal', *New York Times*, 5 October 2007, available at: http://www.nytimes.com/2007/10/05/nyregion/05charlotte.h tml?_r=0. Today it is completely unrecognisable, a tree lined street with residential ranch homes. See 'Then and Now: 'The Worst Slum in America', *CNN*, 10 November 2009. Available online at: http://money.cnn.com/galleries/2009 /real_estate/0911/gallery.charlotte_street/index.html.

201. Miriam Greenberg, *Branding New York: How a City in Crisis*

was Sold to the World (London: Routledge, 2008).

202. T.J. English, *The Savage City: Race, Murder, and a Generation on the Edge* (New York: William Morrow, 2011), p. xxi.

203. This is literally the case with John Carpenter's *Assault on Precinct 13* (1976), which was originally conceived as a Western. Its relatively paltry $100,000 budget forced Carpenter to set the film in the present (in South Central Los Angeles). Shifting the Western onto the new lawless frontier of New York City had been done six years previously in Don Seigel's *Coogan's Bluff*, where Clint Eastwood plays an Arizona sheriff sent to New York to extradite a prisoner. Later, *The Exterminator* (1980), paired the 'urban jungle' with the real jungles of Southeast Asia as a returning Vietnam-vet-cum-vigilante hunts down criminals.

204. *Branding New York*, p. 153. This is certainly disputable for *The Warriors*, which is weirdly redemptive about 'good' gangs, and a could also be challenged for a number of the other 'exploitation' films, which do not necessarily just repeat and reinforce these stereotypes.

205. *Branding New York*, p. 157. Greenberg's not so rigorous list of New York exploitation films also includes Carpenter's *Assault on Precinct 13*, which as noted is actually set in Los Angeles. The 2005 sequel to *Assault on Precinct 13* is set in Detroit.

206. Roger Ebert, 'Wolfen', *Chicago Sun-Times*, 1 January 1981, available at: http://www.rogerebert.com/reviews/wolfen-1981.

207. 'Glory Days', *New York Times*, 2 January 2005, available at: http://www.nytimes.com/2005/01/02/nyregion/thecity/02gold.html?pagewanted=2.

208. For comparison's sake: another dystopian New York film from the area, *Soylent Green* (dir. R. Fleischer, 1973), takes place fifty years in the future, while even *Children of Men* (dir. A. Cuarón, 2006) – which has been lauded for

presenting a future Britain governed under a permanent state of emergency as a distressingly plausible outgrowth of present trends – is set in 2027.

209. Living in Manhattan during the blackout that followed Hurricane Sandy, it was striking how much the skyline of lower Manhattan resembled this shot.

210. John Avlon, 'Chicago Murder Rate Surges as New York's Drops to Record Low', *The Daily Beast*, 7 February 2012, available at: http://www.thedailybeast.com/articles/2012/07/02/chicago-murder-rate-surges-as-new-york-s-drops-to-record-low.html.

201. Joshua B. Freeman, *Working Class New York* (New York: The New Press, 2000), pp. 55-71.

202. Robert Fitch, *The Assassination of New York* (London: Verso, 1993), p. vii.

213. See Fitch, *The Assassination of New York*; Freeman, *Working Class New York*; Kim Moody, *From Welfare State to Real Estate: Regime Change in New York City, 1974 to the Present* (New York: The New Press, 2007); William Tabb, *The Long Default*, (New York: Monthly Review Press, 1982).

214. See Tabb, *The Long Default*.

215. Quoted in Moody, *From Welfare State to Real Estate*, p. 30.

216. *From Welfare State to Real Estate*, p. 15.

217. Quoted in *From Welfare State to Real Estate*, p. 17.

218. Toni Negri, *Revolution Retrieved: Writings on Marx, Keynes, Capitalist Crisis and New Social Subjects (1967-83)* (London: Red Notes, 1988). In a collection of prison letters, Negri writes fondly of the 1977 New York blackout as a moment of proletarian appropriation: *Pipeline. Lettere da Rebibbia* (Turin: Einaudi, 1982).

219. *From Welfare State to Real Estate*, p. 24.

220. David Harvey, *A Brief History of Neoliberalism* (Oxford: Oxford University Press, 2007), p. 45.

221. Deborah Wallace and Rodrick Wallace, *A Plague on Your Houses: How New York Was Burned Down and National Health Crumbled* (London: Verso, 1998), p. 18.

222. *A Plague on Your Houses*, p. xvi; Chang, *Can't Stop Won't Stop*, pp. 14-5.

223. Tabb, *The Long Default*, p. 104.

224. Wallace and Wallace, *A Plague on Your Houses*, p. 24.

225. Miriam Greenberg, *Branding New York*, p. 140.

226. Quoted in Fitch, *The Assassination of New York*, p. viii. The furore around this statement and his articulation of planned shrinkage led to Starr's resignation, but not a shift in city policy.

227. Joe Conason and Jack Newfield, quoted in Chang, *Can't Stop Won't Stop*, p. 14.

228. Quoted in Chang, *Can't Stop Won't Stop*, p. 16.

229. Georg Simmel, 'The Ruin', *Essays on Sociology, Philosophy and Aesthetics*, ed. Kurt Wolff (New York: Harper & Row, 1965), p. 265.

230. 'Ibid., p. 262.

231. The phrase is from William Gilpin's *Observations on the River Wye* (1782) and is quoted by Brian Dillon, *Ruin Lust: Artists' Fascination with Ruins, from Turner to the Present Day* (London: Tate, 2014), the essay accompanying the *Ruin Lust* exhibition he curated at the Tate Britain (4 March-18 May 2014). Dillon rightly notes the disparate cultural meanings accorded to ruins. We would argue however that here, as in most matters relating to the production of space, the economic 'last instance' is preponderant.

232. See the chapter 'Fabulous Ruin' in Mark Binelli, *The Last Days of Detroit* (New York: Vintage, 2014), pp. 268-87.

233. In fact, *Wolfen's* narrative might have been more plausibly set in a city like Detroit, where population density is far less than New York City, and long declining.

234. A preoccupation with ruins has accompanied photography

throughout its history, sometimes recording revolutionary and counter-revolutionary destruction, as in the Paris Commune images of Charles Marville, at others immortalising structures doomed by economic and social change, as in the work of the Society for Photographing Relics of Old London. See Dillon, *Ruin Lust*, p. 28.

235. Evan Calder Williams, *Combined and Uneven Apocalypse* (Winchester: Zero Books, 2011), p. 232-3. This church is apparently the largest exterior set ever built in New York City. See CEJ, 'Wolfen...'.

236. James Bennet, 'A Tribute to Ruin Irks Detroit', *The New York Times*, 10 December 1995, available at: http://www.nytimes.com/1995/12/10/us/a-tribute-to-ruin-irks-detroit.html. See also Binell, *The Last Days of Detroit*, pp. 269-72.

237. Jameson, *The Geopolitical Aesthetic*, p. 83 note 15.

238. Anecdotally, Ronald Reagan was an immense fan of the film, going as far as to telephone the lead actor Michael Beck after screening it at Camp David. Allen Barra, '*The Warriors* fights on', *Salon*, 28 November 2005, available at: http://www.salon.com/2005/11/28/warriors_2/.

239. *The Geopolitical Aesthetic*, p. 83 note 15.

240. See the extraordinary documentary *Flyin' Cut Sleeves* (dir. Henry Chalfant and Rita Fecher, 1993).

241. *Flyin' Cut Sleeves.*

242. Tanyanika Samuels, 'Former Bronx gang members...', *New York Daily News*, 8 December 2011, available at: http://articles.nydailynews.com/2011-12-08/news/30492575_1_gang-violence-melendez-gang-war.

243. Eric Schneider, *Vampires, Dragons and Egyptian Kings: Youth Gangs in Postwar New York* (Princeton: Princeton University Press, 2001), p. 243.

244. Chang, *Can't Stop Won't Stop*, p. 13; Schneider, *Vampires, Dragons and Egyptian Kings*, pp. 243-4.

245. *Vampires, Dragons and Egyptian Kings*, pp. 222-3.

246. Jill Jonnes, *South Bronx Rising: The Rise, Fall, and Resurrection of an American City* (New York: Fordham University Press, 2002), p. 237.

247. Arguably, what is unsatisfying about *Wolfen* is its attempt to *explain* the horrors. The genre is much more affective when the reasons behind the attacks can only be speculated upon, as in *Cloverfield* (dir. Matt Reeves, 2008), by contrast with a film like *The Happening* (dir. M. Night Shyamalan, 2008), which throws up a pseudo-scientific explanation.

248. In the book on which the film is based, there is nothing supernatural about the wolfen. While in Wadleigh's film their sudden appearance in Van Der Veer's penthouse might enjoy a spectral quality, in the book this is accounted for by their ability to leap from balcony to balcony.

249. Having the Native Americans working on high steel is not a strange conceit. Since as early as the 1880s Mohawk ironworkers from the Kahnawake reservation outside of Montreal, so-called 'Skywalkers' or 'Ironwalkers', have worked on bridges and skyscrapers throughout North America, participating in the building of the Empire State Building, World Trade Center, and countless other structures. Around 200 Mohawk are currently taking part in building World Trade Center One, commuting back to Quebec to be with their families on the weekends. In this sense, the traces of indigenous people are not just buried beneath the modern city; their toil is stamped on the quintessential urban skyline. Two Canadian documentaries give a sense of this indigenous working class, its strivings and its politics: Don Owen's 1965 documentary short *High Steel*, available at: https://www.nfb.ca/film/high_steel/; and Alanis Obomsawin's 1997 documentary *Spudwrench*, which links the steel workers to the 1990 'Oka crisis', available at: https://www.nfb.ca/film/spudwrench_kahnawake_man.

250. The werewolf also often functions to symbolise the volatility

and uncontrollability of the body, and has often been seen as an allegory of puberty or menstruation. See Chantal Bourgault du Coudray, *The Curse of the Werewolf: Fantasy, Horror and the Beast Within* (London: I.B. Tauris, 2006).

251. This aspect of the story features more heavily in Strieber's novel than the film.

252. *Capital, Vol. 1*, trans. B. Fowkes, p. 342. See also Mark Neocleous, 'The Political Economy of the Dead: Marx's Vampires', *History of Political Thought* XXXIV, 4 (2003), pp. 668-84.

253. *Capital, Vol. 1*, trans. S. Moore and E. Aveling, p. 291.

254. Franco Moretti, 'Dialectic of Fear', in *Signs Taken for Wonders: Essays in the Sociology of Literary Forms*, rev. ed. (London: Verso, 1988), p. 84.

255. See Annie McClanahan's excellent 2012 essay for the *Post45* online journal, 'Dead Pledges: Debt, Horror, and the Credit Crisis', which covers a dimension of post-2008 crisis cinema we neglect here, that of crisis horror. Available at: http://post45.research.yale.edu/2012/05/dead-pledges-debt-horror-and-the-credit-crisis/

256. 'Man is a Wolf to Man: An Appreciation of Wolfen', *Unemployed Negativity* blog, 13 September 2009, available at: http://www.unemployednegativity.com/2009/09/man-is-wolf-to-man-appreciation-of.html.

257. See Loïc Wacquant, *Prisons of Poverty* (Minneapolis: University of Minnesota Press, 2009).

258. Tabb, *The Long Default*, pp. 4-5.

259. Gus Lubin, '14 Shocking Stats on the Rise of Inequality in New York', *Business Insider*, 19 January 2011, available at: http://www.businessinsider.com/new-york-inequality-2011-1?op=1.

260. Sam Roberts, 'One in Five New York Residents Living in Poverty', *The New York Times*, 22 September 2011, available at: http://www.nytimes.com/2011/09/22/nyregion/one-in-

five-new-york-city-residents-living-in-poverty.html.

261. Harvey, *A Brief History of Neoliberalism*, p. 47.

262. David Harvey, *The Enigma of Capital* (London: Profile, 2011), p. 172

263. It is instructive to compare the production of a narrative and social space in *The Wire*, with Roberto Schwarz's eloquent analysis of another claustrophobic epic of urban violence, Paulo Lins's *Cidade de Deus* (1997), set in the favelas of Rio de Janeiro. The following passage could be usefully transposed onto Simon's Baltimore: 'What are the frontiers of this dynamic? The action takes place within the closed world of the City of God, with only a few forays outside—mainly to prisons, following characters' destinies. Events are portrayed on a grand scale but the space in which they unfold is far more limited than the social premises on which they rest. The higher spheres of drug- and arms-trafficking, and the military and political corruption that protect them, do not appear; their local agents, if not gangsters themselves, are scarcely any different. The real-estate specu-lators and public administration that ensure the favela's segregation from the rest of the city barely figure either, save for odd glimpses—though these are quite enough to suggest that they, too, are all the same. This limited compass functions as a strength in literary terms, dramatizing the blindness and segmentation of the social process'. 'City of God', *New Left Review*, II/12 (2001), p. 107. An analogous observation is made by Ericka Beckman about another Latin American novel, this time from the beginning of the century, José Eustasio Rivera's 1924 *La vorágine* (The Vortex): 'the closer the novel moves into the jungle, the closer it gets to the origins of the commodity as produced by human labor. By the same token, however, the deeper this perspective moves into the "real" of extraction, the less it is able to visualize the circuits outside of the jungle that are actually

governing the production of the export commodity'. *Capital Fictions*, p. 186.

264. See Sudhir Alladi Vankatesh, *Off the Books: The Underground Economy of the Urban Poor* (Cambridge, MA: Harvard University Press, 2006).

265. David Simon, 'Prologue', in Rafael Alvarez, *The Wire: Truth Be Told* (Edinburgh: Canongate Books, 2009), p. 30.

266. Margaret Talbot, 'Stealing Life: The Crusader Behind *The Wire*', *The New Yorker*, 22 October 2007, available at: http://www.newyorker.com/reporting/2007/10/22/071022fa_fact_talbot.

267. Simon himself has referred to the show as a 'visual novel'. 'Prologue', p. 23. The filmmaker Peter Greenaway has polemically repeated that we have not seen any cinema yet, only filmed Victorian novels. *Peter Greenaway: Interviews*, ed. V. Gras and M. Gras (Jackson: University Press of Mississippi, 2000), p. 152. One could argue that *The Wire* is a rare case where Greenaway's formalist slight is flipped into a wholesale ambition.

268. Much has been written about the 'authenticity' of the casting, with several of the actors having similar backgrounds to the characters they play. A remark by Jameson seems apropos: 'the star system is fundamentally, structurally, irreconcilable with neo-realism'. *Signatures of the Visible* (London: Routledge, 2007), p. 51.

269. On the hegemony of a distinctly American 'central conflict theory' in filmic narratives, see Raúl Ruiz, *Poetics of Cinema* (Paris: Dis Voir, 1995), pp. 9-23.

270. Importantly, the show refuses to give any deep psychological motivation to McNulty's drive. Occasionally it is portrayed as part of his competitive and confrontational personality, sometimes it appears motivated by a genuine desire for justice in the face of scores of drug-related murders. The dishevelled, conflicted hero is an all-too

common theme but *The Wire* doesn't, for the most part, pander to treating its principal characters as noble creatures of sacrifice, or moral, responsible subjects.

271. Simon, 'Prologue', p. 3.

272. All the music, beyond the seasonal variations on the distinctive credit theme, is diegetic, playing in car sound systems or dance clubs; knowledge of the local music scene is even at one point used as a way to identify and kill rival dealers from New York. See Andrew Devereaux, ''What Chew Know About Down the Hill?': Baltimore Club Music, Subgenre Crossover, and the New Subcultural Capital of Race and Space', *Journal of Popular Music Studies*, 19.4 (2007), pp. 311-41.

273. Meghan O'Rourke, 'Interviewing the Man behind *The Wire*', *Slate*, 1 December 2006, available online at: http://www. slate.com/articles/news_and_politics/interrogation/2006/ 12/behind_the_wire.html.

274. There is definitely a sense in which *The Wire* is *barely* a television series. While it may have been produced and originally aired as such, an argument could probably be made that its liminal status in terms of both genre and platform coincides with changes in the broadcast mode of television. We have yet to come across anyone, among the many people we know who have seen the show in its entirety, who watched it on television when originally broadcast.

275. John Kraniauskas, 'Elasticity of Demand: Reflections on *The Wire*', *Radical Philosophy*, 154 (2009), p. 27.

276. Loïc Wacquant, *Urban Outcasts: A Comparative Sociology of Advanced Marginality* (London: Polity, 2008), p. 3.

277. Ibid., p. 4.

278. Ibid., p. 9.

279. David Simon, interview with Lauren Laverne, *Culture Show*, BBC 2, 15 July 2008. A reviewer critical of the show's

reformist illusions and its abiding 'policing prism', has not been able to resist the Marxian chiasmus, suggesting that it is also 'a cop show masquerading as a political tract'. Tom Jennings, 'Wired for Sound and Fury', *Freedom*, 70.9 (2009), available at: https://libcom.org/library/wire-david-simon-ed-burns-bbc-2.

280. Bret McCabe, 'Under *The Wire*' (interview with David Simon), *City Paper*, 28 May 2003, available at: http://www.citypaper.com/eat/story.asp?id=3336.

281. David Harvey, *Spaces of Hope* (Edinburgh: Edinburgh University Press, 2000), p. 133.

282. 'Neoliberal Grotesque,' *I Hear A New World* blog, 30 January 2008, available at: http://ihearanewworld.blogspot.com/2008/01/neoliberal-grotesque.html. The moralism pervading this labour nostalgia is indicted by Adolph Reed, Jr., in a devastating appraisal of *Tremé* (2010-13), as the reason for the New Orleans-based show fell for the 'touristic narrative of cultural authenticity', and wholly severs black politics from class politics. See 'Three Tremés', *nonsite.org*, 4 July 2011, available at: http://nonsite.org/editorial/three-tremes.

283. Simon himself often disavows any such allegiances: 'You're not looking at a Marxist here', he quips at a talk.

284. Karl Polanyi, *The Great Transformation: The Political and Economic Origins of Our Time* (Boston: Beacon Press, 2001 [1944]), p. 60.

285. Fred Block, 'Introduction', in *The Great Transformation*, pp. xxv.

286. The talk is available at: http://www.youtube.com/watch?v=k8E8xBXFLKE&feature=kp.

287. 'Cognitive Mapping', pp. 352-3.

288. See Harvey, *The New Imperialism* (Oxford: Oxford University Press, 2005), pp. 27-33.

289. Conor Friedersdorf, '*The Wire* Isn't a Critique of Capitalism',

The Huffington Post, 18 January 2008, available at: http://www.huffingtonpost.com/conor-friedersdorf/the-wire-isnt-a_b_82222.html.

290. Liam Kennedy and Stephen Shapiro, 'Tale of the Neoliberal City: The Wire's Boundary Lines', in *The Wire: Race, Class, and Genre*, ed. L. Kennedy and S. Shapiro (Ann Arbor: The University of Michigan Press, 2012), p. 150. The very character who for Kennedy and Shapiro embodies the petty-bourgeois guild-consciousness that the show can't extricate itself from, Freamon, is for Jameson (see 'Realism and Utopia in *The Wire*') one of the bearers of its utopian impulse. The 'embedding' of the narrative, in this case not in the police but in the military, is incidentally one of the deep flaws in Simon's 2008 *Generation Kill*, whose moments of astute social observation all involve Simon's obsession with 'the hell of middle management' as the pivot of America's ills.

291. Alberto Toscano, 'Culture and Admin', *Radical Philosophy*, 182 (2013), pp. 40-3.

292. 'Cognitive Mapping', p. 356. See also 'Totality as Conspiracy', in *The Geopolitical Aesthetic*, pp. 7-84.

293. Simon, 'Prologue', p. 5.

294. Vincenzo Ruggiero, *Economie sporche. L'impresa criminale in Europa* (Turin: Bollati Boringhieri, 1996), p. 208.

295. Meghan O'Rourke, 'Interviewing the Man behind *The Wire*'.

296. 'The Wire is really not interested in Good and Evil; it's interested in economics, sociology and politics' (David Simon, DVD commentary). It 'is not an individual criminal responsible for an enigmatic crime, but rather a whole society that must be opened up to representation and tracked down, identified, explored, mapped like a new dimension or a foreign culture'. Jameson, 'Realism and Utopia in *The Wire*', p. 362.

297. This is reminiscent of Žižek's claim that capital can be

thought of as the Lacanian Real. See, among others, *Contingency, Universality, Hegemony* (London: Verso, 2000) and *The Fragile Absolute* (London: Verso, 2001). Perhaps this is why depictions of capital's silent compulsion inevitably seem to be figured on the level of fantasy: ex-special forces hitmen capable of extreme stealth and exemplary efficiency as the (reassuring) secret behind successful corporations.

298. Kraniauskas, 'Elasticity of Demand', p. 27.

299. Jameson, 'Realism and Utopia in *The Wire*', p. 361.

300. Harvey, *Spaces of Hope*, p. 148.

301. David Harvey, *Spaces of Global Capitalism: Towards a Theory of Uneven Geographical Development* (London: Verso, 2006), p. 86.

302. One can recall in this regard a scene from episode 53 where Marlo Stanfield, the young and ruthless leader of an outfit that has scrambled the fronts of the drug wars, travels to the Antilles to assure himself that the money he has been 'cleaning' there is actually, physically there. 'I came to see my account.' 'Y'all got my money in here?' 'It's mine. Y'all got my money,' he tells an uncomprehending teller. In this vision, the deeply financialised character of the drug trade does not percolate down to the street.

303. Gilles Deleuze, *Cinema 2: The Time-Image*, trans. H. Tomlinson and R. Galeta (Minneapolis: University of Minnesota Press, 1989), p. 244.

304. Kraniauskas, 'Elasticity of Demand', p. 26.

305. David Harvey, 'A view from Federal Hill', in *Spaces of Capital: Towards a Critical Geography* (Edinburgh: Edinburgh University Press, 2001), pp. 147-50.

306. Quoted in Margaret Talbot, 'Stealing Life: The Crusader Behind *The Wire*'. Simon goes on to say: 'But the guys we were stealing from in *The Wire* are the Greeks. In our heads we're writing a Greek tragedy, but instead of the gods being petulant and jealous Olympians hurling lightning bolts

down at our protagonists, it's the Postmodern institutions that are the gods. And they are gods. And no one is bigger.'

307. It could be remarked that in light of comments such as these, the 'postmodern institutions' are remarkably... Fordist, in the sense that, following Ruggiero's suggestion, this 'crime as work' depends on the classic capitalist division of labour between programming and execution – dramatized in the show by the closely guarded distance between leader of the gang, Avon Barksdale, and the 'hoppers' on the street.

308. David Simon, Talk at the University of Southern California, 3 March 2008, available at: http://www.youtube.com/watch?v=k8E8xBXFLKE. Simon's political vision is a curious kind of social-democratic tragic-existentialism: 'my faith in individuals to rebel against rigged systems and exert for dignity, while at the same time doubtful that the institutions of a capital-obsessed oligarchy will reform themselves short of outright economic depression (New Deal, the rise of collective bargaining) or systemic moral failure that actually threatens middle-class lives (Vietnam and the resulting, though brief commitment to rethinking our brutal foreign-policy footprints around the world)'. Intervention by Simon in the comment thread to Matthew Yglesias, 'David Simon and the Audacity of Despair', *The Atlantic*, 2 January 2008. available online at: http://matthewyglesias.theatlantic .com/archives/2008/01/david_simon_and_the_audacity_o.p hp#comment1068461.

309. Ignorance of suitable cases in non-Anglo-American cinema; the social and symbolic proximity of the UK/US film industries to the sites of the financial crisis; and the way in which 'the crisis' in salient respects finds its origins in the US (New York, Washington, the suburbs) and London (the City), explains why this survey only touches on 'Atlantic' visions of the crisis. Comparative work on representations of crisis across national contexts – for instance contrasting the recent

spate of US documentaries on the crisis with Fernando E. Solanas combative take on the Argentinian crisis of December 2001, *Memoria del Saqueo / Social Genocide* (2003) – would be a worthwhile undertaking. Despite the title and date, Genestal's *Krach* (2010), with its improbable plot about predicting stock market fluctuations with climate change models, rehashes much of the visual and narrative clichés of modern finance without tackling the crisis itself.

310. In a more experimental vein, several film works in the contemporary art scene have provided a sharper and more reflexive focus on systemic concerns. See, for example, Hito Steyerl's *In Free Fall* (2010), Superflex's *The Financial Crisis* (2009), and Melanie Gilligan's *Crisis in the Credit System* (2008) and *Popular Unrest* (2010). Gilligan's intensively researched work is particularly stimulating in its capacity to stage, with more than a hint of Brechtian comedy, the languages of finance and to foreground the enigmatic character of financial capital (one of her traders in *Crisis*, 'the Oracle', is essentially a medium, while in *Popular Unrest* all social and economic relations are mediated by a system called 'the Spirit').

311. Morris Dickstein, *Dancing in the Dark: A Cultural History of the Great Depression* (New York: Norton, 2009), p. 10.

312. In a 1930 lecture, Eisenstein declared 'I will attempt to film *Capital* so that the humble worker or peasant can understand it'. Quoted in Samuel Brody, 'Paris hears Eisenstein', *Jump Cut*, 14 (1977), pp. 30-31, available at: http://www. ejumpcut.org/archive/onlinessays/JC14folder/Paris%20Hea rs%20E.html.

313. Fredric Jameson, 'Marx and Montage', *New Left Review*, 58 (2009), p. 113. According to Jameson, in *Kuhle Wampe* Brecht and Dudow tried 'to trace the visible symptoms back to their absent (or untotalizable) causes' (114).

314. For a magisterial interpretation of these films, see Jameson's

'Conspiracy as Totality', in *The Geopolitical Aesthetic.*

315. Consider this claim by critic Rex Reed in *The New York Observer*: 'In my father's day, people were proud of where they worked, and there were rewards for loyalty and longevity. Now the job market is ruled by companies that care more about their stockholders than the dignity, respect and self-esteem of their employees.' Rex Reed, 'Up the Creek Without a Paycheck: *The Company Men* Paints a Moving, Nuanced Picture of Life After Layoffs', *New York Observer*, 7 December 2010, available at: http://www.observer.com/20 10/culture/creek-without-paycheck-company-men-paints-moving-nuanced-picture-life-after-layoffs.

316. Jacques Le Goff, *Your Money or Your Life: Economy and Religion in the Middle Ages*, trans. P. Ranum (New York: Zone Books, 1998), p. 30.

317. Telis Demos, 'Oliver Stone: Life After *Wall Street*', *Fortune*, 21 September 2007, available at: http://money.cnn.com/2007/09/ 20/news/newsmakers/oliver_stone.fortune/index.htm

318. This replicates visualisations of the 'skyscraper index', the hypothesis that booms in the construction of massively tall buildings are predictive of crises.

319. Joshua Clover, 'The Future in Labor', *Film Quarterly*, 63.1 (2009), available at: http://www.filmquarterly.org/2009 /09/the-future-in-labor-2/.

320. Eric Eisenberg, 'Creators of *The Other Guys* End Credits', *CinemaBlend.com*, 13 August 2010, available at: http:// www.cinemablend.com/new/Exclusive-Interview-Creators-Of-The-Other-Guys-End-Credits20143.html.

321. 'Oliver Stone: Life After *Wall Street*'.

322. See, for example, the case between Procter & Gamble and Banker's Trust in 1995, one of the first to shed light on the dangers of so-called over the counter derivatives. 'The Bankers Trust Tapes', *Business Week*, 16 October 1995, available at: http://www.businessweek.com/1995/42/b34461

.htm.

323. This can be seen in contrasted to a film like *The Take* (Avi Lewis, 2004), which followed a group of workers outside of Buenos Aires who collectivized their factory after it shut down following the Argentine economic collapse in 2001.

324. This runs in contrast to the tendency of many contemporary political thrillers to be almost ostentatiously international in both plot and location – films like *Traffic, Syriana, The International*, the *Bourne* films, and so on, come to mind.

325. The literature is vast and growing, but for a compelling Marxist intervention that also critically reviews some alternative explanation of the crisis, see David McNally, *Global Slump: The Economics and Politics of Crisis and Resistance* (Oakland: PM Press, 2010).

326. See Donald MacKenzie's writings in the *London Review of Books*, for a fine example of this approach: http://www.lrb.co.uk/contributors/donald-mackenzie.

327. Shahien Nasiripour, 'Financial Crisis Panel in Turmoil as Republicans Defect; Plan to Blame Government for Crisis', *Huffington Post*, 15 December 2010, available at: http://www.huffingtonpost.com/2010/12/14/financial-crisis-panel-wall-street_n_796839.html.

328. *The Geopolitical Aesthetic*, p. 3.

329. Louis Althusser, 'Cremonini, Painter of the Abstract', in *Lenin and Philosophy and Other Essays*, trans. B. Brewster (New York: Monthly Review, 1971).

330. Isaac Julien, *Riot* (New York: Museum of Modern Art, 2013).

331. 'It is unclear whether these sequences are intended to be ironic. Nevertheless, they induce one thing: a sense of Arab kitsch—a view of the Arab world told through mediated, distanced eyes. Indeed, this scene differs little from the innumerable portrayals of Arab sites to be found in hegemonic culture, where the men are abstract, oppressive figures, the women forced into labor, and the visual and

sonic tapestry is one that evokes Orientalism'. Omar Kholeif, 'Isaac Julien's "Playtime"', *art agenda*, 10 February 2014, available at: http://art-agenda.com/reviews/isaac-julien%E2%80%99s-%E2%80%9Cplaytime%E2%80%9D/. See also William S. Smith, 'Isaac Julien', *Art in America*, 5 February 2014, available at: http://www.artinamericam-agazine.com/reviews/isaac-julien/.

332. Bertolt Brecht, 'The Threepenny Trial: A Sociological Experiment', in *German Essays on Film*, ed. R. McCormick and A. Guenther-Pal (New York: Continuum, 2004).

333. Sergio Bologna, 'L'undicesima tesi', in *Ceti medi senza futuro? Scritti, appunti sul lavoro e altro* (Rome: DeriveApprodi, 2007), p.84.

334. Marc Levinson, *The Box: How the Shipping Container Made the World Smaller and the World Economy Bigger* (Princeton: Princeton University Press, 2008), pp. 171-88.

335. A cinematic trace of this process can be found in the scene from *Apocalypse Now Redux* in which Willard is imprisoned in 'conex box' and read *Time Magazine* by Kurz/Brando.

336. Terence K. Hopkins and Immanuel Wallerstein, 'Commodity Chains in the World-Economy Prior to 1800', *Review*, 10.1 (1986), pp. 157-70.

337. For an attempt to encompass these films in a novel generic category, see Andrew deWaard, 'The Global Social Problem Film', *Cinephile*, 3.1 (2007), pp. 12-18. DeWaard cites this astute reflection from Rogert Ebert's enthusiastic review of *Syriana*: 'The movie's plot is so complex we're not really supposed to follow it, we're supposed to be surrounded by it. Since none of the characters understand the whole picture, why should we?' His effort to link this to Deleuze and Guattari's theory of the rhizome is less persuasive. It is worth noting that the source for Soderbergh's *Traffic*, the superior British TV mini-series *Traffik* (dir. Alastair Reid, 1989), is among the films – in our view, by far the more

successful – that Jameson has mentioned as cognitive mappings of globalising capital. See Ian Buchanan, *Fredric Jameson: Live Theory* (London: Continuum, 2006), p. 113.

338. See Jonathan Lamb, 'The Implacability of Things' (2012), *The Public Domain Review*, available online at: http://public-domainreview.org/2012/10/03/the-implacability-of-things/. For an example, see Joseph Addison's 'The Adventures of a Shilling' (1710), available at: http://essays.quotidiana. org/addison/adventures_of_a_shilling/. An important twentieth-century communist variant of this genre is Ilya Ehrenburg's 1929 *The Life of the Automobile*.

339. There is of course a dense narrative prehistory to such 'hyperlinks', which on closer attention have little that is new about them when they are extracted from their contrast with the conservatism of most cinematic plots. See, for instance, Jameson's comments on the theme of the 'web' in George Eliot's novels. 'The Experiments of Time', p. 227.

340. Alissa Quart, 'Networked', *Film Comment*, 41.4 (2005), pp. 48–5, available at: http://www.alissaquart.com/articles/2005 /08/networked_don_roos_and_happy_e.html.

341. See T.J. Demos, 'Moving Images of Globalization', *Grey Room*, 37 (Fall 2009), pp. 6-29. See also his *The Migrant Image: The Art and Politics of Documentary During Global Crisis* (Durham, NC: Duke University Press, 2013).

342. As an aside, it's worth noting that these networks may not only be complex, but perhaps literally impossible to trace; many of the links or even pivots of a global commodity chain will be shrouded by illegality or clandestinity. R.T. Naylor evocatively describes the process of diamonds traveling from mine to consumer thus: 'The diamond begins its commercial life in mines rife with theft; crosses borders in smugglers' pouches or, what is often the same thing, diplomatic luggage; comes briefly into daylight again in cutting and polishing centres whose practitioners, more

often than not, grant themselves a general tax exemption; re-enters underground freight channels via informal bourses where deals have traditionally been done in cash and sealed with a handshake; sneaks again across borders to dodge import duties or excise taxes; then finally arrives in a retail marketing network replete with commercial fraud. En route the diamond might pass through the hands of impoverished diggers and backwoods traders, career criminals and corrupt functionaries, spies and insurgents, counterfeiters and money-launderers, and investment sharks and telemarketing scam artists before coming to rest around an especially elegant neck or a languorously beckoning finger - at least until some enterprising jewel thief thinks differently'. R.T. Naylor, 'The Political Economy of Diamonds', *Counterpunch*, 16-18 March 2007, available at: http://www.counterpunch.org/2007/03/16/the-political-economy-of-diamonds/.

343. Quoted in Beckman, *Capital Fictions*, p. 188.

344. China Miéville, 'Blood & Diamonds', *rejectamentalist manifesto* blog, 6 August 2010, available at: http://chinamieville.net/post/910506879/blood-ice.

345. See: http://www.phonestory.org/.

346. Peter T. Drucker, *Innovation and Enterpreneurship* (London: Routledge, 2007), p. 28.

347. As we'll explore further in the next chapter, this is particularly evident in photography – for instance, in the work of Edward Burtynsky, or in a more reflexive vein, Isabelle Grosse. But we could also consider the monumental use of the container in Balka's Unilever commission for the Tate Modern, *How It Is* (2009). Aside from the sadly ubiquitous use of container for pop-up shops and galleries, and the sundry architectural projects that celebrate it as the architecture of crisis and survival, there are some more thoughtful exemplars of container-related artwork, among

them Paolo Tamburella's *Djahazi*, his entry for Comoros Islands to the 2009 Venice Biennale, or Phyllida Barlow's sprawling installation at the Tate Britan, *dock* (2014).

348. *Fish Story*, p. 12.

349. Roberto Saviano, *Gomorra* (Milan: Mondadori, 2006), pp. 11-25. Alberto Toscano's translation.

350. See the polemical study by the Italian sociologist Alessandro Dal Lago, *Eroi di carta. Il caso Gomorra e altre epopee* (Rome: manifestolibri, 2010).

351. Luca Rastello, *I Am the Market: How to Smuggle Cocaine by the Ton and Live Happily*, tr. J. Hunt (London: Granta, 2010).

352. Keller Easterling, *Enduring Innocence: Global Architecture and its Political Masquerades* (Cambridge, MA: The MIT Press, 2007), p. 102.

353. Ibid., p. 104.

354. Ibid., pp. 111, 113. On the grid, see Rosalind Krauss, *The Originality of the Avant-Garde and Other Modernist Myths* (Cambridge, MA: The MIT Press, 1985). The essay was originally published as 'Grids', *October*, 9 (1979), pp. 50–64.The logistics fantasy, and its application, is also shadowed by an informal, vernacular use of the container as architectural unit. Not logistics as a virtual matrix, but the disjecta of logistics as the basis for a permanently-temporary use of built space: 'Outside in the streets, informality characterizes the built environment itself. Much of the city is an architecture of shipping containers. Around the corner from the Mustafa Hotel, across from the bus station, shipping containers act as storefronts. One sawdust-filled container acts as a furniture-making workshop. Another is a kebab restaurant. An Internet café is built into another. This is an architecture of flexibility and impermanence. A shipping container might host a business, a storage space, even a prison as the situation on the ground changes. In any case, the containers can be quickly and

easily abandoned'. Paglen, *Blank Spots on the Map*, p. 245.

355. *Enduring Innocence*, p. 119.

356. Fredric Jameson, *Valences of the Dialectic* (London: Verso, 2010), pp. 421-2.

357. Allan Sekula, 'The Instrumental Image: Steichen at war', *Artforum*, 14.4 (1975), p. 30. Sekula perspicuously notes that for this spiritualisation of abstract landscape to be effective, the author-function of the photographer – the separation and sublimation of his intellectual labour – needs to be affirmed. See also a later statement, according to which 'the ideological force of photographic art in modern society may lie in the apparent reconciliation of human creative energies with a scientifically guided process of mechanization, suggesting that despite the modern industrial division of labour, and specifically despite the industrialization of cultural work, despite the historical obsolescence, marginal-ization, and degradation of artisanal and manual modes of representation, the category of the artist lives on in the exercise of a *purely mental*, imaginative command over the camera'. 'The Traffic in Photographs', *Art Journal*, 41.1 (1981), pp. 15-16.

358. Jacques Rancière, 'Notes on the Photographic Image', *Radical Philosophy*, 156 (2009), p. 12.

359. Jacques Lacan, *The Seminar of Jacques Lacan. Book XI: The Four Fundamental Concepts of Psychoanalysis*, trans. A. Sheridan (New York: W.W. Norton, 1981), p. 115.

360. Friedrich Dürrenmatt's novella *The Assignment: Or, on the Observing of the Observer of the Observers* (1986), is an incisive allegory of this predicament.

361. For an illuminating historical and theoretical reflection on aftermath photography, touching on Norfolk's work, which places it within a broader conjuncture of image-production, see John Roberts, 'Photography after the Photograph: Event, Archive and the Non-Symbolic', *Oxford Art Journal*, 3.2.

(2009), pp. 281–98.

362. 'The Instrumental Image', p. 27.

363. Ibid., p. 28.

364. Ibid., p. 32.

365. Ibid., p. 34.

366. '[B]oth modern science and modernist art tend to end up worshipping in floating cathedrals of formal, abstract, mathematical relations and "laws". Perhaps the fundamental question to be asked is this: can traditional photographic representation, whether symbolist or realist in its dominant formal rhetoric, transcend the pervasive logic of the commodity form, the exchange abstraction that haunts the culture of capitalism? Despite its origins in a radical refusal of instrumental meaning, symbolism appears to have been absorbed by mass culture, enlisted in the spectacle that gives imaginary flesh to the abstract regime of commodity exchange'. Allan Sekula, 'The Traffic in Photographs', p. 16.

367. Here Sekula cuts off the path to the ambiguous metaphysics of technology driving Paul Virilio's account of the logistics of perception in *War and Cinema: The Logistics of Perception*, trans. P. Camiller (London: Verso, 1989), which cites Sekula's writing on Steichen.

368. Quoted in Sekula, 'The Traffic in Photographs', pp. 21-2.

369. Sekula, 'The Traffic in Photographs', p. 22.

370. Farocki quoted in Georges Didi-Huberman, 'How to Open Your Eyes', in *Harun Farocki: Against What? Against Whom?*, ed. A. Ehmann and K. Eshun (Berlin: Walther König, 2009), p. 47.

371. 'That the US Army command showed operational images during the Gulf War, images that were produced for operational reasons and not for edification or instruction, is also an incredible displacement and is also conceptual art. I, too, only wish to arrive at art incidentally'. Harun Farocki,

'Cross Influence/Soft Montage', in *Harun Farocki: Against What? Against Whom?*, p. 74.

372. Didi-Huberman, 'How to Open Your Eyes', p. 47.

373. Ibid., p. 48.

374. Grégoire Chamayou, *Théorie du drone* (Paris: La Fabrique, 2013), pp. 57-68.

375. See Laura Kurgan, *Close Up at a Distance*.

376. T.J. Clark, 'Lowry's Other England', in T.J. Clark and Anne M. Wagner, *Lowry and the Painting of Modern Life* (London: Tate, 2013), pp. 38-9.

377. Though it should be noted that some of Lowry's views of formless industrial landscapes, especially those featuring polluted waters – Industrial Landscape, Wigan (1925), River Scene (Industrial Landscape) (1935), The Lake (1937), River Scene (1950) – bear comparison with the zones of devastation of contamination of *Stalker* (dir. Andrei Tarkovsky, 1979), the provincial wastes in which many of Béla Tarr's films are set, or, more to the point, the Chinese rust belt in Wang Bing's epic documentary of deindustrialisation, *West of the Tracks* (2003). For an appreciation of the latter, see Owen Hatherley's 'Future Ruins', in *Leaving the Factory: Wang Bing's Tie Xi Qu/West of the Tracks*, ed. S. Sandhu (New York: Texte und Töne, 2009).

378. Quoted in T.J. Clark, 'Lowry's Other England', p. 37.

379. John Berger, 'Lowry', in *The Moment of Cubism and other essays* (London: Weidenfeld and Nicolson, 1969), p. 102.

380. 'Lowry's Other England', p. 62.

381. Ibid., p. 61.

382. Berger, 'Lowry', pp. 104-5. It would be interesting to consider the figure of O.G.S. Crawford, pioneer of landscape archaeology and communist castigator of interwar British capitalism, as an acerbic and immoderate counterpart to Lowry, in his attentiveness to the mutations of the landscape, but also in his 'satirical archaeology' of an

obsolescent regime of accumulation, as registered in the often unfetishisable commodities that made English urban life not just drab but shoddy. See Kitty Hauser's captivating *Bloody Old Britain: O.G.S. Crawford and the Archaeology of Modern Life* (London: Granta, 2009).

383. Commissioned but never shown by Channel 4. See also Keiller's essay 'The Dilapidated Dwelling' in *The View from the Train: Cities & Other Landscapes* (London: Verso, 2013).

384. Originally published in the 1960s in the *New Left Review*, the key statements of the Nairn-Anderson theses were later collected in Tom Nairn, *The Break-up of Britain* (London: New Left Books, 1977) and Perry Anderson, *English Questions* (London: Verso, 1992). For a broader panorama of 1990s British cultural production in light of the theses, see Paul Dave, 'The Bourgeois Paradigm and Heritage Cinema', *New Left Review* 224 (1997), pp. 111-26, and, for an expanded take on the arguments of that essay, Dave's *Visions of England: Class and Culture in Contemporary Cinema* (Oxford: Berg, 2006).

385. *The View from the Train*, pp. 6 and 88, on the influence of 'declinist scenarios' on the making of *London*.

386. Perry Anderson, 'Diary', *London Review of Books*, 23 January 2014, p. 38.

387. Tom Nairn, 'The British Political Elite', *New Left Review* 23 (1964), p. 22.

388. The forensic character of this exercise is marked by a sardonic quip taken from *The Adventures of Sherlock Holmes*: 'It is my belief, Watson', said Holmes, 'founded upon my experience, that the lowest and vilest allies in London do not present a more dreadful record of sin than does the smiling and beautiful countryside'. Patrick Keiller, *Robinson in Space* (Reaktion, 1999), p. 11.

389. On the Robinson films as both repurposing and refutation of *A Tour through the Whole Island of Great Britain*, see Robert

Mayer, 'Not Adaptation but "Drifting": Patrick Keiller, Daniel Defoe, and the Relationship between Film and Literature', *Eighteenth-Century Fiction*, 16.4 (2004), pp. 803-27.

390. W.G. Hoskins, *The Making of the English Landscape* (London: Penguin, 1955), p. 299.

391. 'Today's urban landscape in Britain – the undistinguished modern architecture, the neglect of public services and amenities from the arts to transportation, the general seediness – is not an invention of Thatcherism alone but belongs to a longer pattern of capitalist development and the commodification of all social goods, just as the civic pride of Continental capitals owes much to the traditions of burgher luxury and absolutist ostentation as to the values of modern urbanism and advanced welfare capitalism'. Ellen Meiksins Wood, *The Pristine Culture of Capitalism: A Historical Essay on Old Regimes and Modern States* (London: Verso, 1991), pp. 108-9. For Keiller's endorsement of Wood, as well as his suggestion that London may be seeing the emergence of a 'latterday burgherdom', see 'London in the 1990s', in *The View from the Train*, pp. 93-5; also, Nina Power's interview with Keiller, 'Ghost of the Fields', *Film Quarterly*, 64.2 (2010), p. 49.

392. Patrick Wright, 'A Conversation with Patrick Keiller', in *Robinson in Space*, p. 232.

393. Ibid., p. 90.

394. 'The Robinson Institute', in *The View from the Train*, p. 119.

395. *Robinson in Space*, p. 220.

396. Patrick Keiller, *The Possibility of Life's Survival on the Planet* (London: Tate, 2012).

397. 'Port Statistics', in *The View from the Train*, p. 47.

398. See the crucial essay 'Port Statistics' in *The View from the Train*, which details some of Keiller's research into what happens when 'economic activity … no longer takes place in

cities' (p. 35). This comment is particularly apropos: 'Like many people with a tourist's familiarity with the waterfronts of Liverpool and Birkenhead, I took the spectacular dereliction of the docks to be symptomatic of a past decline in their traffic, and Liverpool's impoverishment to be a result of this decline in its importance as a port. In fact, in September 1995, when the images of Liverpool in the film [*Robinson in Space*] were photographed, Liverpool's port traffic was greater that at any time in its history' (p. 37).

399. *Robinson in Space*, p. 221.

400. The visual meditations on biophilia in the context of financial crisis in *Robinson in Ruins* further complicate this matter, especially as they displace some of the utopian tonalities in Keiller from history (of revolutions lost) to nature (without or after 'us'). See Mark Fisher, 'English Pastoral: Robinson in Ruins', available at: http://old.bfi. org.uk/sightandsound/feature/49663 (and in the booklet accompanying the DVD/Blu-Ray edition of the film). See also Paul Dave, '*Robinson in Ruins*: New materialism and the archaeological imagination', *Radical Philosophy* 169 (2011), pp. 22-34; 'Ghost of the Fields', p. 45.

401. 'Urbanism as Will and Representation' [*Internationale situationniste* 9 (August 1964)], in *The Situationists and the City*, ed. Tom McDonough (London: Verso, 2009), p. 208.

402. G.P. Lomazzo, *Trattato dell'arte della pittura, scultura e architettura* (1585), quoted in E.H. Gombrich, 'The Renaissance Theory of Art and the Rise of Landscape', in *Norm and Form: Studies in the Art of the Renaissance* (London: Phaidon, 1966), p. 120.

403. The show *New Topographics: Photographs of a Man-Altered Landscape*, curated by William Jenkins, was on display the International Museum of Photography at George Eastman House in Rochester, NY, in January 1975. The photographers included in the exhibition were Robert Adams, Lewis

Baltz, Joe Deal, Frank Gohlke, Nicholas Nixon, John Schott, Stephen Shore, Henry Wessel, Jr., and Bernda and Hilla Becher.

404. Takuma Nakahira, 'Why an Illustrated Botanical Dictionary', in *Setting Sun: Writings by Japanese Photographers*, ed. I. Vartanian et al. (New York: Aperture, 2006), p. 127. 'For even atrocities might seem to us today to belong rather to the malignant properties of evil or cursed landscapes than to the savagery of an individual actor'. Fredric Jameson, 'War and Representation', in *The Antinomies of Realism*, p. 240. For a superb reflection on this and many of the themes of this chapter, with reference to Joseph Losey's uncanny gem *Figures in a Landscape* (1970), see Evan Calder Williams, 'Figures in a Threatscape', *La Furia Umana*, 17, available at: http://www.lafuriaumana .it/index.php/29-archive/lfu-17/33-evan-calder-williams-figures-in-a-threatscape

405. 'Takuma Nakahira, 'Rebellion Against the Landscape: Fire at the Limits of my Perpetual Gazing...', in *For a Language to Come* (Tokyo: Osiris, 2010).

406. On *fûkeiron* in film, see Yuriko Furuhata's impressive monograph, *Cinema of Actuality: Japanese Avant-Garde Filmmaking in the Season of Image Politics* (Durham, NC: Duke University Press, 2013), which is particularly enlightening on the manner in which reference to 'landscape' is part of an attempt 'to diagramatically map – and make visible – the invisible yet ubiquitous relations of power' (p. 170).

407. Allan Sekula, 1982 postscript to 'School is a Factory' (1978/1980), in *Allan Sekula: Performance Under Working Conditions*, ed. Sabine Breitweiser (Berlin: Hatje Cantz, 2003), p. 252.

408. Ibid., p. 251.

409. Lewis Baltz, 'American Photography in the 1970s: Too Old to Rock, Too Young to Die' (1985), in *Lewis Baltz Texts*

(Göttingen: Steidl, 2012), p. 63.

410. Quoted in Cathy Curtis, 'The Wasteland', *Los Angeles Times*, 29 March 1992, available at: http://articles.latimes.com/1992-03-29/entertainment/ca-372_1_photographer-lewis-baltz.

411. Baltz, 'American Photography in the 1970s', p. 69.

412. Baltz, *Lewis Baltz Texts*, p. 16.

413. 'Notes on *Park City*' (1980), in *Lewis Baltz Texts*, p. 45.

414. 'The mostly windowless factory buildings were erected as gigantic speculation objects in suburban zones optimized for traffic infrastructure. Printed without an introduction, devoid of commentary, Baltz's fifty-one photographs of these uniform structures reveal nothing beyond the structural facades. The focus lies upon the texture of the surfaces and the grid-like structure of the architectural ensemble. No single element is accentuated more than another. … Is not the lack of commentary itself a commentary on this serialized, suburban conformity? Whereas someone like Allan Sekula documents the transformation of the working environment under the auspices of a global economy, these causalities remain invisible in Baltz's case, as indeed does every form of production behind factory gates.' Vanessa Joan Müller, 'Between Representation and Reality: Reflections on a Film Installation by Mario Pfeifer', in *Reconsidering The New Industrial Parks near Irvine, California by Lewis Baltz, 1974, by Mario Pfeifer, 2009* (Berlin: Sternberg Press, 2011), pp. 83, 84. Pfeifer's installation returns to the site of one of Baltz's photographs, to document it from within.

415. 'Rebellion Against the Landscape: Fire at the Limits of my Perpetual Gazing…', p. 9.

416. See Chris Balaschak, 'New World: Lewis Baltz and a Geography of Aesthetic Decisions', in *Reconsidering…*

417. Karl Marx, 'Economic Manuscripts of 1861-63', *Marx and*

Engels Collected Works, Volume 34 (London: Lawrence & Wishart, 1993), p. 30.

418. *Representing Capital*, pp. 101, 102.

419. 'Popular Science', *The View from the Train*, pp. 66-7.

420. See Alain Badiou, *Theory of the Subject*, trans. B. Bosteels (London: Continuum, 2009), Part VI: 'Topics of Ethics'.

421. Thomas Hobbes, *Leviathan* (London: Penguin, 1985), p. 167. This passage is discussed in Carlo Ginzburg, *Paura reverenza terrore. Rileggere Hobbes oggi* (Parma: Monte Università Parma, 2008). On the visual in Hobbes, see Horst Bredekamp, 'Thomas Hobbes's Visual Strategies', in *The Cambridge Companion to Hobbes*, ed. P. Springborg (Cambridge: Cambridge University Press, 2007), pp. 29-60.

422. *Postmodernism*, p. 417.

423. 'The reactionary practice of the cinema is that which involves [the] petrification of the spectator in a position of pseudo-dominance offered by the metalanguage. This metalanguage, resolving as it does all contradictions, places the spectator outside the realm of contradiction and action – outside of production'. Colin MacCabe, 'Realism and Cinema', in Theoretical Essays: Film, Linguistics, Literature (Manchester: Manchester University Press, 1985), p. 54.

424. Franco Fortini, 'The Writers' Mandate and the End of Anti-Fascism', *Screen* 15.1 (1974), p. 67. Translation Modified. See also Alberto Toscano, 'The Non-State Intellectual: Franco Fortini and Communist Criticism', in Franco Fortini, *The Dogs of the Sinai*, trans. A. Toscano (Calcutta: Seagull, 2013).

zer0
books

Contemporary culture has eliminated both the concept of the public and the figure of the intellectual. Former public spaces – both physical and cultural – are now either derelict or colonized by advertising. A cretinous anti-intellectualism presides, cheerled by expensively educated hacks in the pay of multinational corporations who reassure their bored readers that there is no need to rouse themselves from their interpassive stupor. The informal censorship internalized and propagated by the cultural workers of late capitalism generates a banal conformity that the propaganda chiefs of Stalinism could only ever have dreamt of imposing. Zer0 Books knows that another kind of discourse – intellectual without being academic, popular without being populist – is not only possible: it is already flourishing, in the regions beyond the striplit malls of so-called mass media and the neurotically bureaucratic halls of the academy. Zer0 is committed to the idea of publishing as a making public of the intellectual. It is convinced that in the unthinking, blandly consensual culture in which we live, critical and engaged theoretical reflection is more important than ever before.